FAIRY

ROYALE

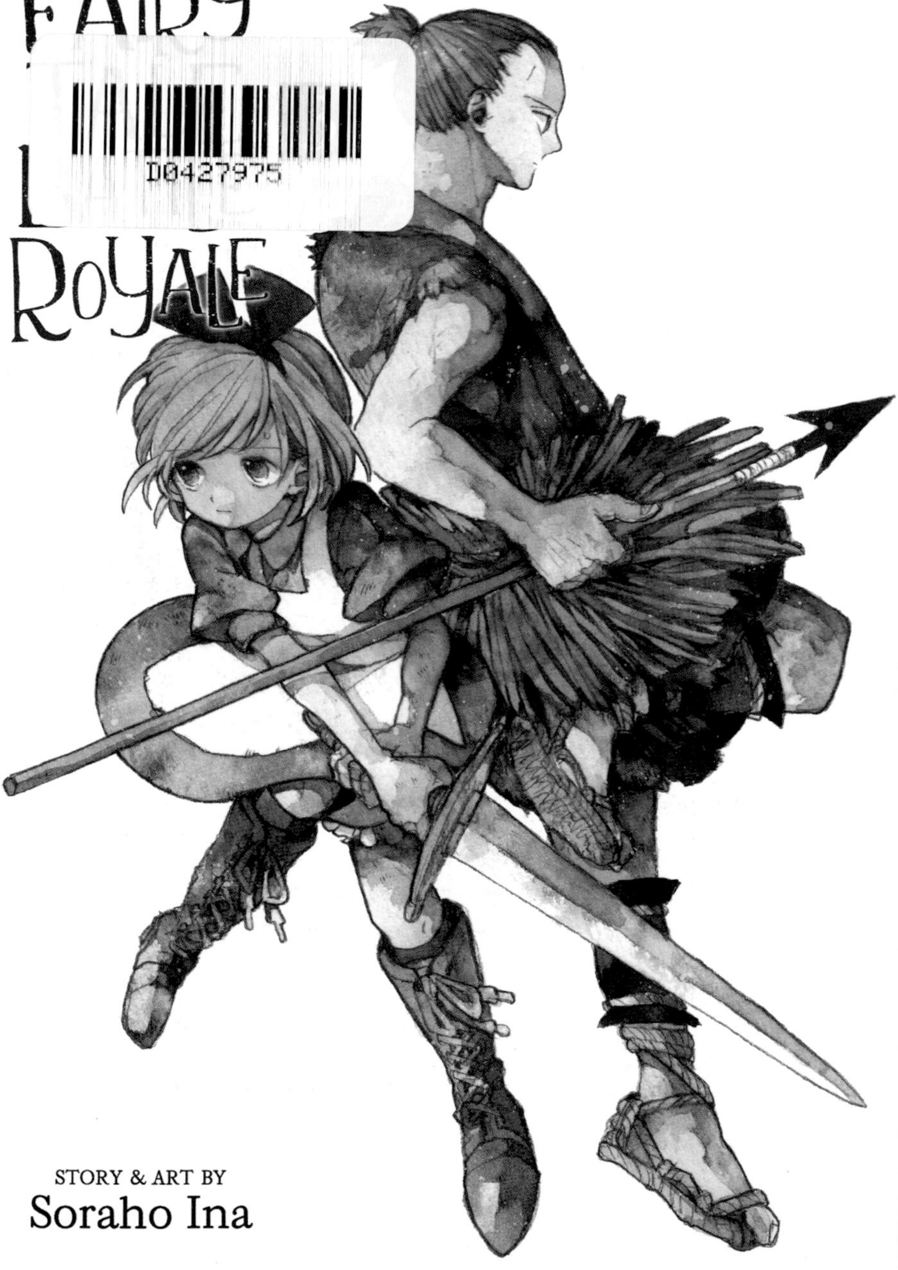

STORY & ART BY

Soraho Ina

Contents

FAIRY
TALE
BATTLE
ROYALE

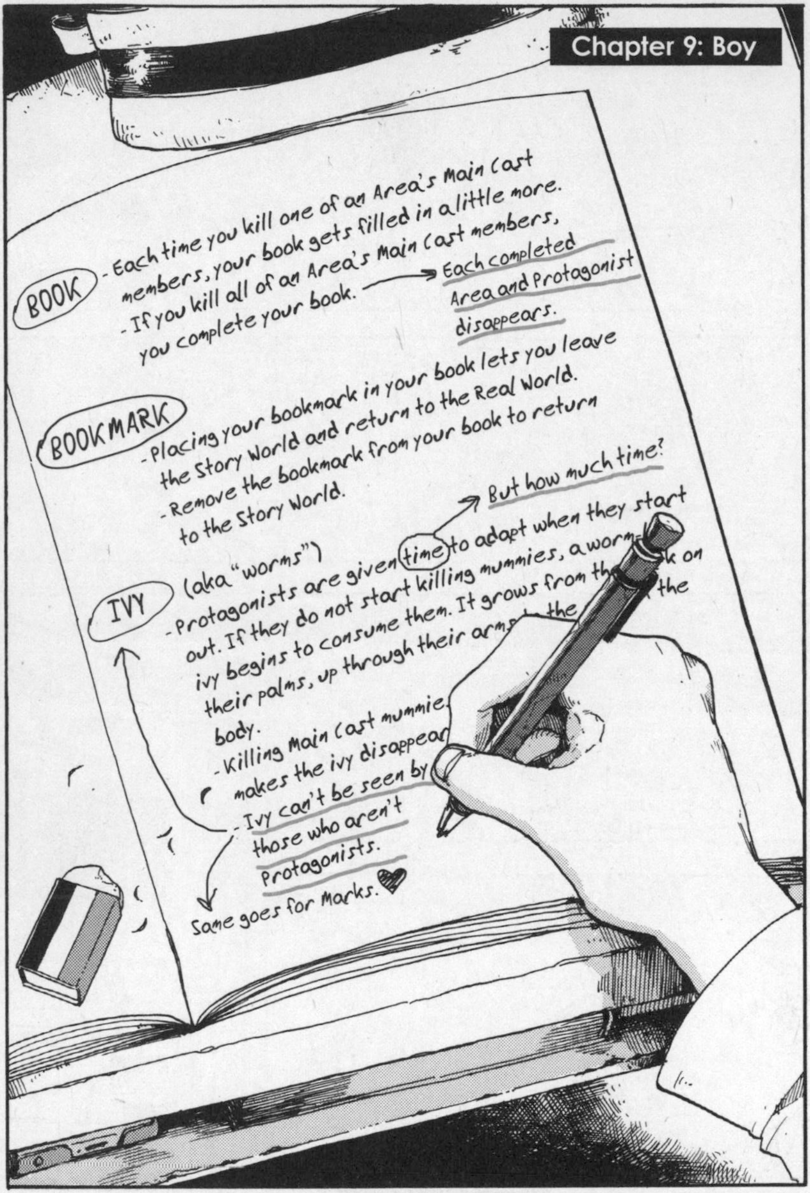

BOOK
- Each time you kill one of an Area's Main Cast members, your book gets filled in a little more.
- If you kill all of an Area's Main Cast members, you complete your book. → Each completed Area and Protagonist disappears.

BOOKMARK
- Placing your bookmark in your book lets you leave the Story World and return to the Real World.
- Remove the bookmark from your book to return to the Story World.

→ But how much time?

IVY   (aka "worms")
- Protagonists are given time to adapt when they start out. If they do not start killing mummies, a worm ck on ivy begins to consume them. It grows from th the their palms, up through their arm the body.
- Killing Main Cast mummie makes the ivy disappea
- Ivy can't be seen by those who aren't Protagonists.

Same goes for Marks. ♥

4

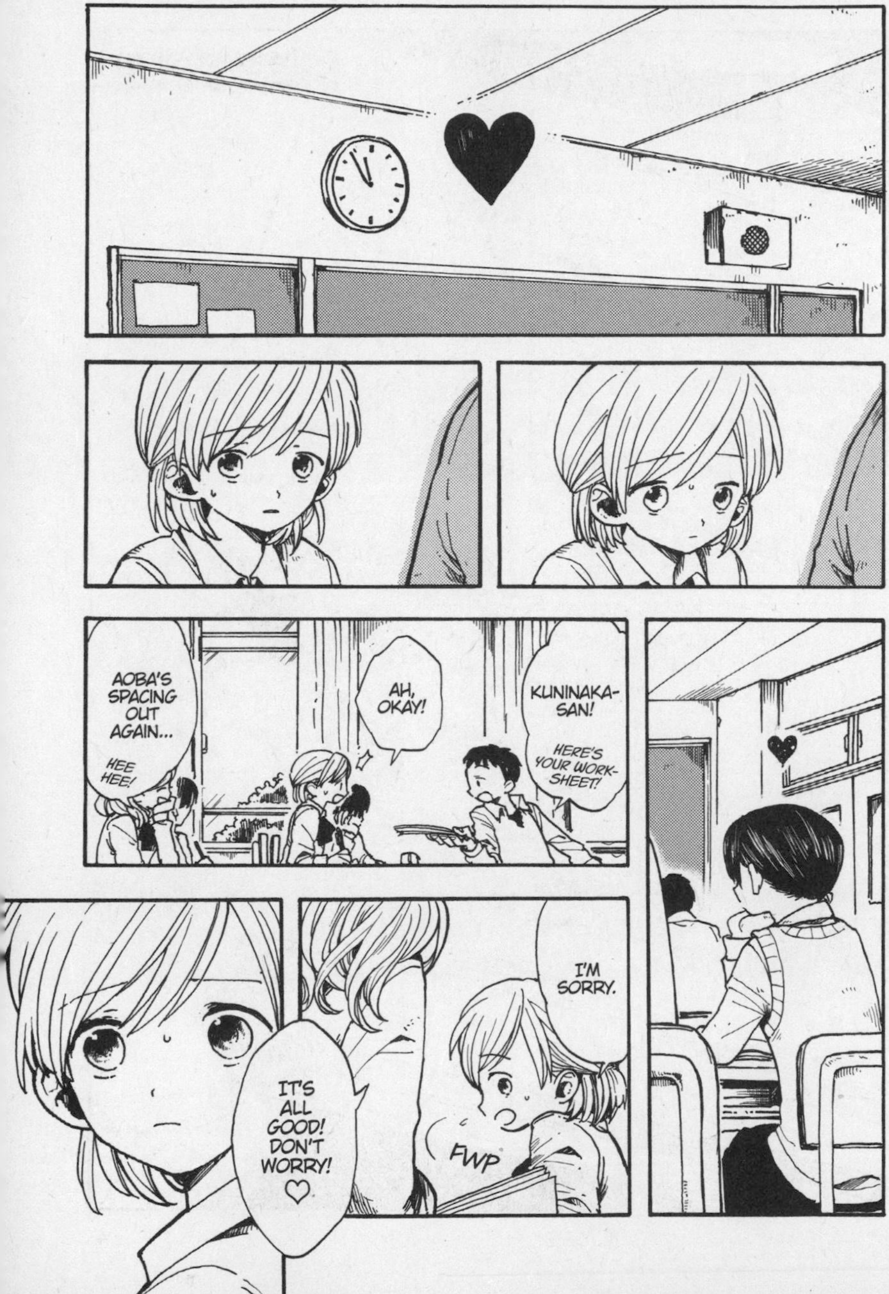
KUNINAKA-SAN!
HERE'S YOUR WORK-SHEET!
AH, OKAY!
AOBA'S SPACING OUT AGAIN...
HEE HEE!
I'M SORRY.
FWP
IT'S ALL GOOD! DON'T WORRY! ♡

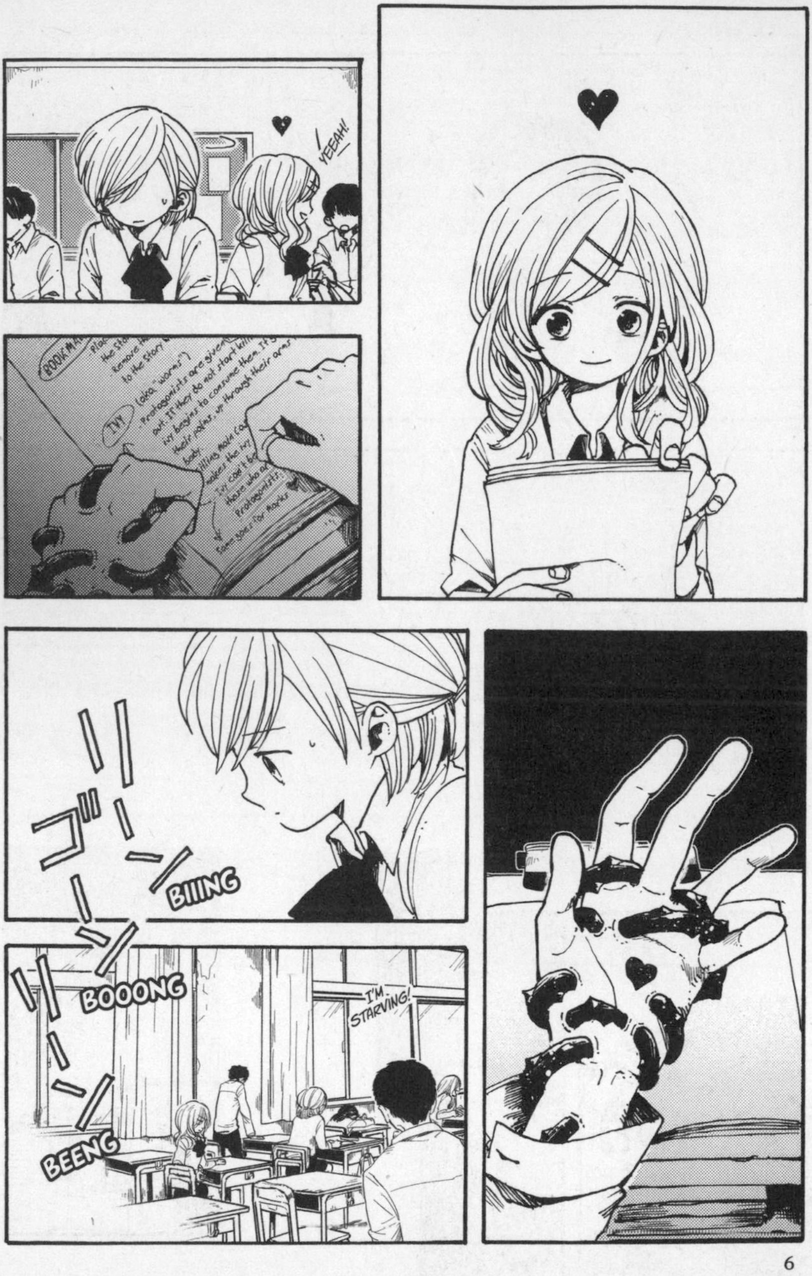
YEEAH!
IVY
(aka "worms")
Protagonists are given
Ivy begins to consume them.
their notes, up through their arms
body.
ゴーン
BIIING
BOOONG
I'M STARVING!
BEENG

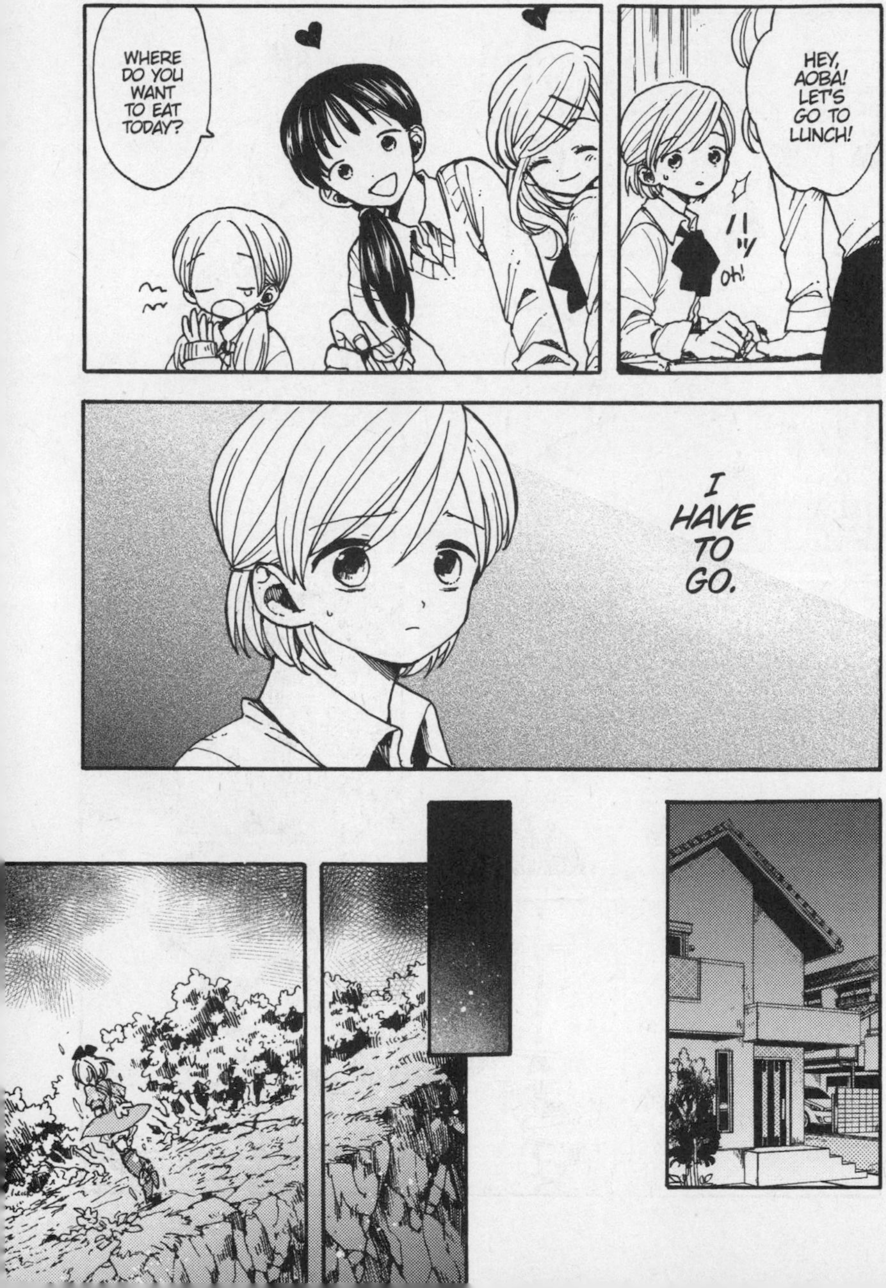
HEY, AOBA! LET'S GO TO LUNCH!
Oh!
WHERE DO YOU WANT TO EAT TODAY?
I HAVE TO GO.

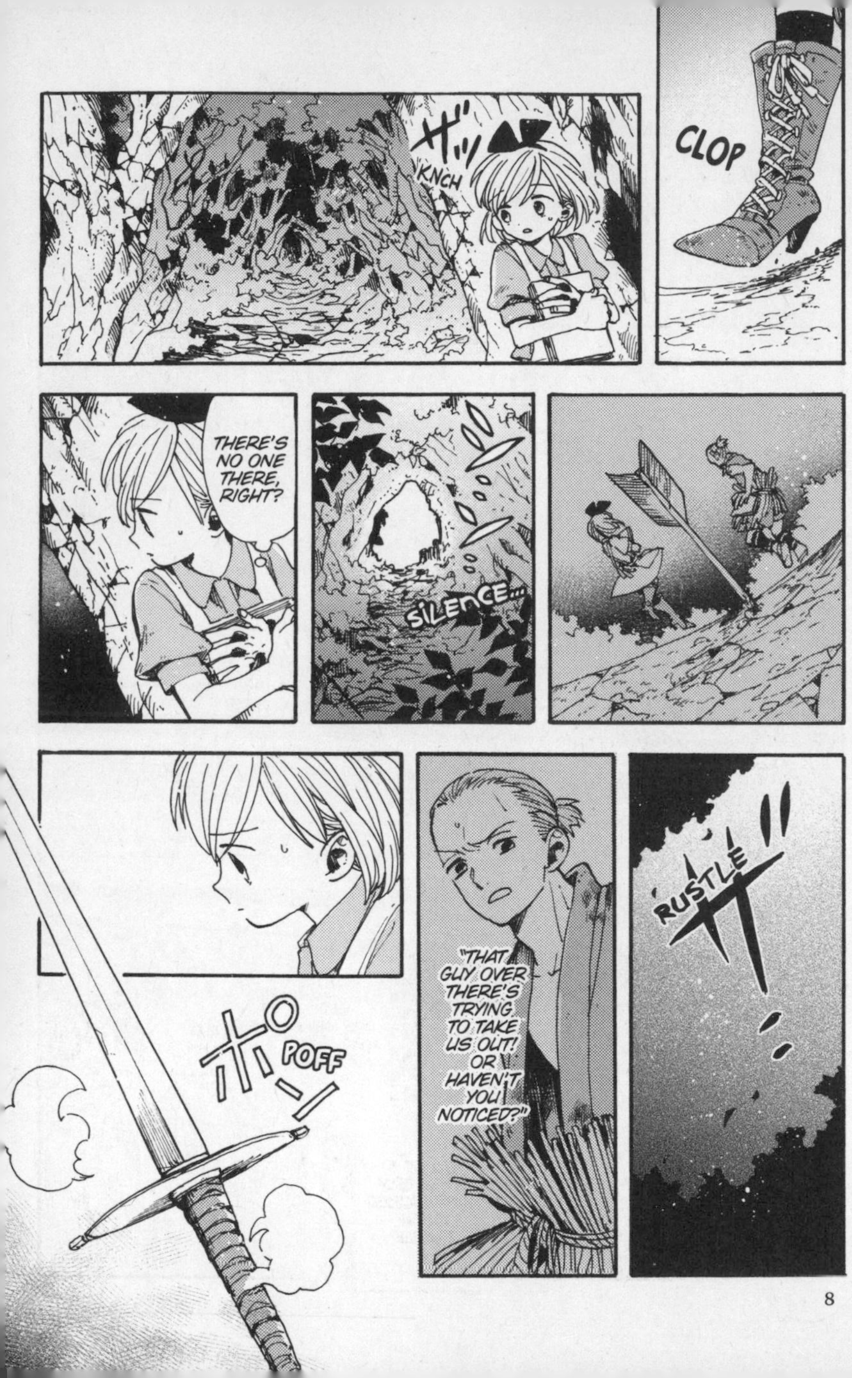
CLOP
ザッ
KNCH
SILENCE...
THERE'S NO ONE THERE, RIGHT?
RUSTLE
"THAT GUY OVER THERE'S TRYING TO TAKE US OUT! OR HAVEN'T YOU NOTICED?"
POFF

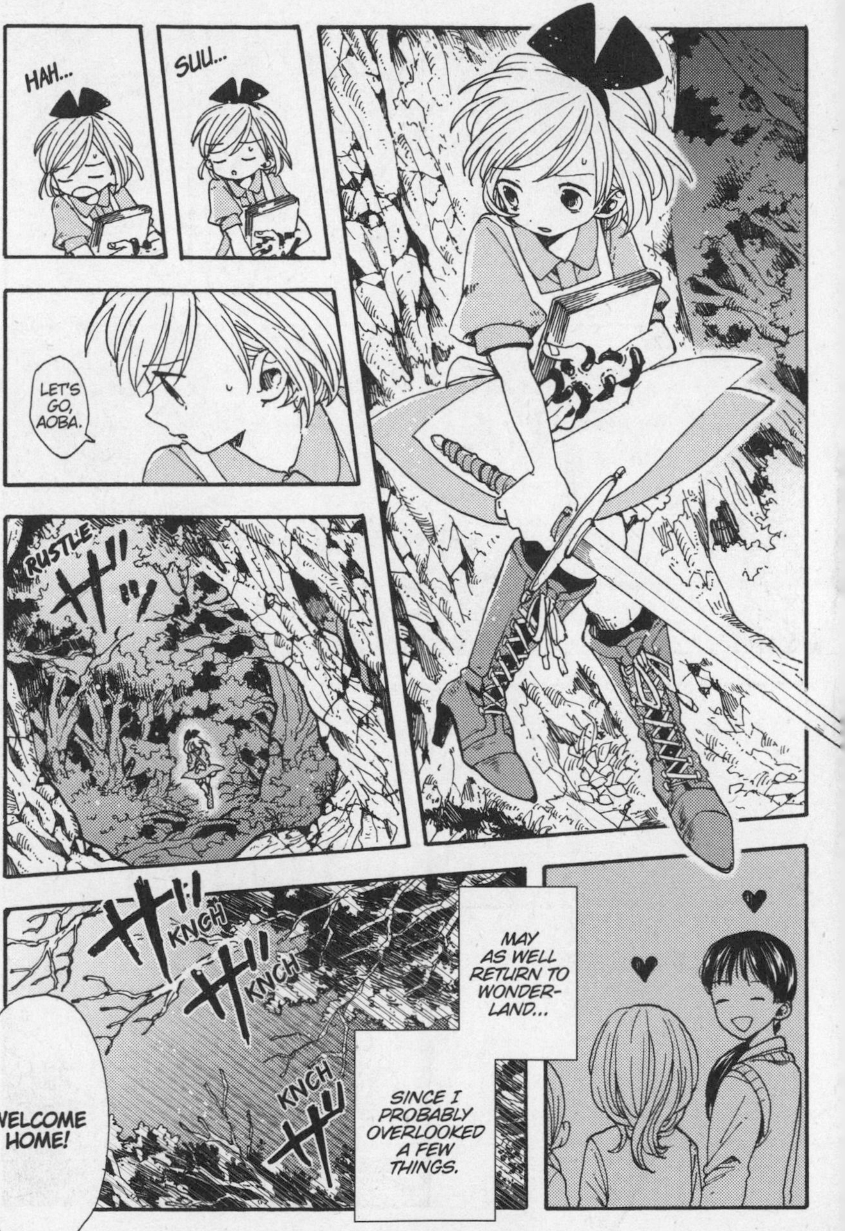
SUU...
HAH...
LET'S GO, AOBA.
RUSTLE
MAY AS WELL RETURN TO WONDER-LAND...
SINCE I PROBABLY OVERLOOKED A FEW THINGS.
KNCH
KNCH
KNCH
WELCOME HOME!

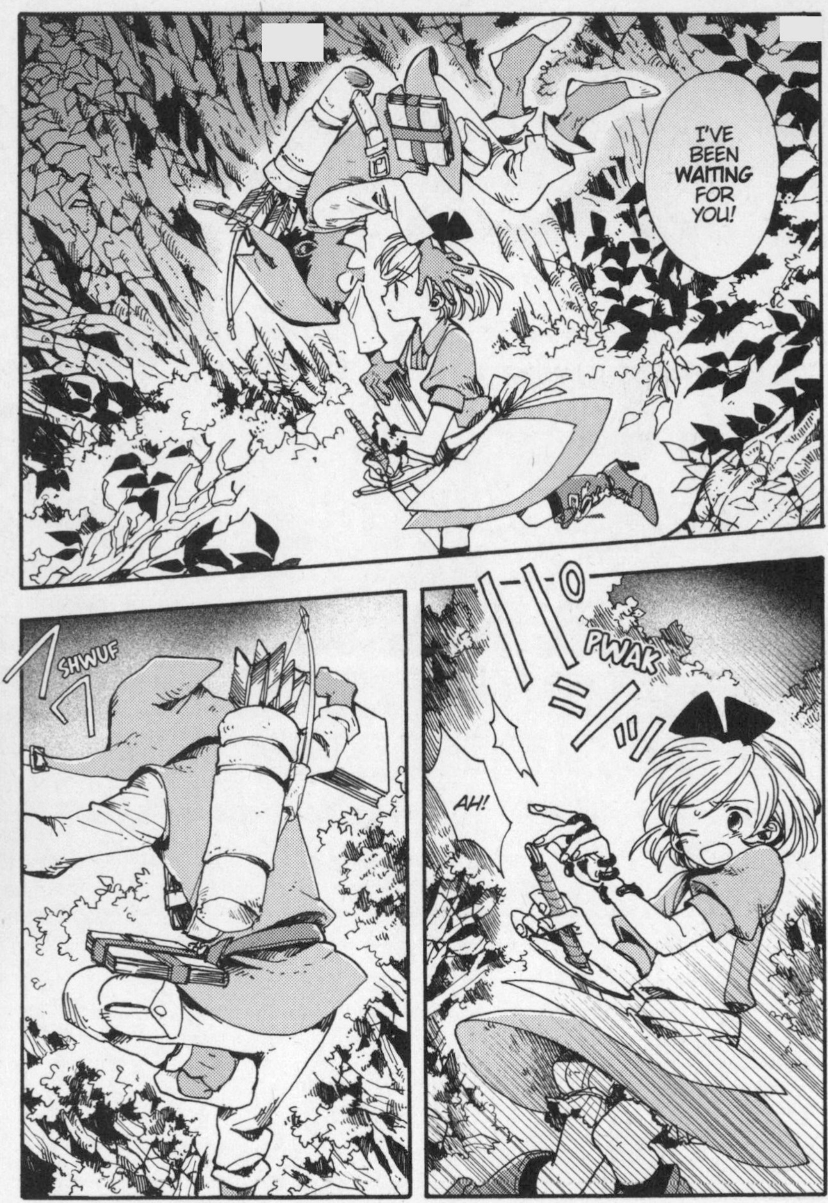
I'VE BEEN WAITING FOR YOU!
PWAK
AH!
SHWUF

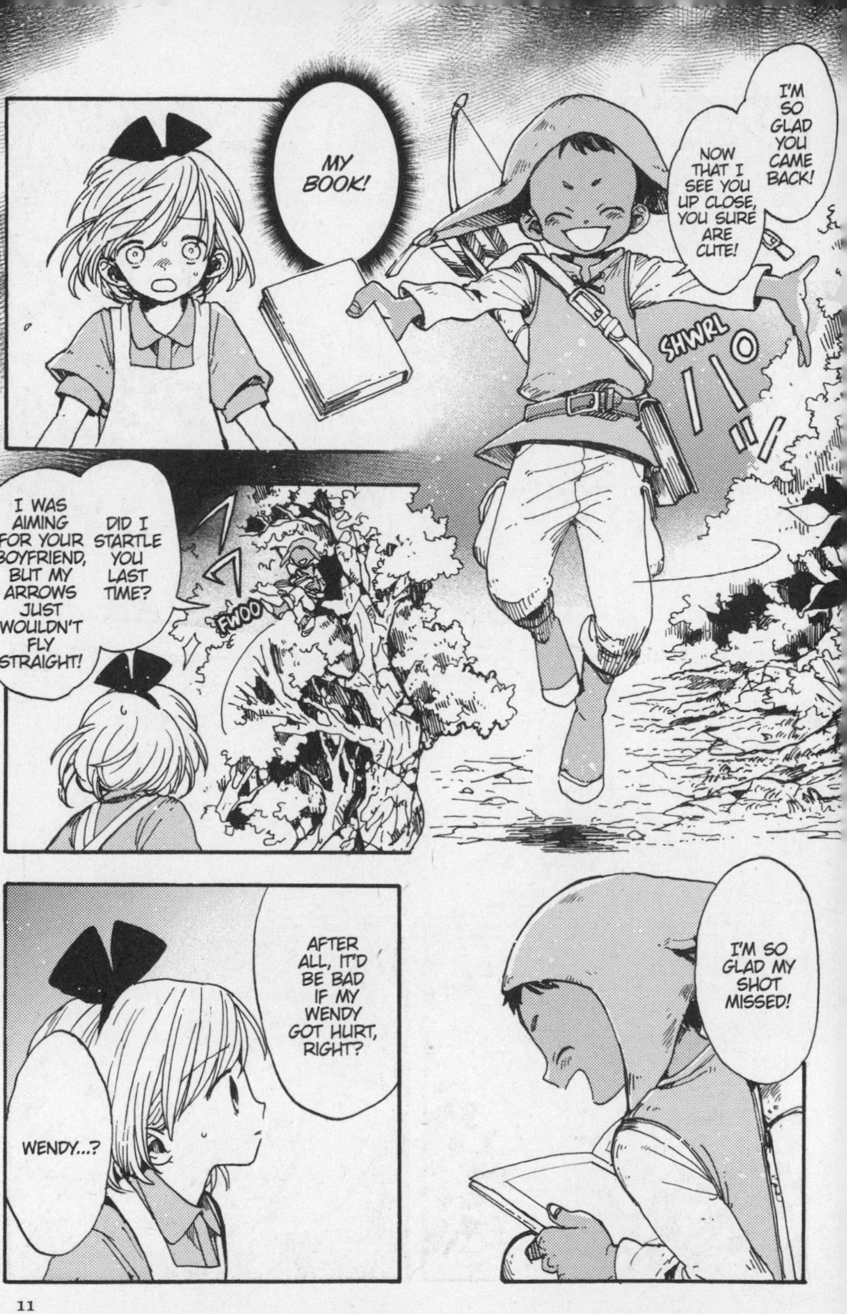
I'M SO GLAD YOU CAME BACK!
NOW THAT I SEE YOU UP CLOSE, YOU SURE ARE CUTE!
SHWRL
MY BOOK!
DID I STARTLE YOU LAST TIME?
I WAS AIMING FOR YOUR BOYFRIEND, BUT MY ARROWS JUST WOULDN'T FLY STRAIGHT!
FWOO
I'M SO GLAD MY SHOT MISSED!
AFTER ALL, IT'D BE BAD IF MY WENDY GOT HURT, RIGHT?
WENDY...?

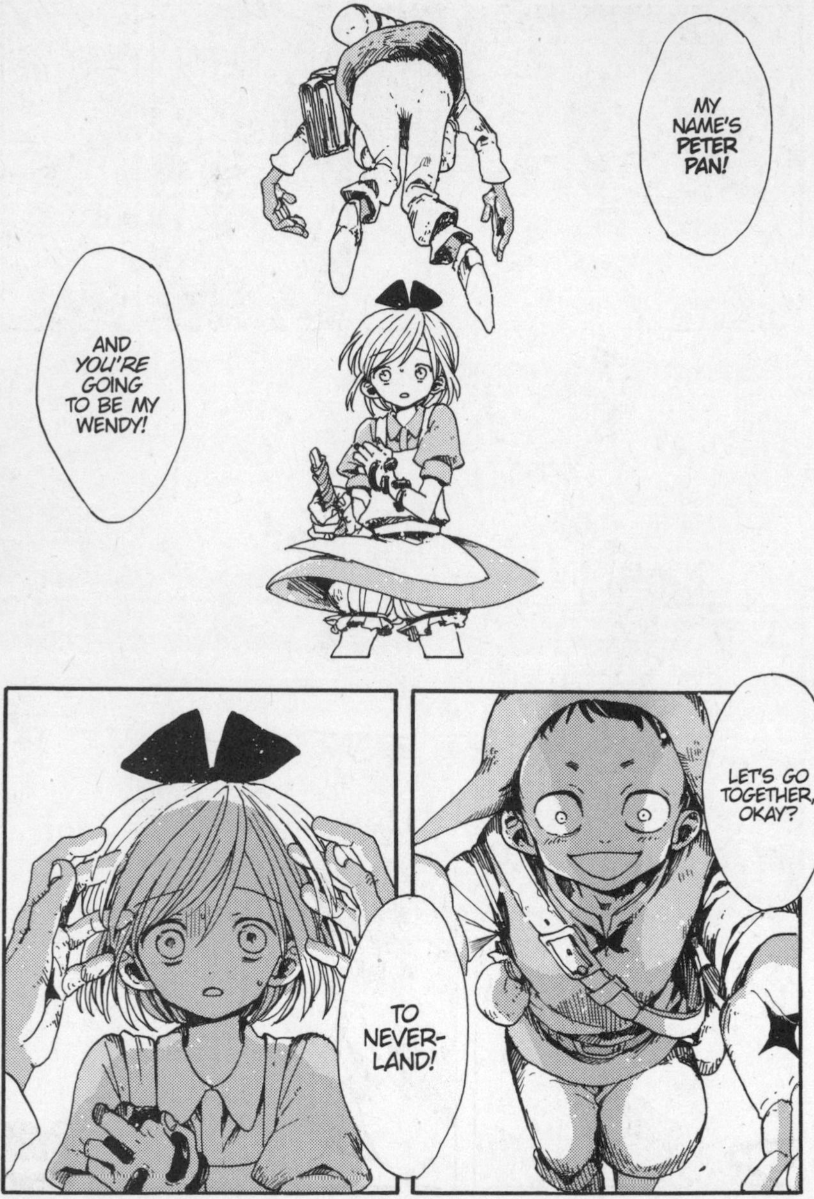
MY NAME'S PETER PAN!
AND *YOU'RE* GOING TO BE MY WENDY!
LET'S GO TOGETHER, OKAY?
TO NEVER-LAND!

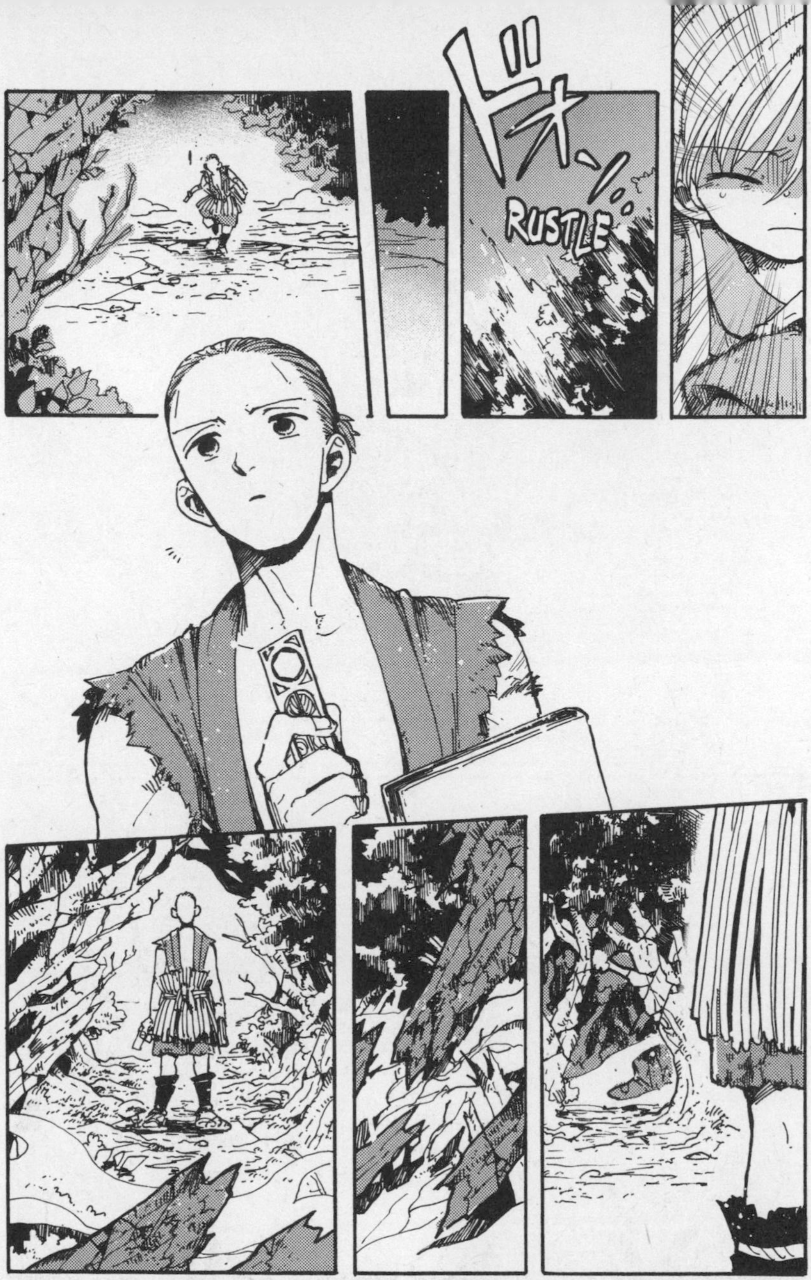
ドォーン…
RUSTLE

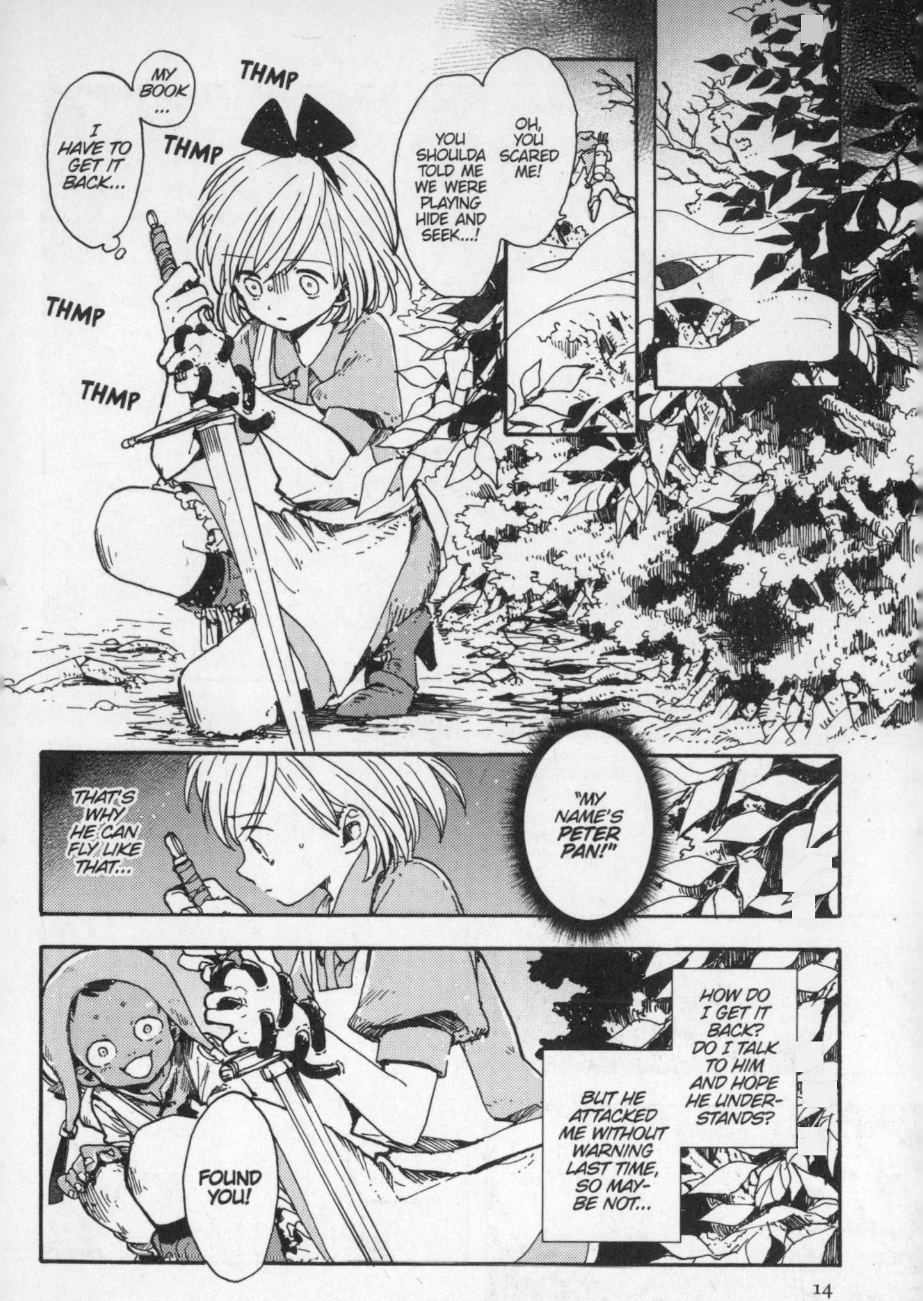
OH, YOU SCARED ME! YOU SHOULDA TOLD ME WE WERE PLAYING HIDE AND SEEK...!
THMP
THMP
MY BOOK...
I HAVE TO GET IT BACK...
THMP
THMP
"MY NAME'S PETER PAN!"
THAT'S WHY HE CAN FLY LIKE THAT...
HOW DO I GET IT BACK? DO I TALK TO HIM AND HOPE HE UNDERSTANDS?
BUT HE ATTACKED ME WITHOUT WARNING LAST TIME, SO MAYBE NOT...
FOUND YOU!

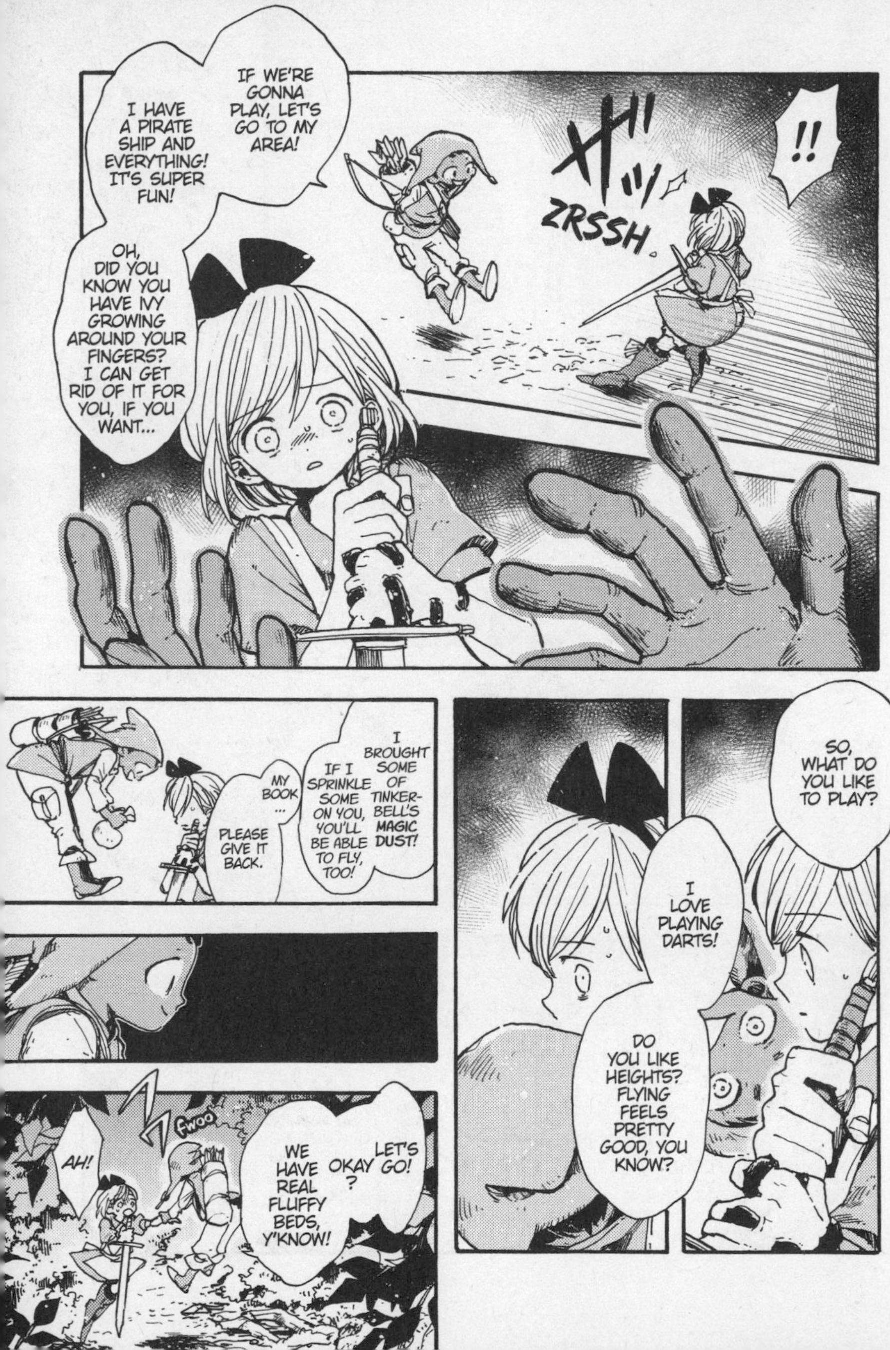
!!
ZRSSH
IF WE'RE GONNA PLAY, LET'S GO TO MY AREA!
I HAVE A PIRATE SHIP AND EVERYTHING! IT'S SUPER FUN!
OH, DID YOU KNOW YOU HAVE IVY GROWING AROUND YOUR FINGERS? I CAN GET RID OF IT FOR YOU, IF YOU WANT...
SO, WHAT DO YOU LIKE TO PLAY?
I LOVE PLAYING DARTS!
DO YOU LIKE HEIGHTS? FLYING FEELS PRETTY GOOD, YOU KNOW?
I BROUGHT SOME OF TINKER-BELL'S MAGIC DUST!
IF I SPRINKLE SOME ON YOU, YOU'LL BE ABLE TO FLY, TOO!
MY BOOK...
PLEASE GIVE IT BACK.
LET'S GO!
OKAY?
WE HAVE REAL FLUFFY BEDS, Y'KNOW!
FWOO
AH!

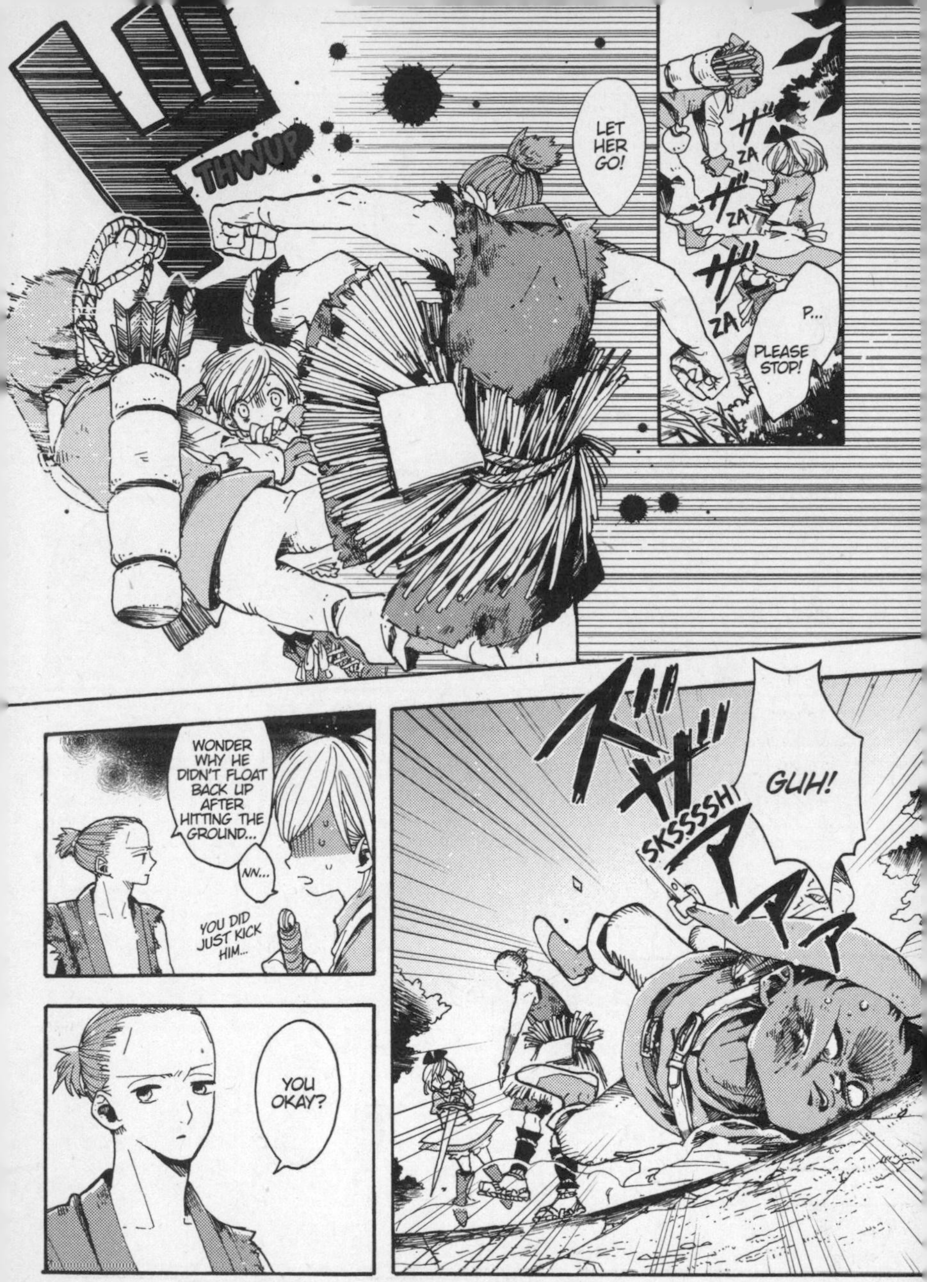
ZA
ZA
ZA
P... PLEASE STOP!
LET HER GO!
THWUP
GUH!
SKSSSSH
WONDER WHY HE DIDN'T FLOAT BACK UP AFTER HITTING THE GROUND...
NN...
YOU DID JUST KICK HIM...
YOU OKAY?

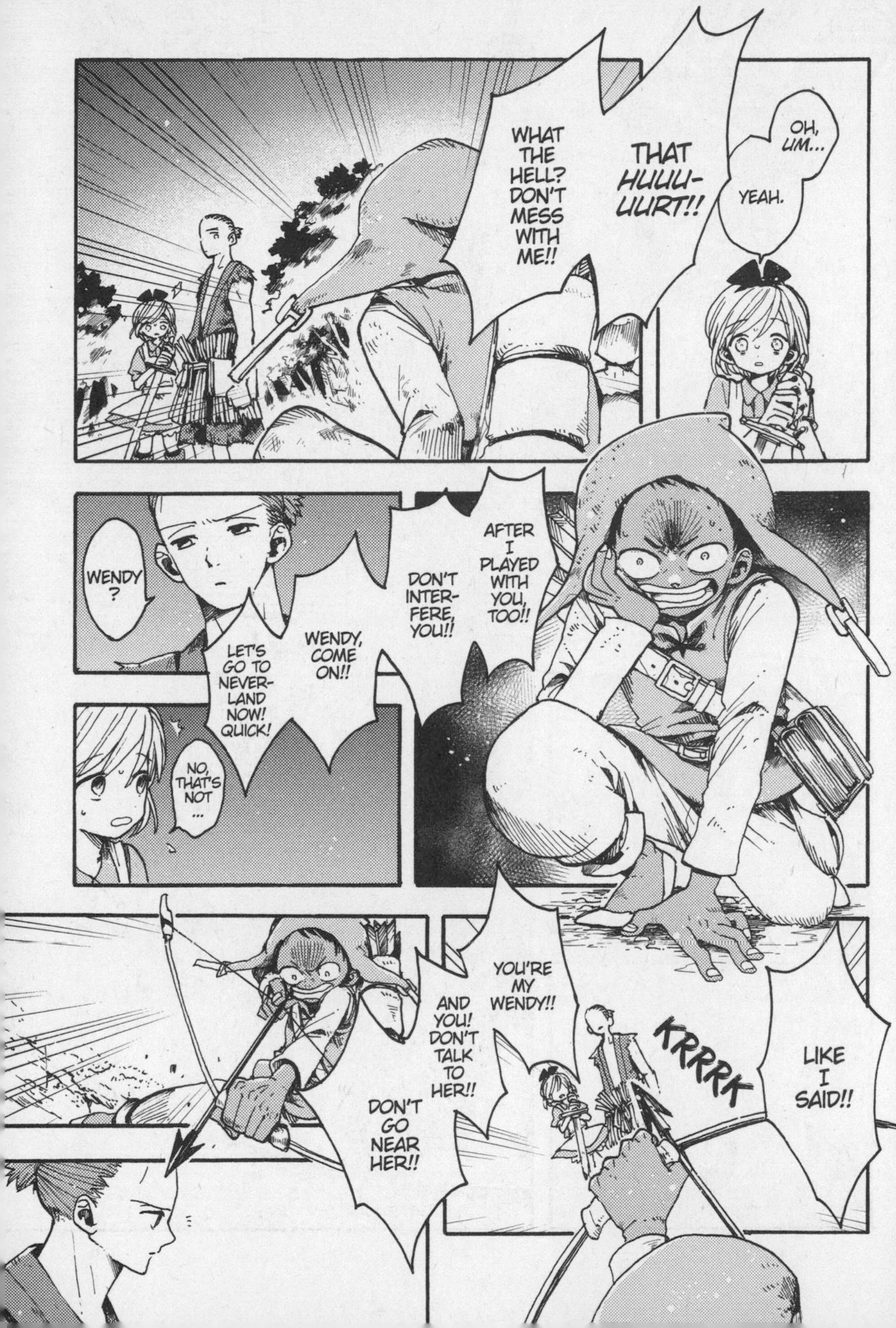
OH, UM...
YEAH.
THAT HUUU-UURT!!
WHAT THE HELL? DON'T MESS WITH ME!!
AFTER I PLAYED WITH YOU, TOO!!
DON'T INTER-FERE, YOU!!
WENDY, COME ON!!
LET'S GO TO NEVER-LAND NOW! QUICK!
WENDY ?
NO, THAT'S NOT ...
LIKE I SAID!!
KRRRK
YOU'RE MY WENDY!!
AND YOU! DON'T TALK TO HER!!
DON'T GO NEAR HER!!

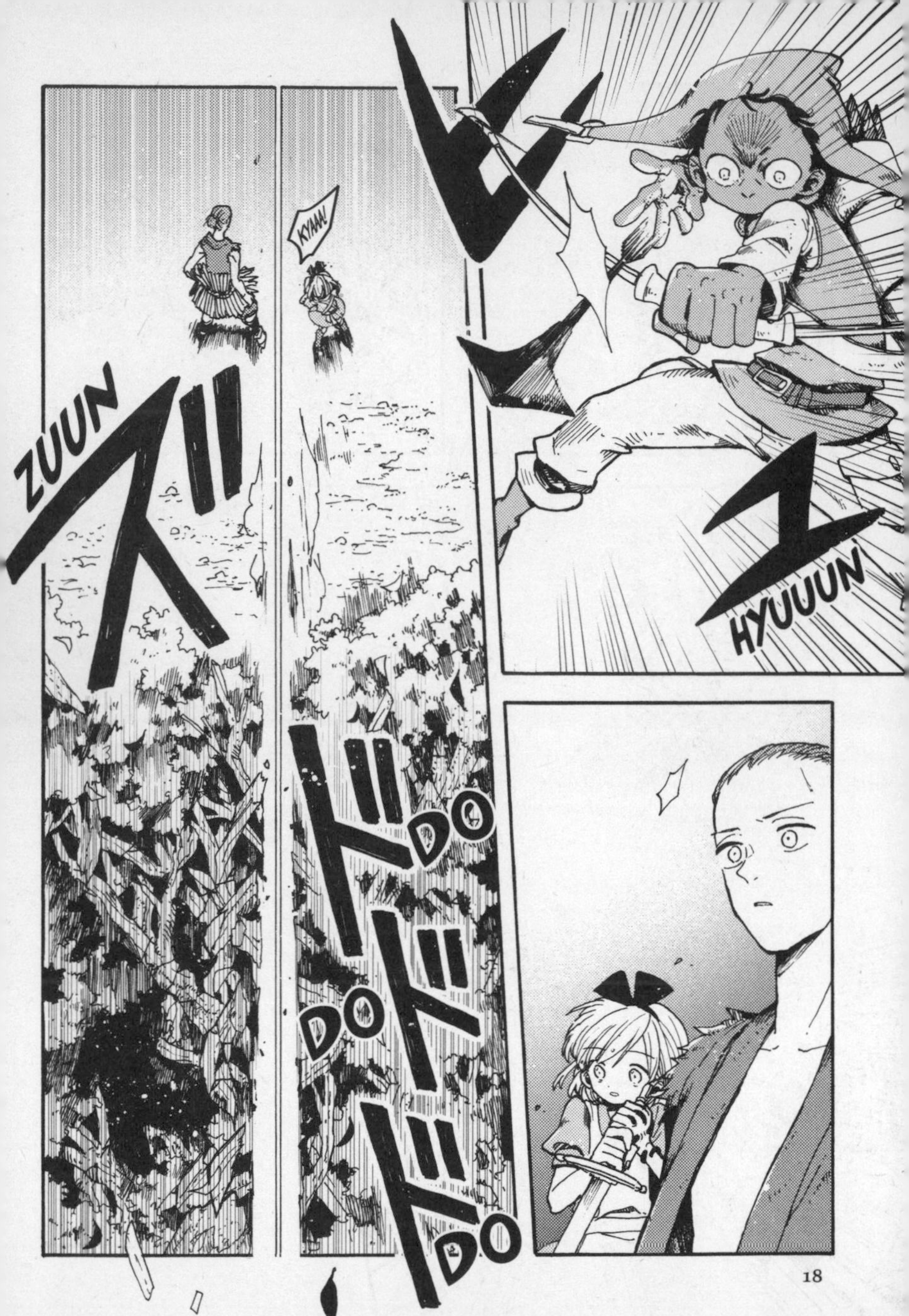
HYUUUN
KYAAA!
DO
DO
DO
ZUUN

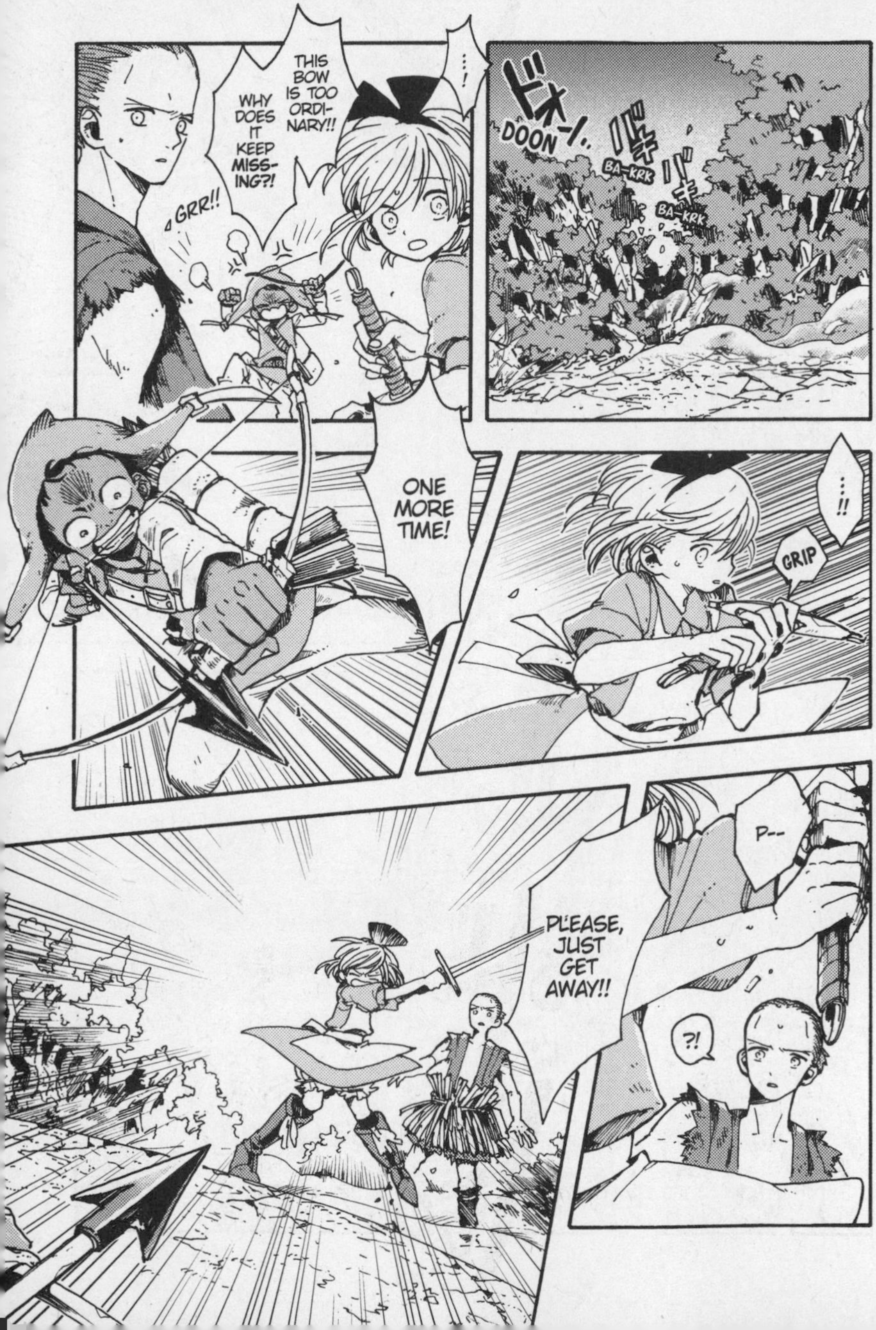
DOON
BA-KRK
BA-KRK
...!
THIS BOW IS TOO ORDINARY!!
WHY DOES IT KEEP MISSING?!
GRR!!
...!!
GRIP
ONE MORE TIME!
P--
PLEASE, JUST GET AWAY!!
?!

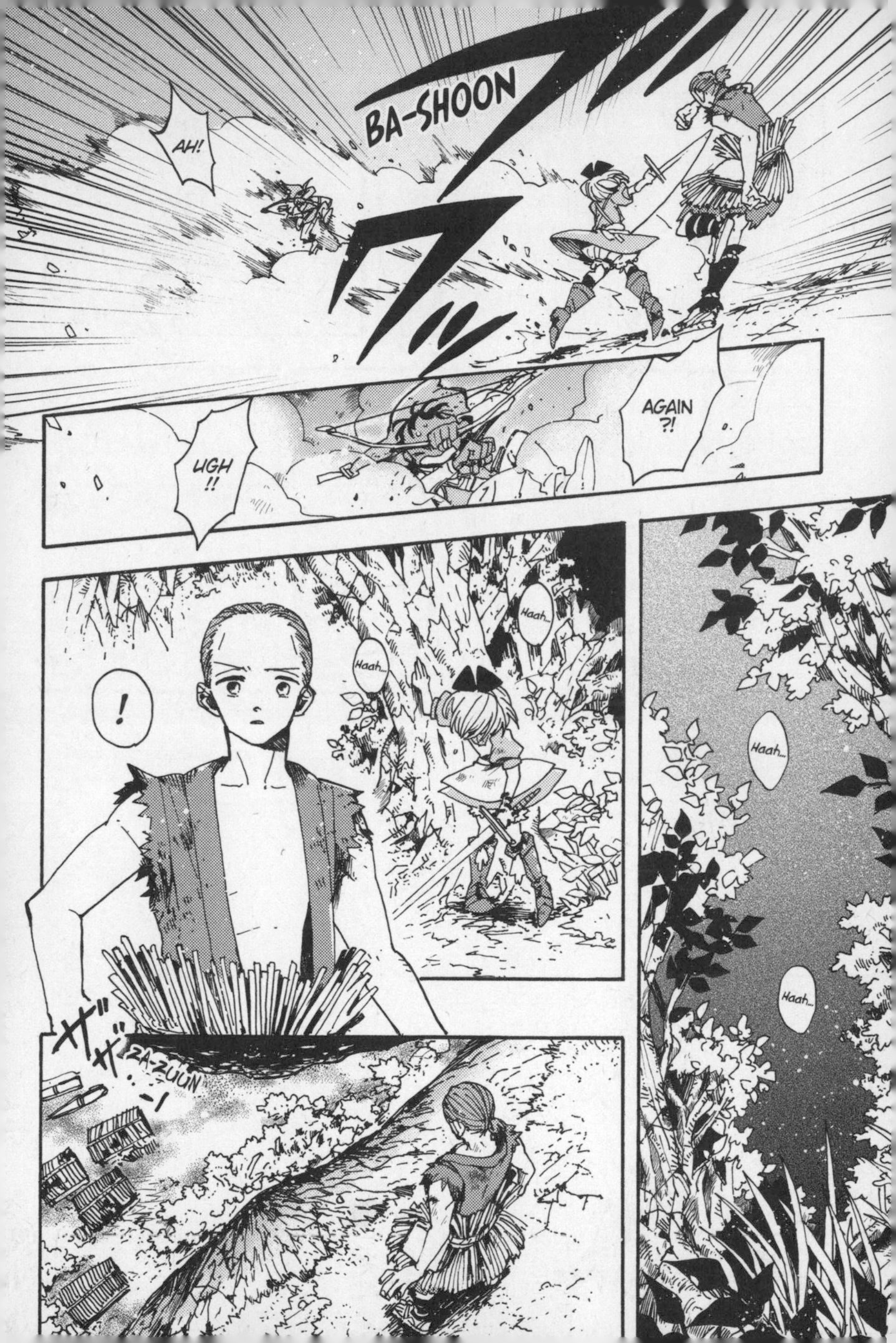
BA-SHOON
AH!
AGAIN ?!
UGH !!
Haah...
Haah...
Haah...
Haah...
!
ZA-ZUUN

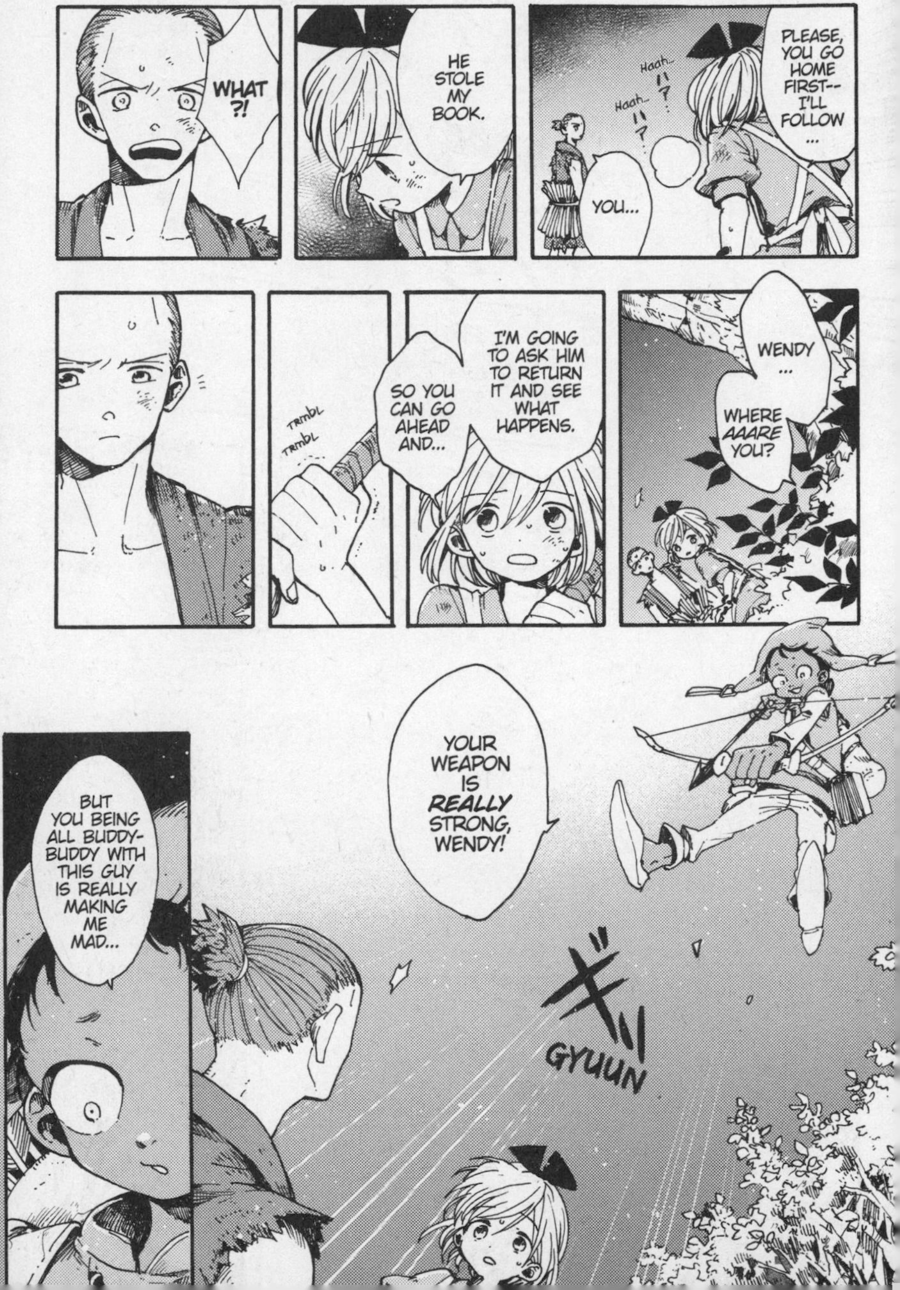
PLEASE, YOU GO HOME FIRST-- I'LL FOLLOW ...
Haah.. ハァ
Haah.. ハァ
YOU...
HE STOLE MY BOOK.
WHAT ?!
WENDY ...
WHERE AAARE YOU?
I'M GOING TO ASK HIM TO RETURN IT AND SEE WHAT HAPPENS.
SO YOU CAN GO AHEAD AND...
Trmbl Trmbl
YOUR WEAPON IS REALLY STRONG, WENDY!
GYUUN
BUT YOU BEING ALL BUDDY-BUDDY WITH THIS GUY IS REALLY MAKING ME MAD...

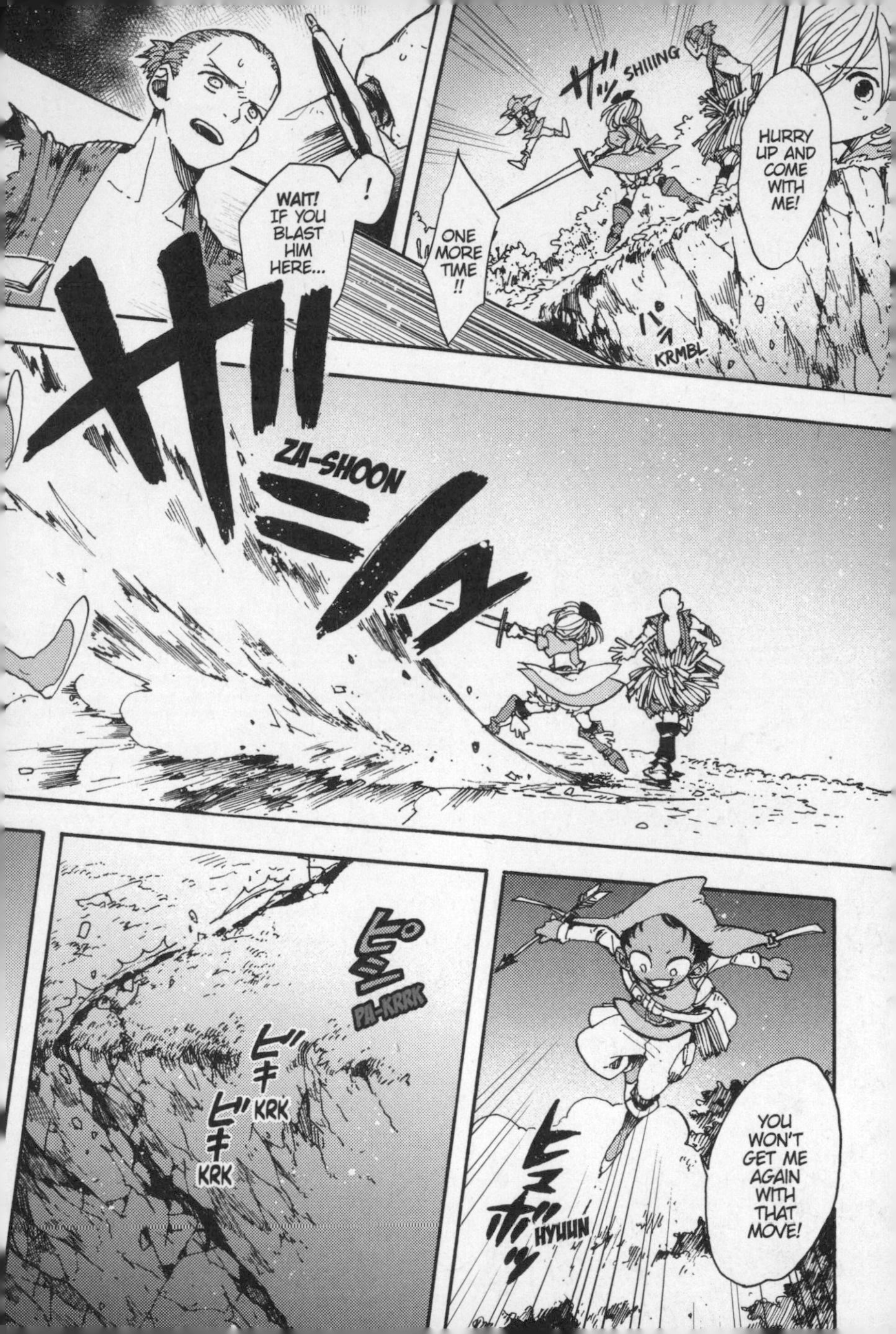

HURRY UP AND COME WITH ME!
SHIIING
ONE MORE TIME!!
KRMBL
!
WAIT! IF YOU BLAST HIM HERE...
ZA-SHOON
YOU WON'T GET ME AGAIN WITH THAT MOVE!
HYUUN
PA-KRRK
KRK
KRK

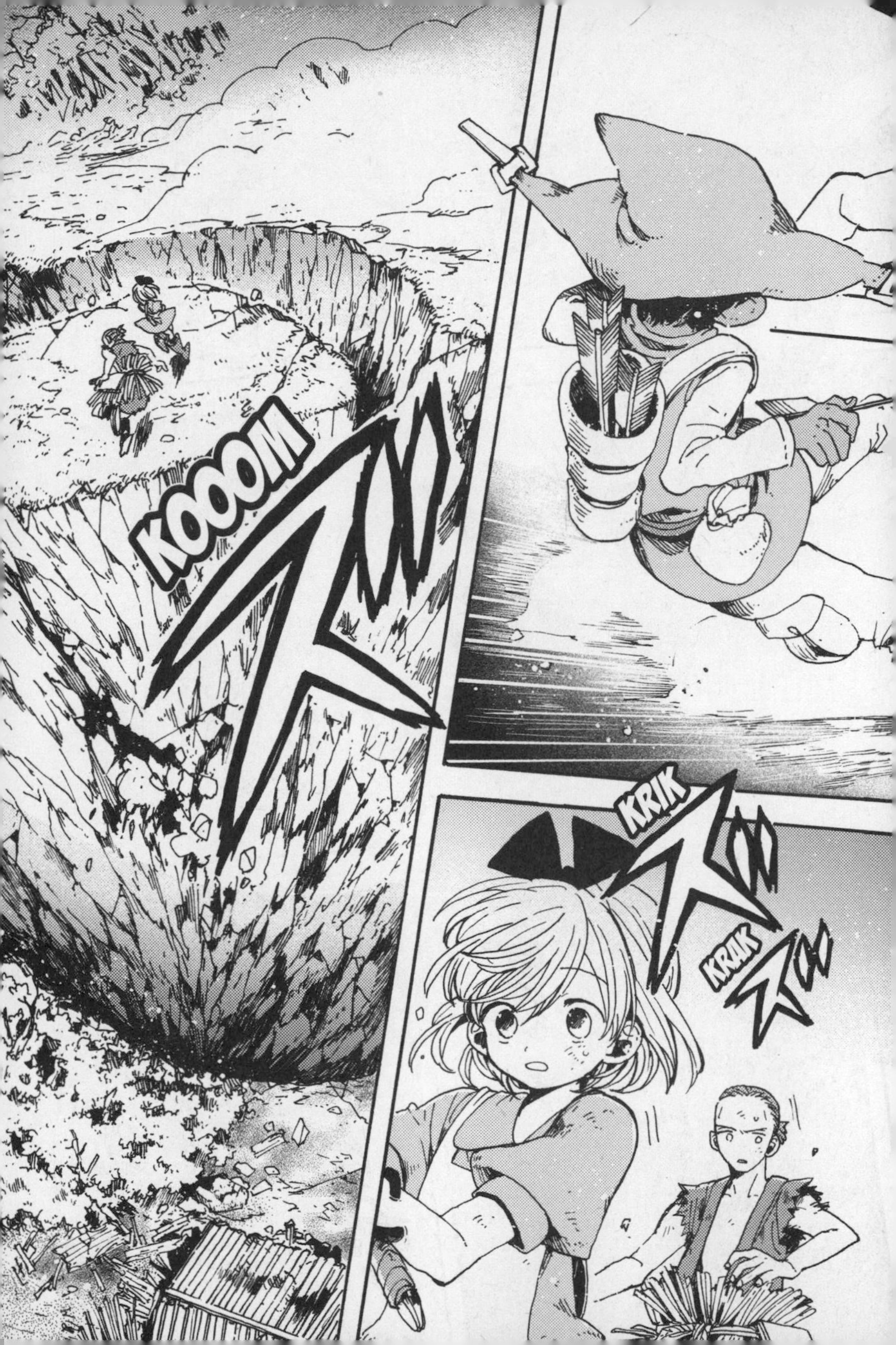
KRIK
KRAK
KOOOM

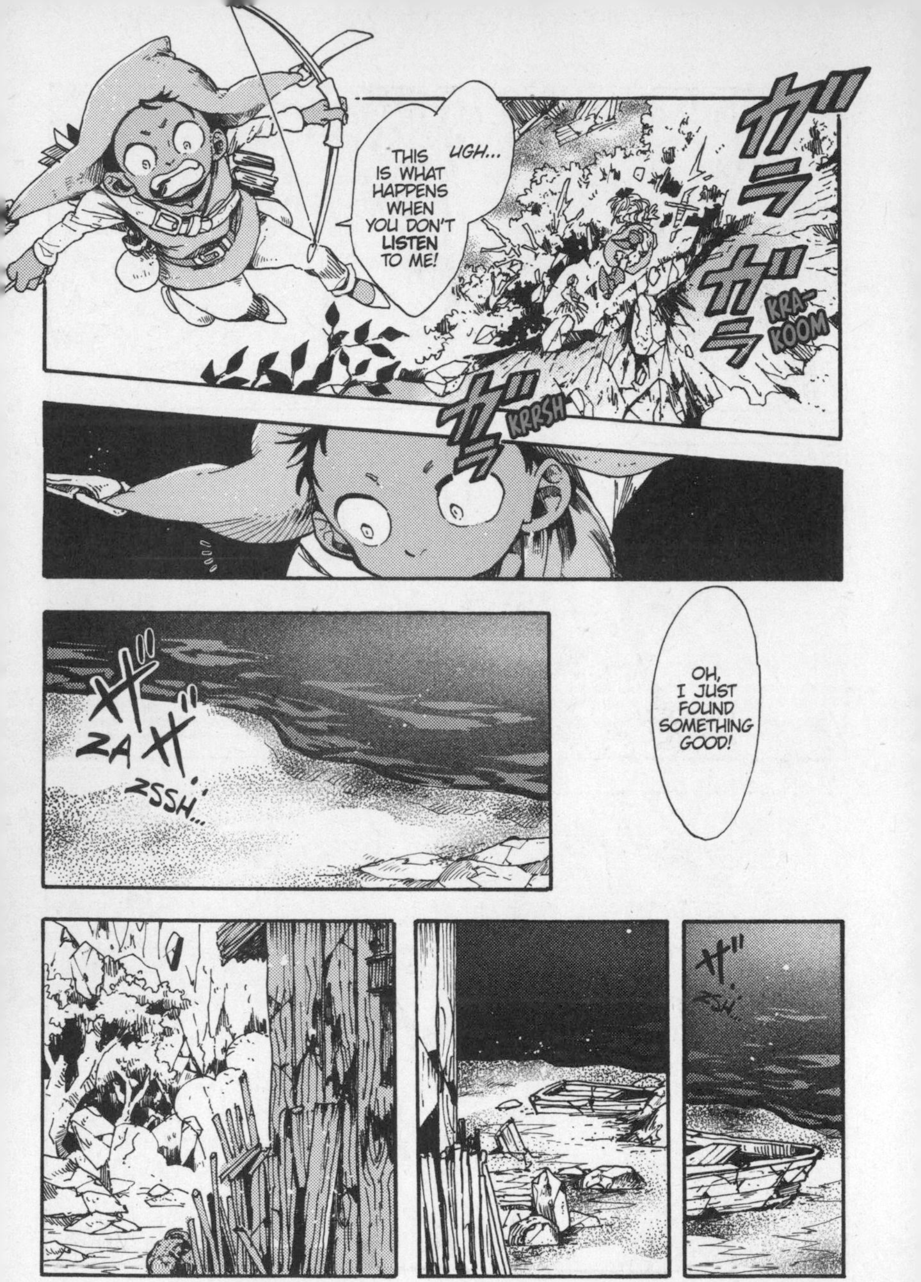
ガラ
ガラ
KRA-KOOM
UGH... THIS IS WHAT HAPPENS WHEN YOU DON'T LISTEN TO ME!
ガ
KRRSH
OH, I JUST FOUND SOMETHING GOOD!
ザザ
ZA
ZSSH...
ザ
ZSH...

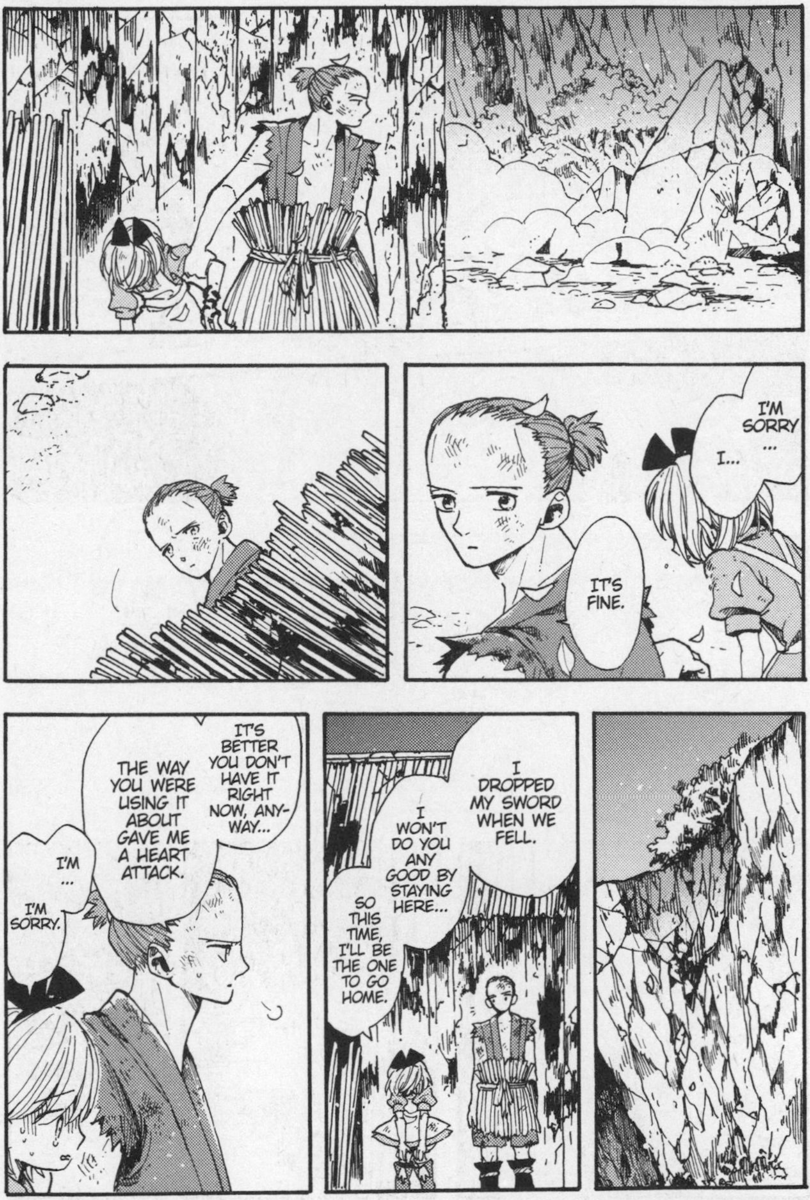
I'M SORRY ... I...
IT'S FINE.
I DROPPED MY SWORD WHEN WE FELL.
I WON'T DO YOU ANY GOOD BY STAYING HERE...
SO THIS TIME, I'LL BE THE ONE TO GO HOME.
IT'S BETTER YOU DON'T HAVE IT RIGHT NOW, ANY-WAY...
THE WAY YOU WERE USING IT ABOUT GAVE ME A HEART ATTACK.
I'M ... I'M SORRY.

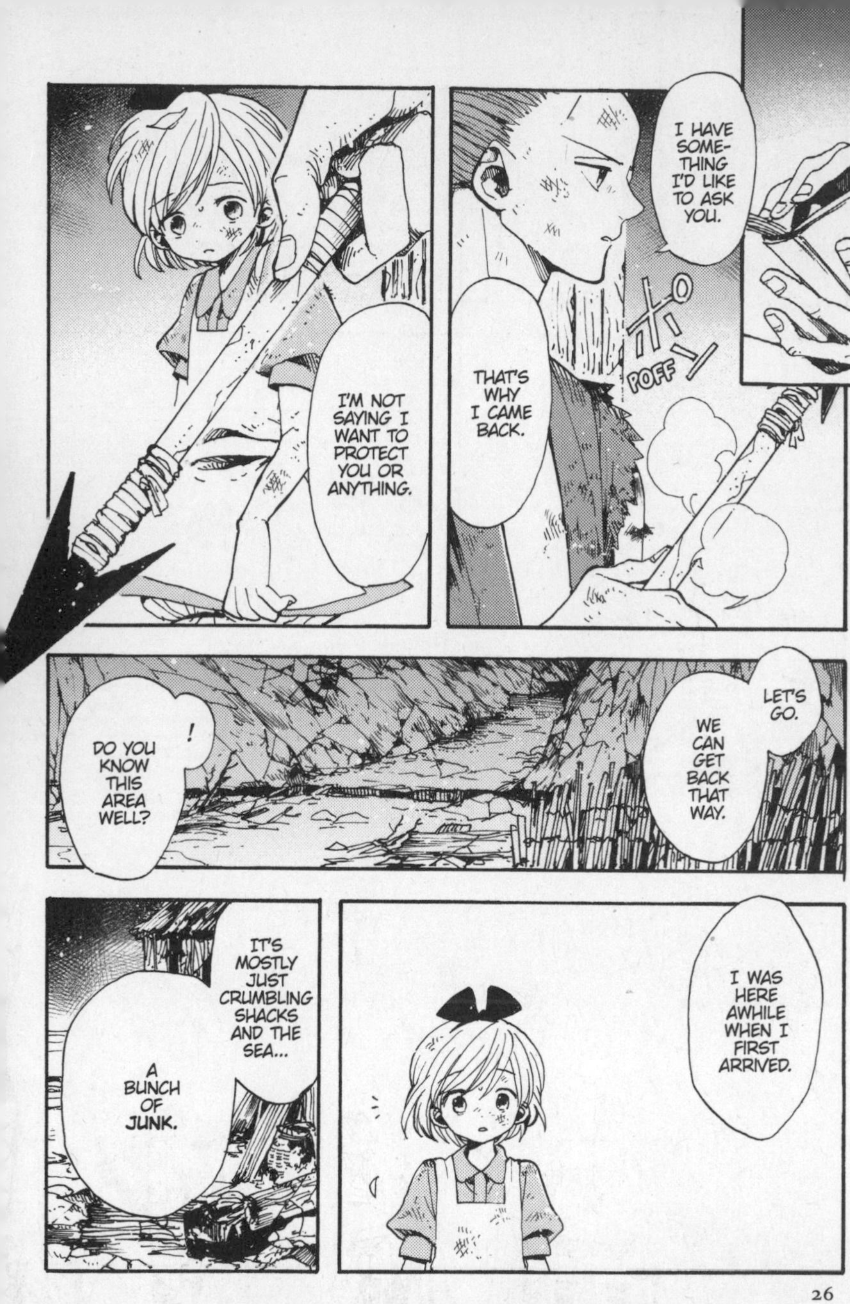
I HAVE SOMETHING I'D LIKE TO ASK YOU.
POFF
THAT'S WHY I CAME BACK.
I'M NOT SAYING I WANT TO PROTECT YOU OR ANYTHING.
LET'S GO.
WE CAN GET BACK THAT WAY.
!
DO YOU KNOW THIS AREA WELL?
I WAS HERE AWHILE WHEN I FIRST ARRIVED.
IT'S MOSTLY JUST CRUMBLING SHACKS AND THE SEA...
A BUNCH OF JUNK.

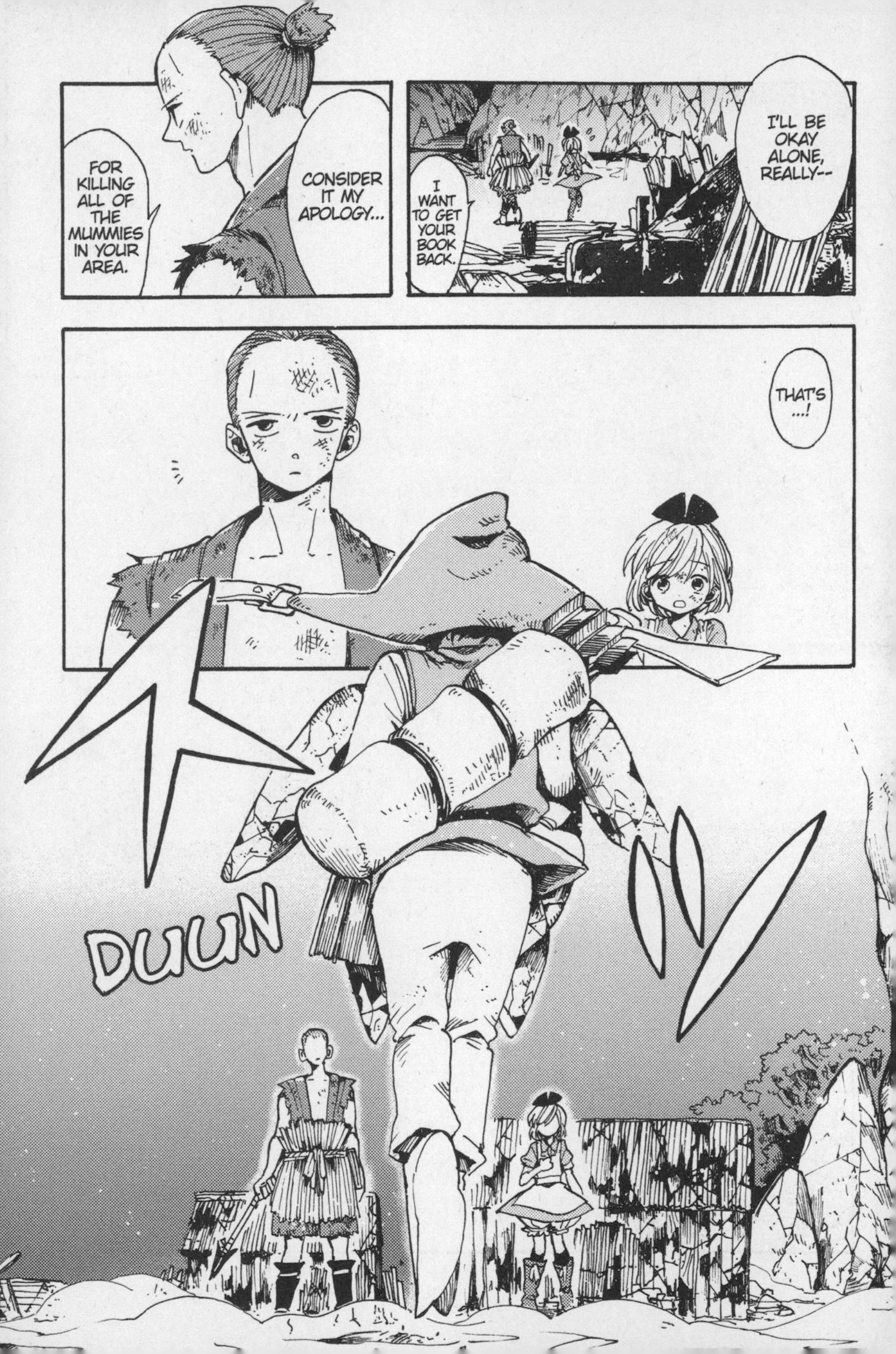
I'LL BE OKAY ALONE, REALLY--
I WANT TO GET YOUR BOOK BACK.
CONSIDER IT MY APOLOGY...
FOR KILLING ALL OF THE MUMMIES IN YOUR AREA.
THAT'S ...!
DUUN

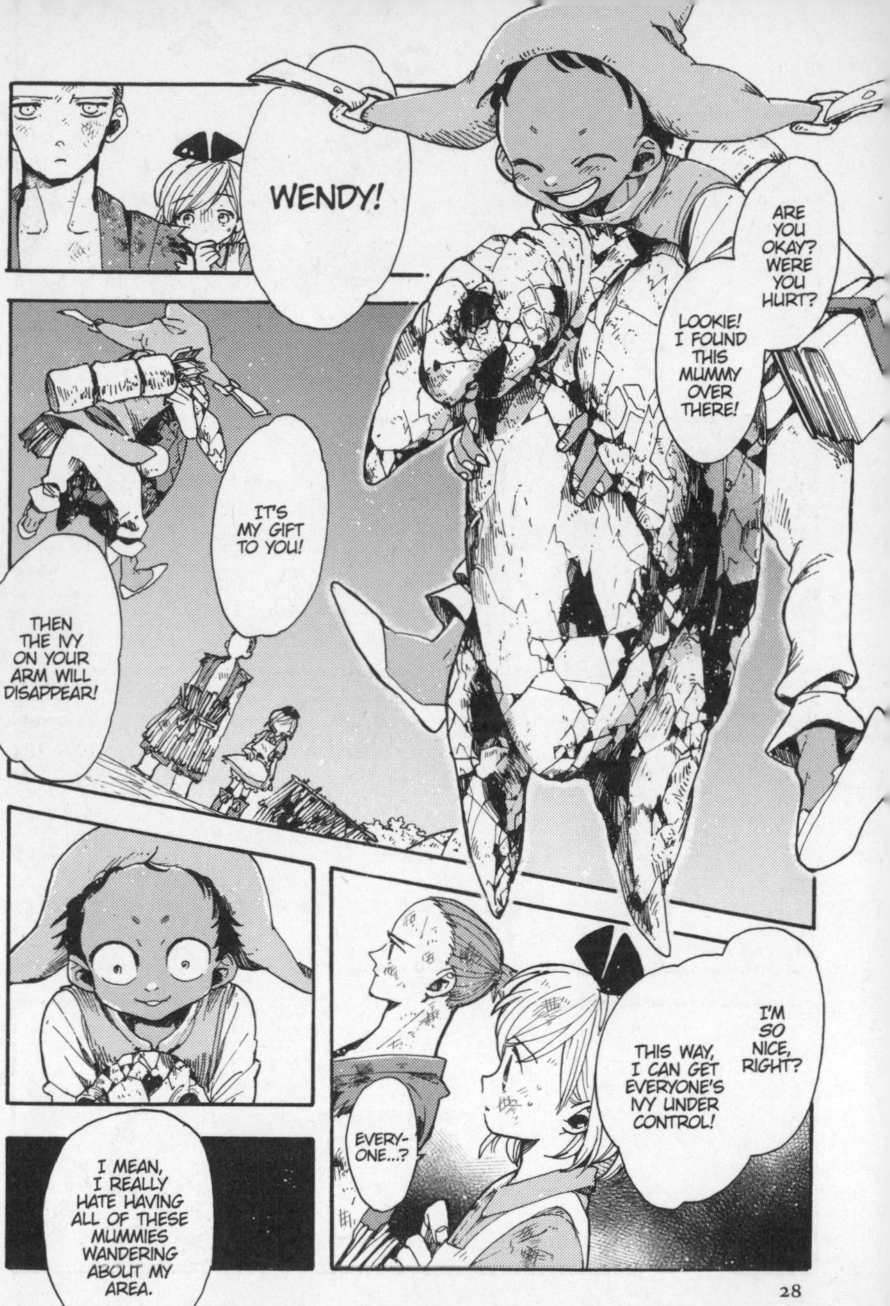
WENDY!
ARE YOU OKAY? WERE YOU HURT?
LOOKIE! I FOUND THIS MUMMY OVER THERE!
IT'S MY GIFT TO YOU!
THEN THE IVY ON YOUR ARM WILL DISAPPEAR!
I'M SO NICE, RIGHT?
THIS WAY, I CAN GET EVERYONE'S IVY UNDER CONTROL!
EVERY-ONE...?
I MEAN, I REALLY HATE HAVING ALL OF THESE MUMMIES WANDERING ABOUT MY AREA.

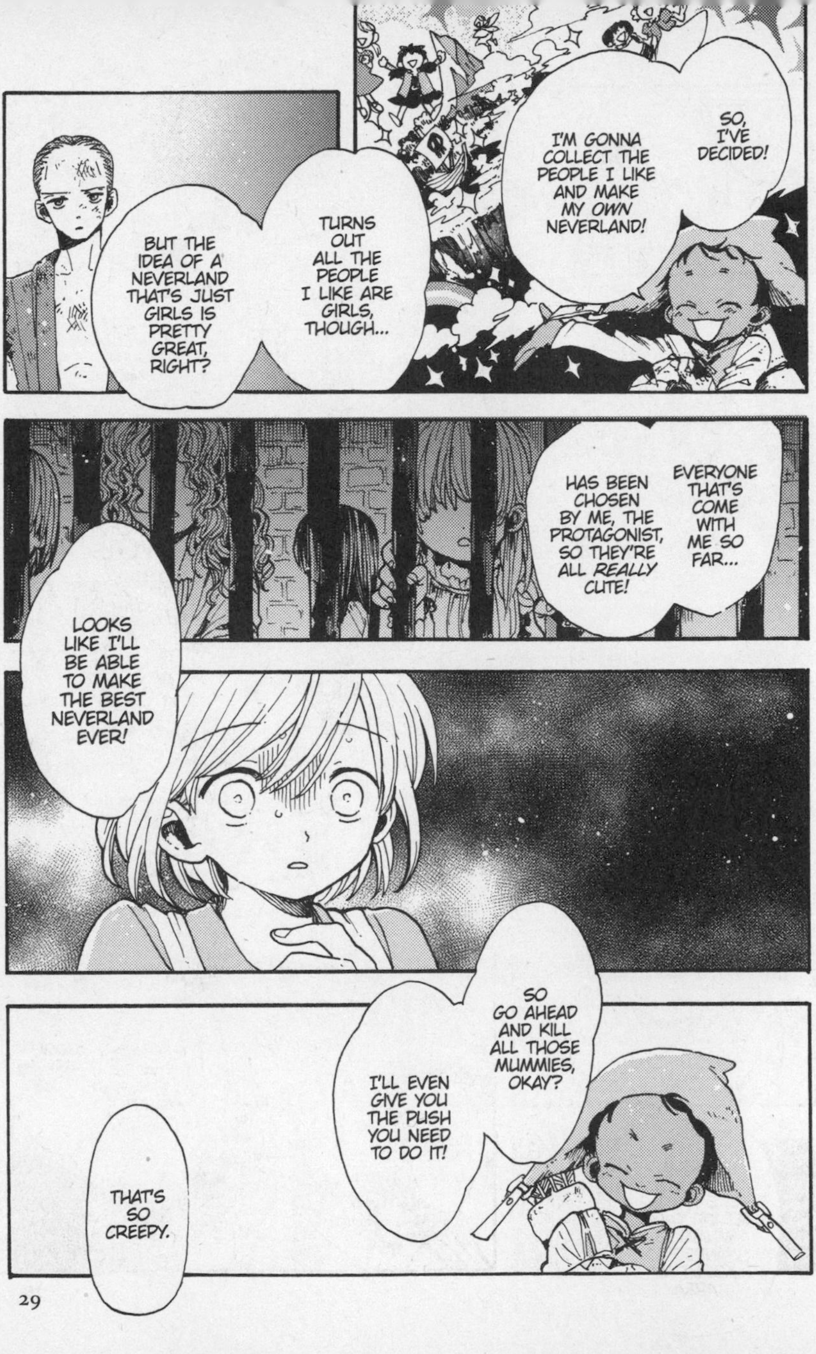
SO, I'VE DECIDED!
I'M GONNA COLLECT THE PEOPLE I LIKE AND MAKE MY *OWN* NEVERLAND!
TURNS OUT ALL THE PEOPLE I LIKE ARE GIRLS, THOUGH...
BUT THE IDEA OF A NEVERLAND THAT'S JUST GIRLS IS PRETTY GREAT, RIGHT?
EVERYONE THAT'S COME WITH ME SO FAR...
HAS BEEN CHOSEN BY ME, THE PROTAGONIST, SO THEY'RE ALL *REALLY* CUTE!
LOOKS LIKE I'LL BE ABLE TO MAKE THE BEST NEVERLAND EVER!
SO GO AHEAD AND KILL ALL THOSE MUMMIES, OKAY?
I'LL EVEN GIVE YOU THE PUSH YOU NEED TO DO IT!
THAT'S SO CREEPY.

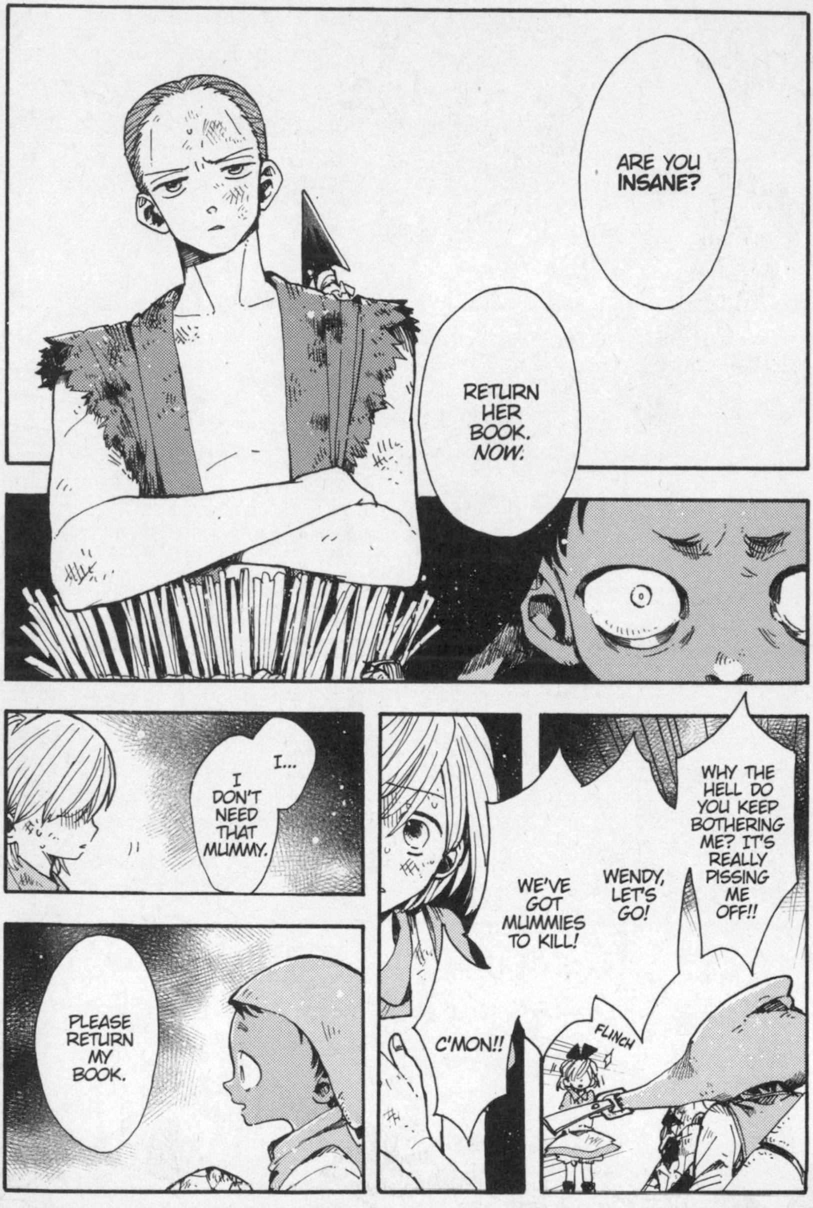
ARE YOU INSANE?
RETURN HER BOOK. NOW.
WHY THE HELL DO YOU KEEP BOTHERING ME? IT'S REALLY PISSING ME OFF!!
WENDY, LET'S GO!
WE'VE GOT MUMMIES TO KILL!
FLINCH
C'MON!!
I... I DON'T NEED THAT MUMMY.
PLEASE RETURN MY BOOK.

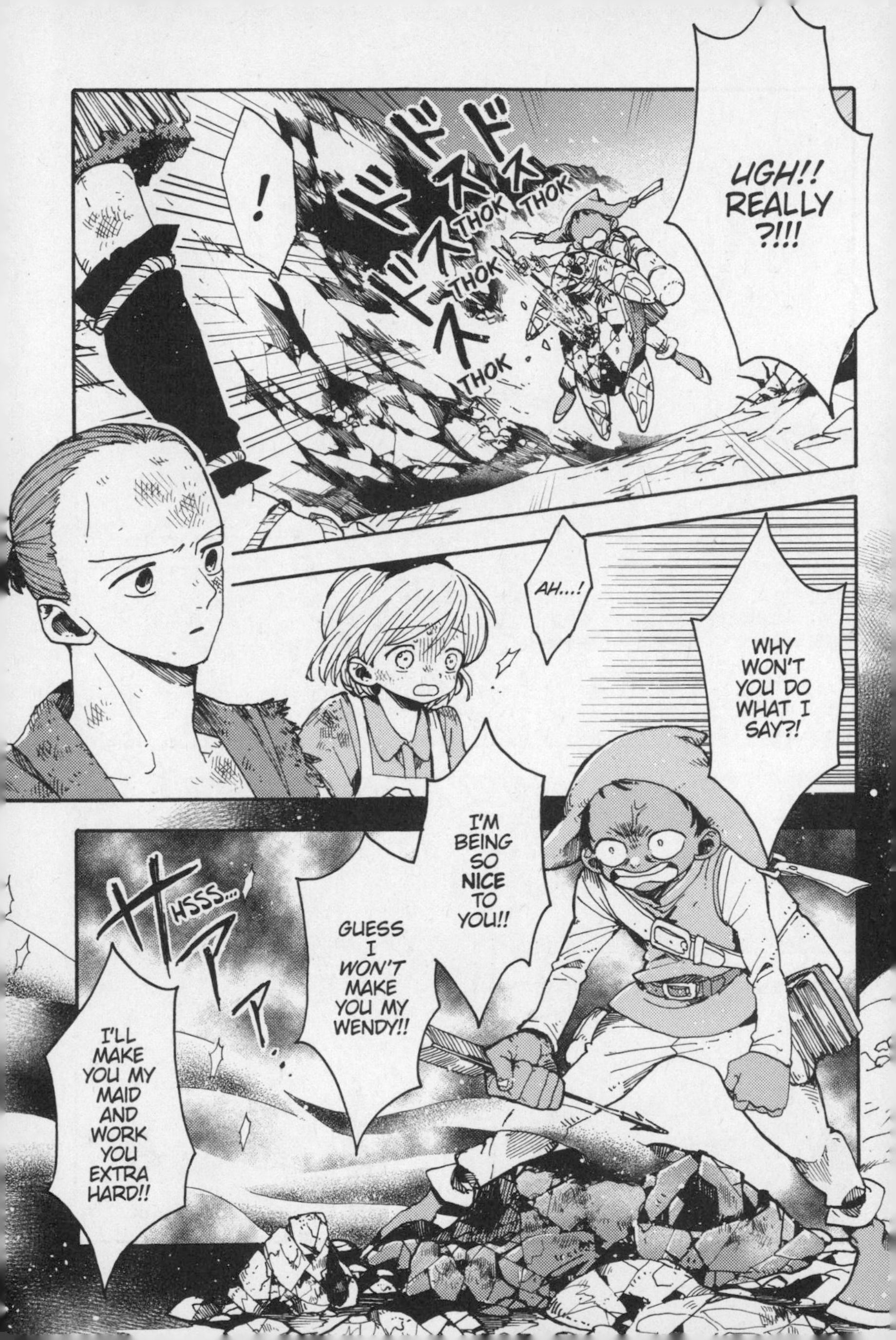
UGH!! REALLY ?!!!
!
THOK THOK THOK THOK
AH...!
WHY WON'T YOU DO WHAT I SAY?!
I'M BEING SO NICE TO YOU!!
GUESS I WON'T MAKE YOU MY WENDY!!
HSSS...
I'LL MAKE YOU MY MAID AND WORK YOU EXTRA HARD!!

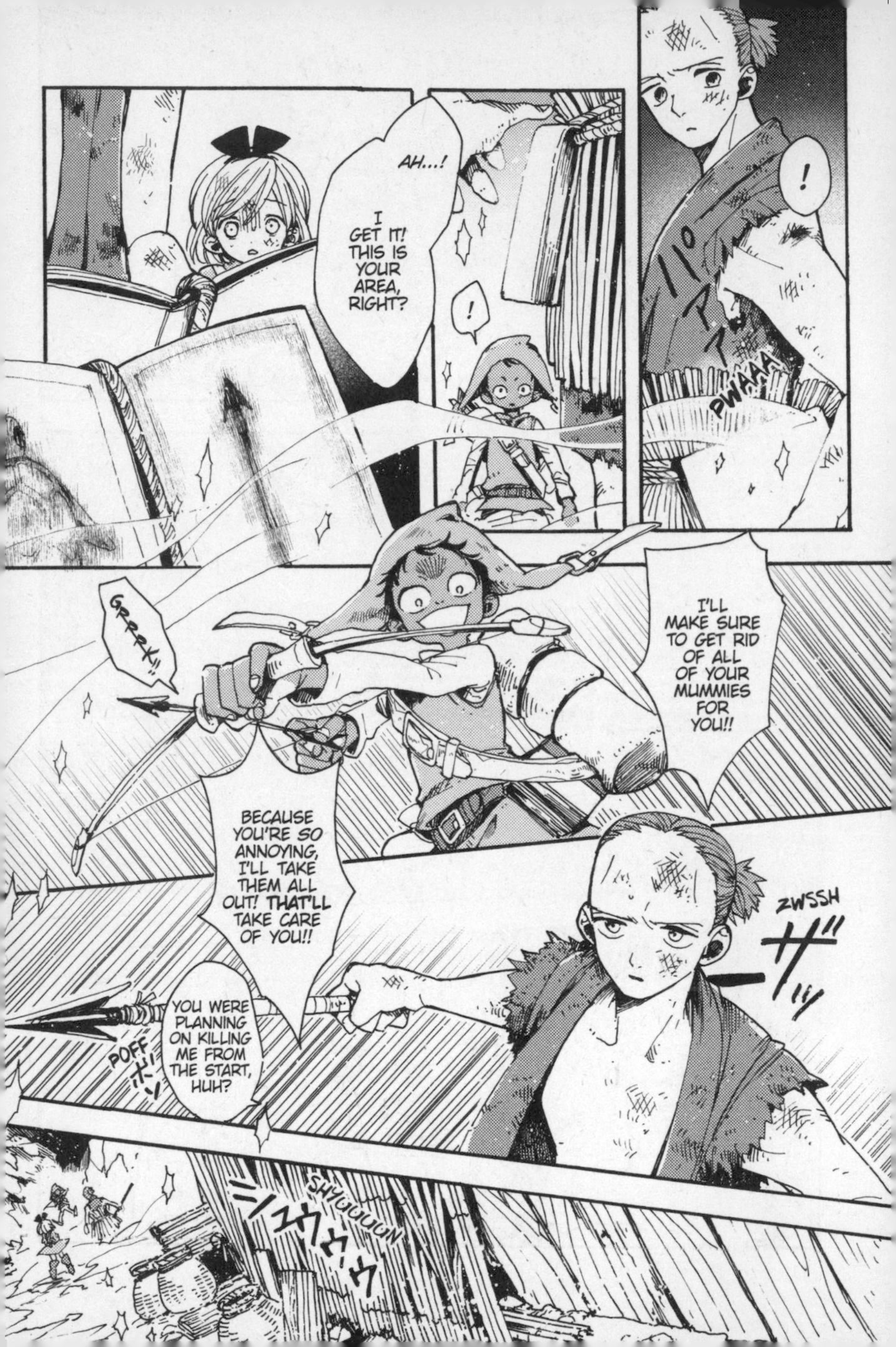
!
PWAAA
!
AH...! I GET IT! THIS IS YOUR AREA, RIGHT?
I'LL MAKE SURE TO GET RID OF ALL OF YOUR MUMMIES FOR YOU!!
GRRRK!!
BECAUSE YOU'RE SO ANNOYING, I'LL TAKE THEM ALL OUT! THAT'LL TAKE CARE OF YOU!!
ZWSSH
YOU WERE PLANNING ON KILLING ME FROM THE START, HUH?
POFF
SHYUUUUN

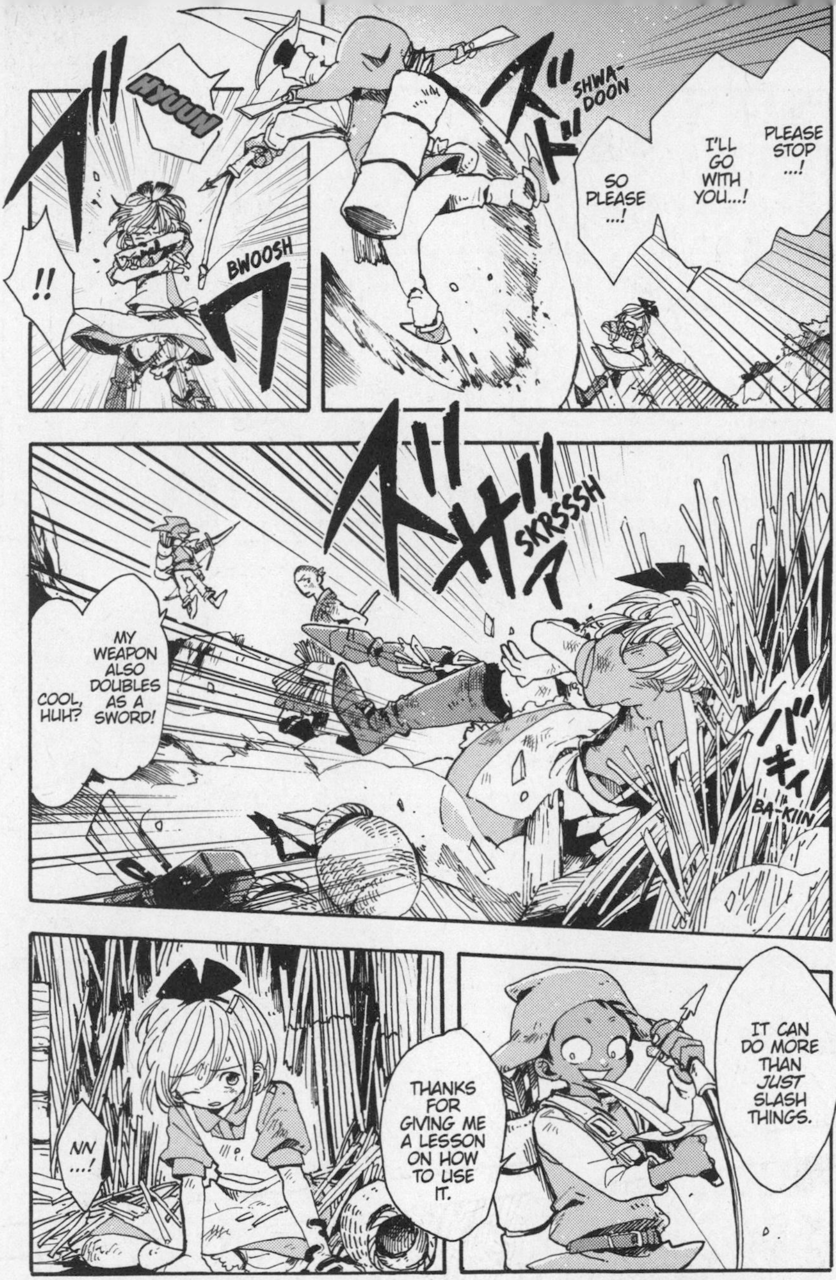
SHWA-DOON
PLEASE STOP ...!
I'LL GO WITH YOU...!
SO PLEASE ...!
HYUUN
BWOOSH
!!
SKRSSSH
BA-KIIN
MY WEAPON ALSO DOUBLES AS A SWORD!
COOL, HUH?
IT CAN DO MORE THAN JUST SLASH THINGS.
THANKS FOR GIVING ME A LESSON ON HOW TO USE IT.
NN ...!

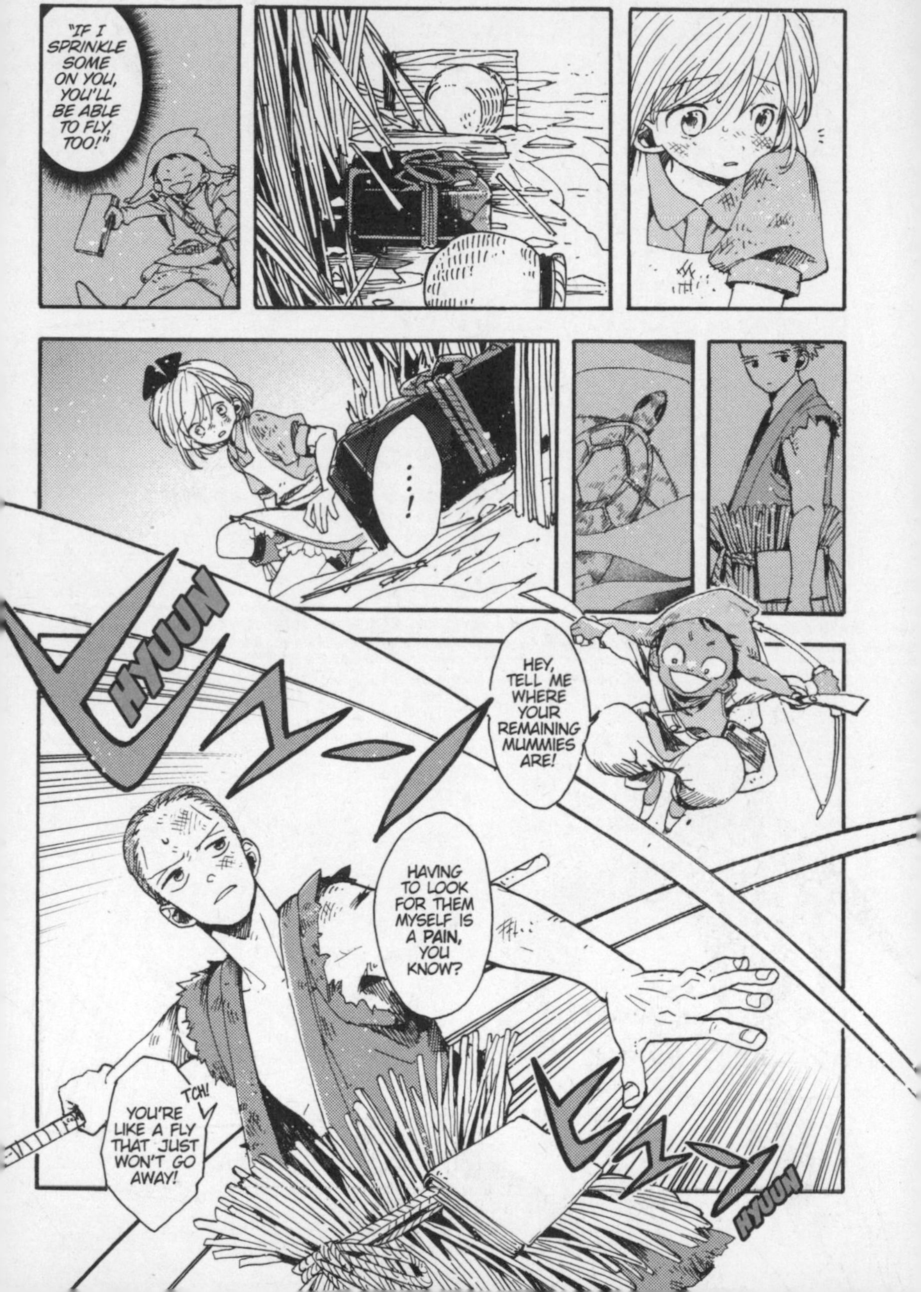
"IF I SPRINKLE SOME ON YOU, YOU'LL BE ABLE TO FLY, TOO!"
...!
HEY, TELL ME WHERE YOUR REMAINING MUMMIES ARE!
HYUUN
HAVING TO LOOK FOR THEM MYSELF IS A PAIN, YOU KNOW?
HYUUN
TCH!
YOU'RE LIKE A FLY THAT JUST WON'T GO AWAY!

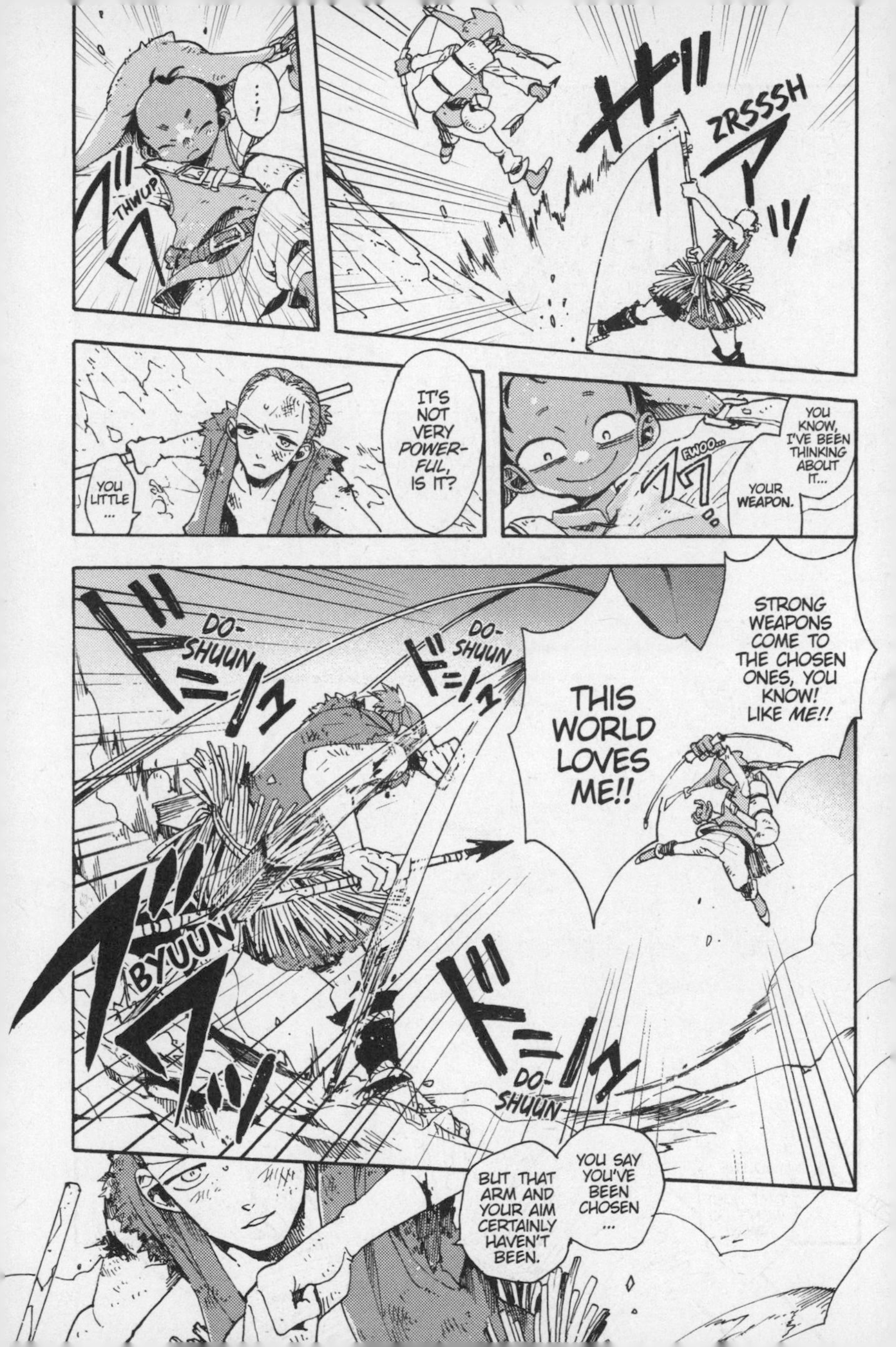
ZRSSSH
THWUP
...!
YOU KNOW, I'VE BEEN THINKING ABOUT IT...
YOUR WEAPON.
FWOO...
IT'S NOT VERY POWERFUL, IS IT?
YOU LITTLE ...
STRONG WEAPONS COME TO THE CHOSEN ONES, YOU KNOW! LIKE ME!!
THIS WORLD LOVES ME!!
DO-SHUUN
DO-SHUUN
BYUUN
DO-SHUUN
YOU SAY YOU'VE BEEN CHOSEN ...
BUT THAT ARM AND YOUR AIM CERTAINLY HAVEN'T BEEN.

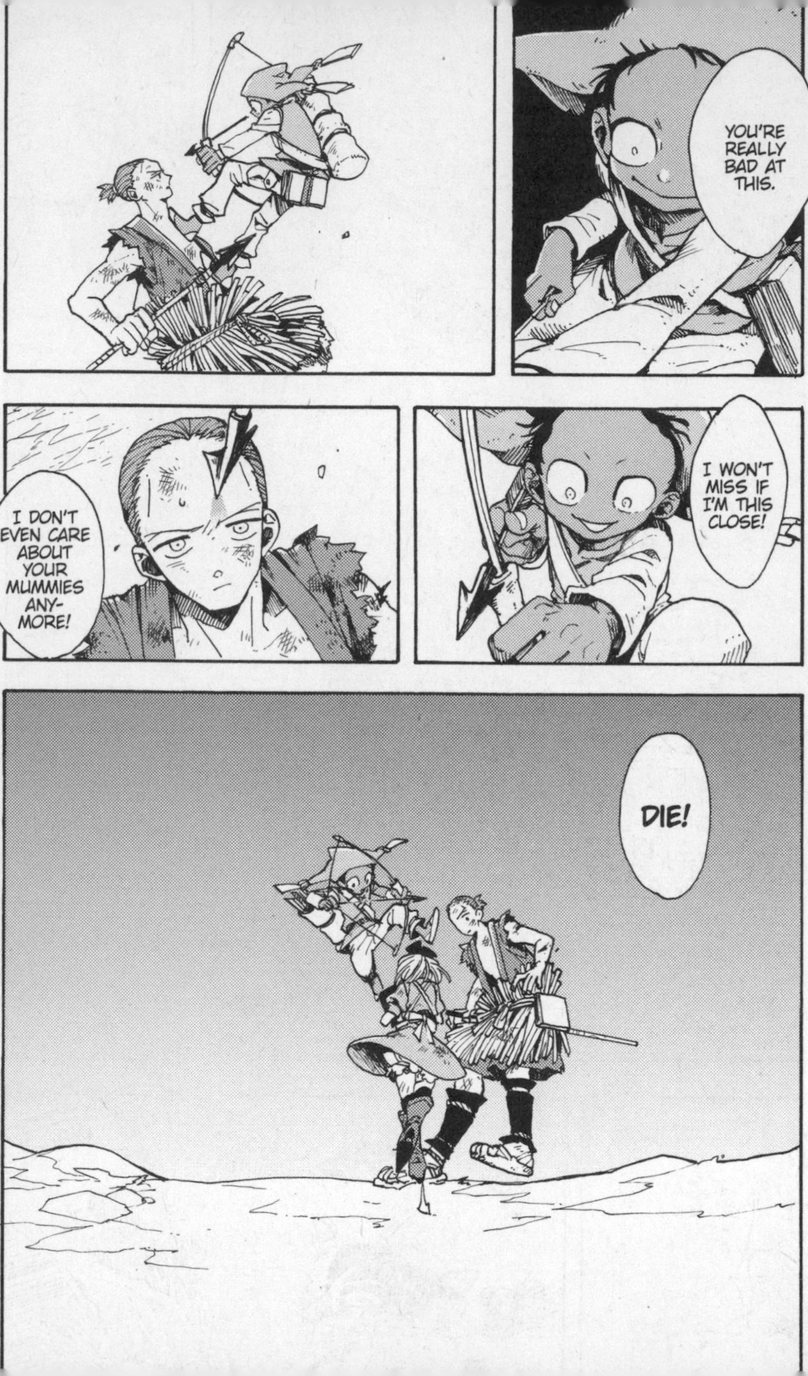
YOU'RE REALLY BAD AT THIS.
I WON'T MISS IF I'M THIS CLOSE!
I DON'T EVEN CARE ABOUT YOUR MUMMIES ANY-MORE!
DIE!

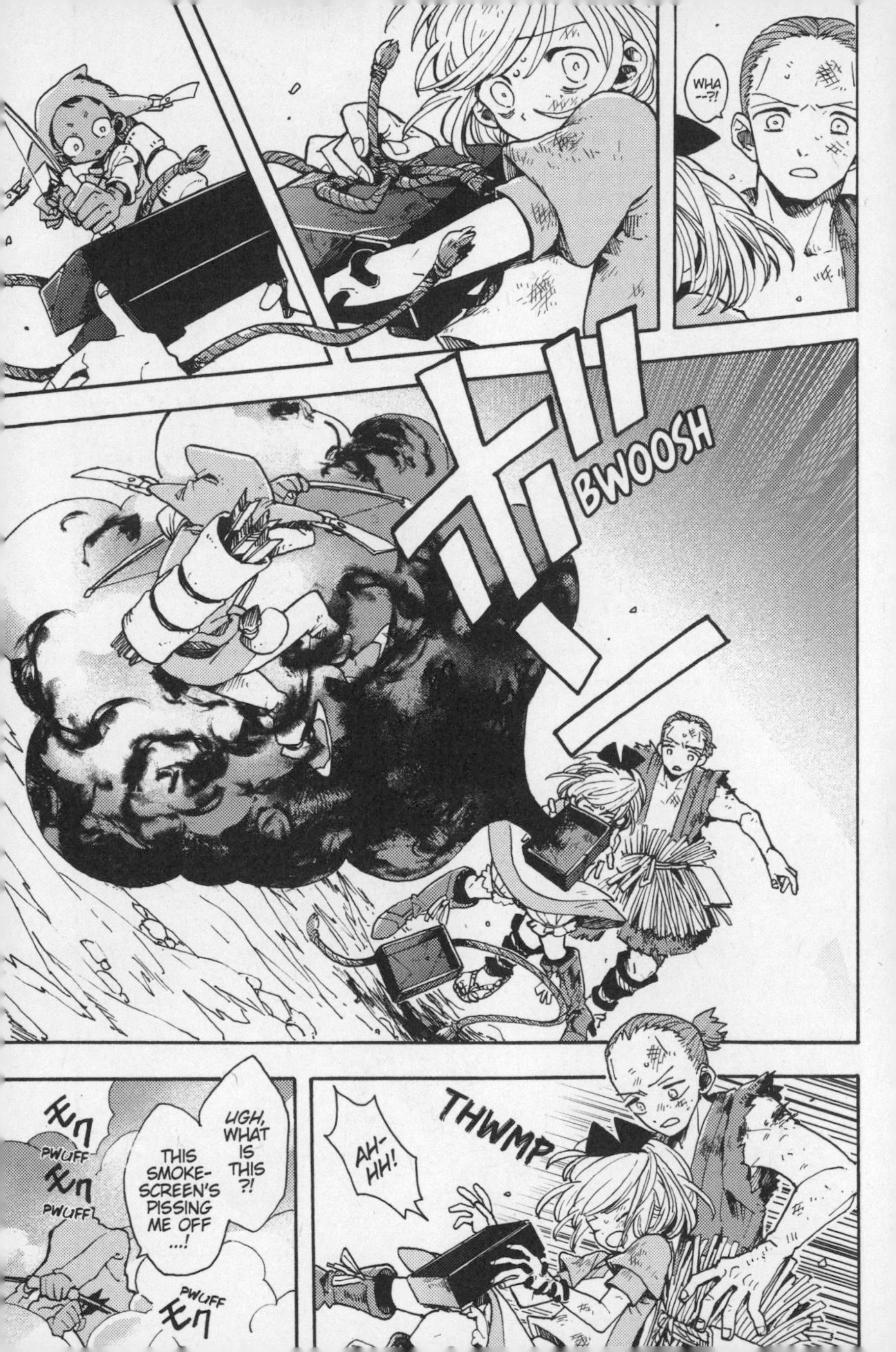
WHA--?!
BWOOSH
THWMP
AH-HH!
UGH, WHAT IS THIS?!
THIS SMOKE-SCREEN'S PISSING ME OFF...!
モク
PWUFF
モク
PWUFF
PWUFF
モク

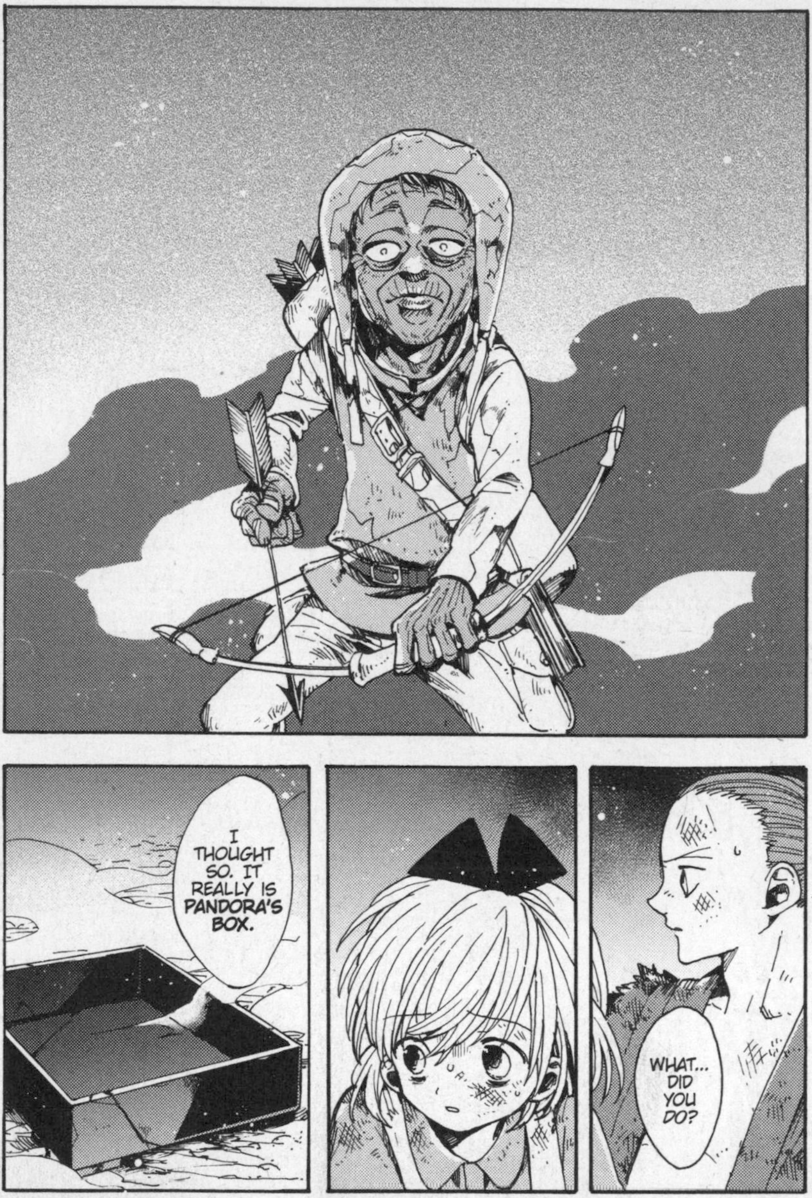
WHAT... DID YOU DO?
I THOUGHT SO. IT REALLY IS PANDORA'S BOX.

FAIRY
TALE
BATTLE
ROYALE

FAIRY
TALE
BATTLE
ROYALE

Chapter 10: Cage

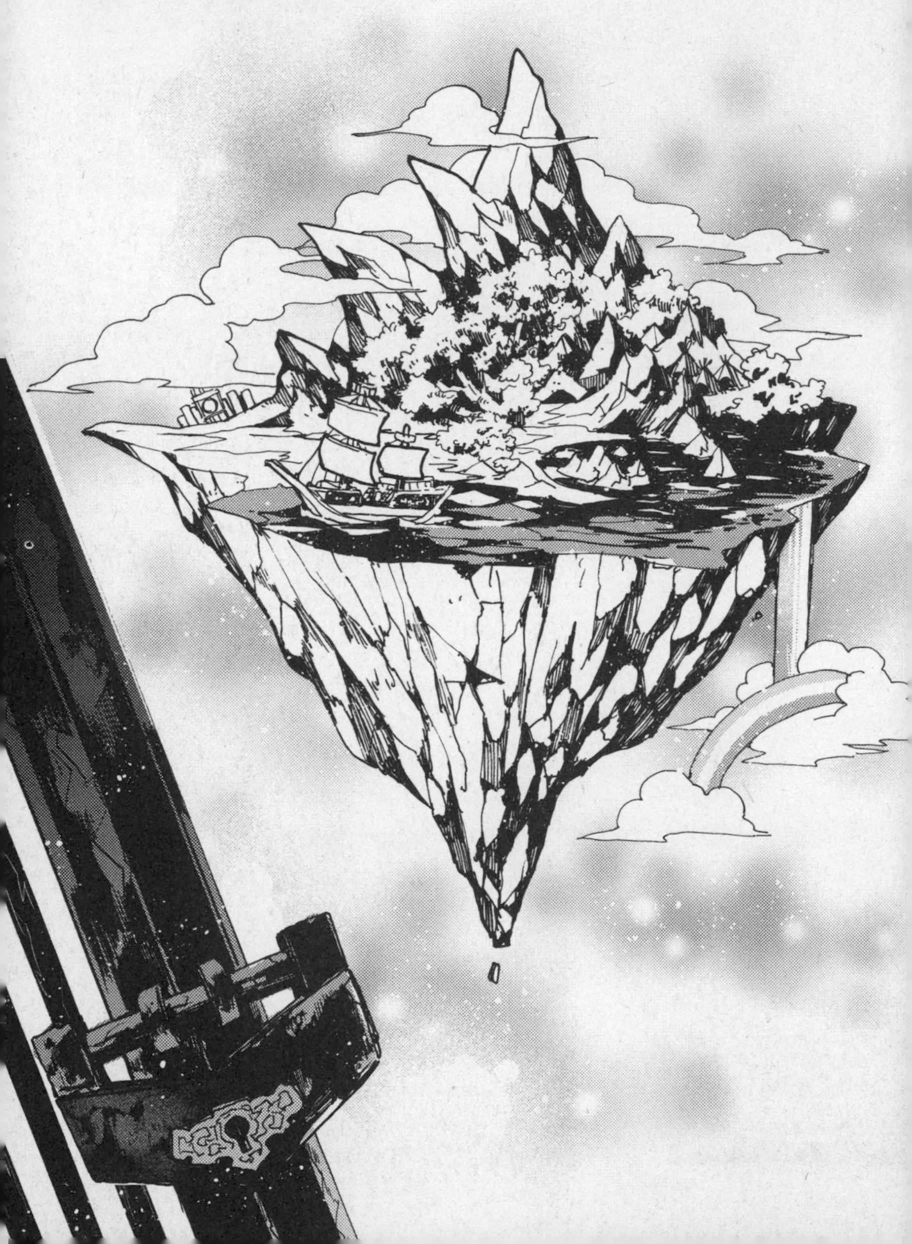

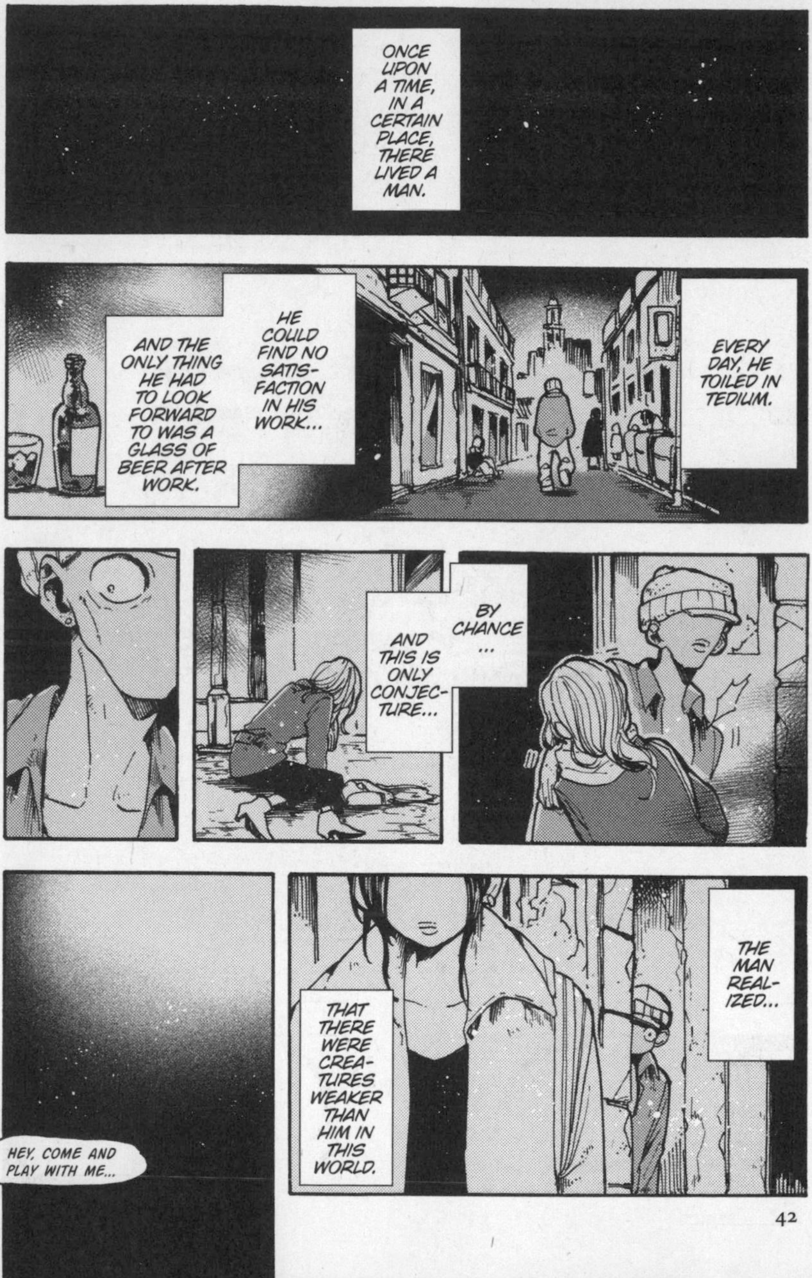
ONCE UPON A TIME, IN A CERTAIN PLACE, THERE LIVED A MAN.
EVERY DAY, HE TOILED IN TEDIUM.
HE COULD FIND NO SATIS-FACTION IN HIS WORK...
AND THE ONLY THING HE HAD TO LOOK FORWARD TO WAS A GLASS OF BEER AFTER WORK.
BY CHANCE ...
AND THIS IS ONLY CONJEC-TURE...
THE MAN REAL-IZED...
THAT THERE WERE CREA-TURES WEAKER THAN HIM IN THIS WORLD.
HEY, COME AND PLAY WITH ME...

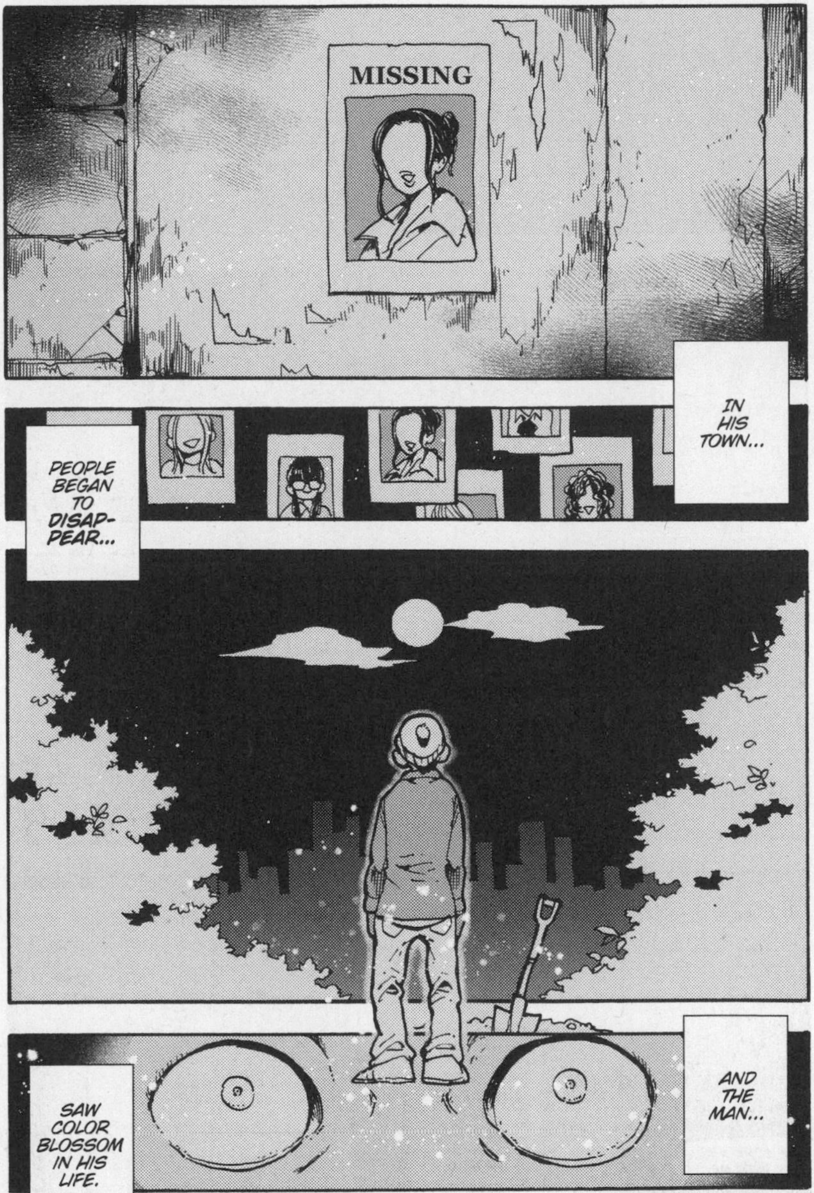
MISSING
IN HIS TOWN...
PEOPLE BEGAN TO DISAP-PEAR...
AND THE MAN...
SAW COLOR BLOSSOM IN HIS LIFE.

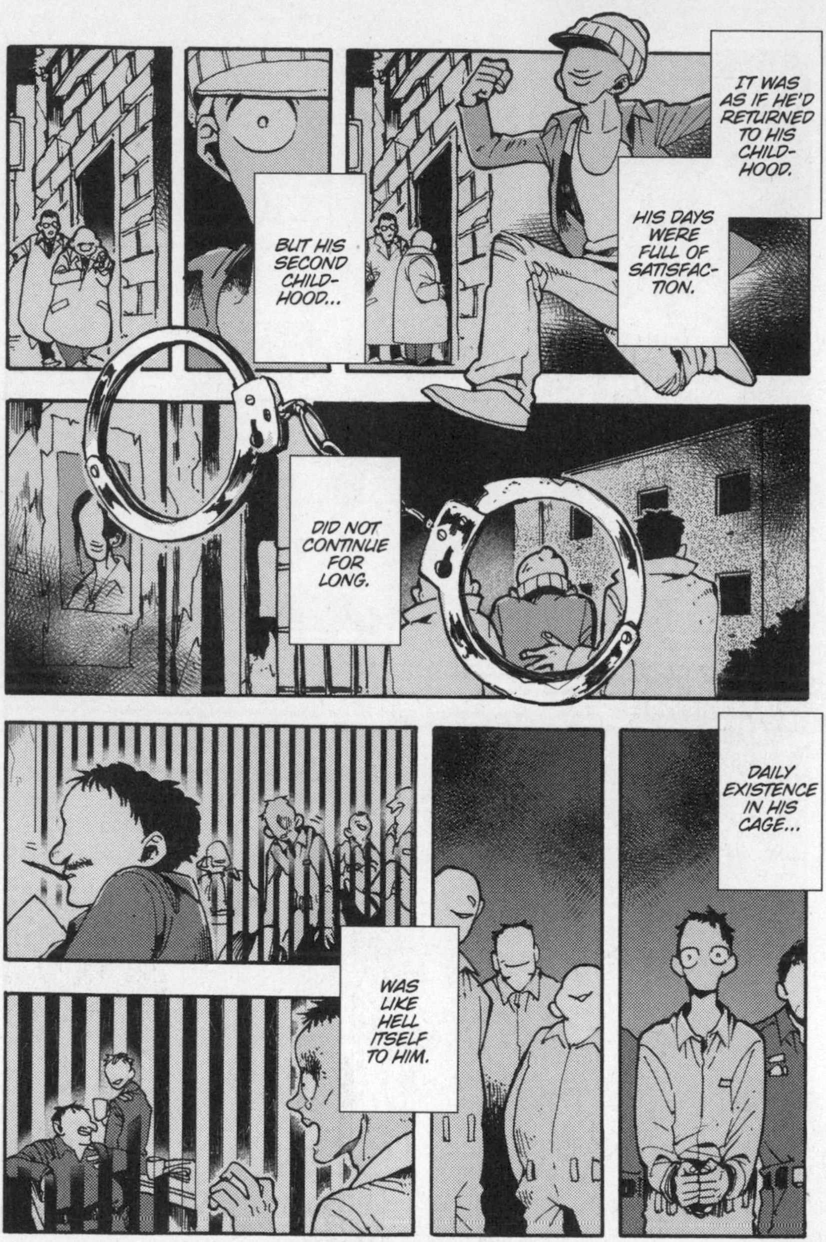
IT WAS AS IF HE'D RETURNED TO HIS CHILD-HOOD.
HIS DAYS WERE FULL OF SATISFAC-TION.
BUT HIS SECOND CHILD-HOOD...
DID NOT CONTINUE FOR LONG.
DAILY EXISTENCE IN HIS CAGE...
WAS LIKE HELL ITSELF TO HIM.

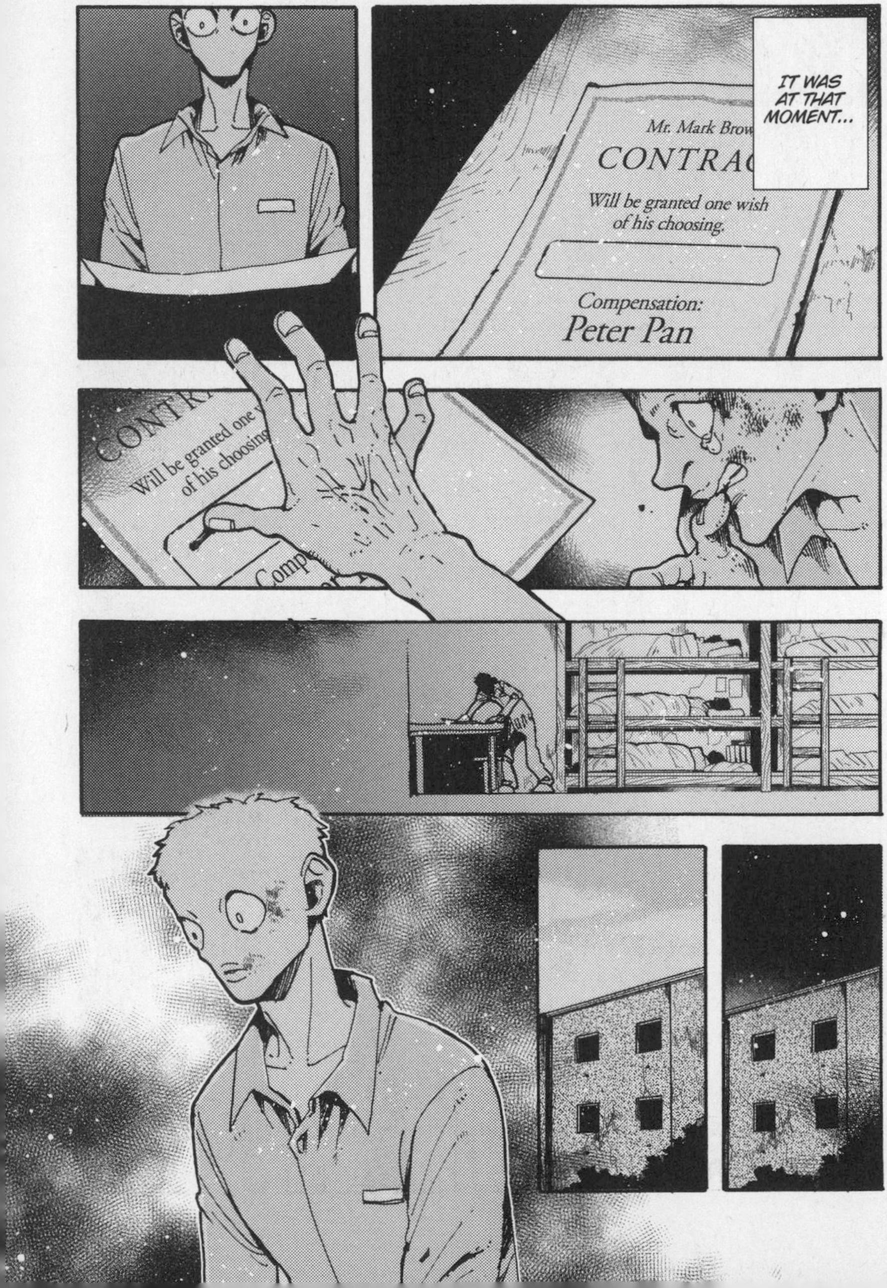
IT WAS AT THAT MOMENT...
Mr. Mark Brow
CONTRAC
Will be granted one wish of his choosing.
Compensation:
Peter Pan
CONTR
Will be granted one
of his choosing
Comp

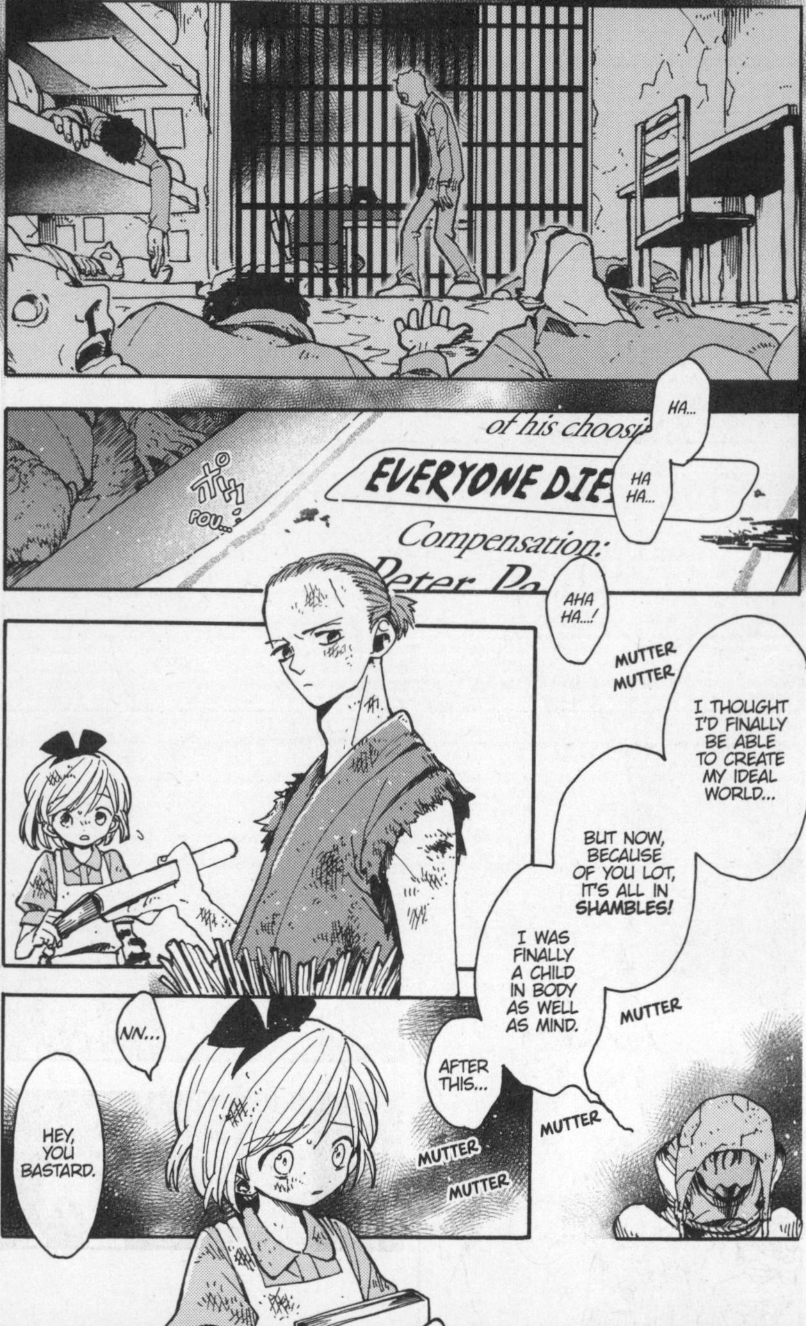

HA...
HA HA...
AHA HA...!
EVERYONE DIE
Compensation:
ポゥ
POU...
MUTTER MUTTER
I THOUGHT I'D FINALLY BE ABLE TO CREATE MY IDEAL WORLD...
BUT NOW, BECAUSE OF YOU LOT, IT'S ALL IN SHAMBLES!
I WAS FINALLY A CHILD IN BODY AS WELL AS MIND.
MUTTER
AFTER THIS...
MUTTER
MUTTER
MUTTER
NN...
HEY, YOU BASTARD.

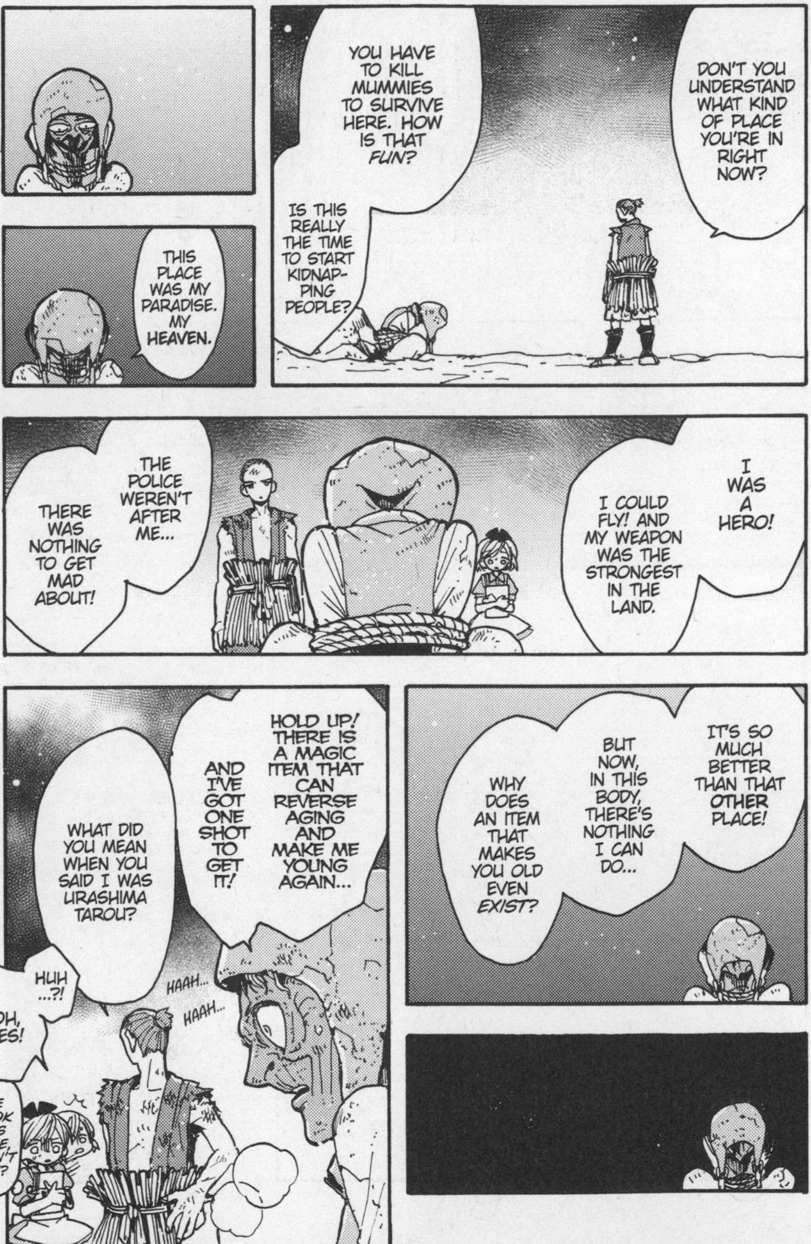
DON'T YOU UNDERSTAND WHAT KIND OF PLACE YOU'RE IN RIGHT NOW?
YOU HAVE TO KILL MUMMIES TO SURVIVE HERE. HOW IS THAT *FUN?*
IS THIS REALLY THE TIME TO START KIDNAP-PING PEOPLE?
THIS PLACE WAS MY PARADISE. MY HEAVEN.
I WAS A HERO!
I COULD FLY! AND MY WEAPON WAS THE STRONGEST IN THE LAND.
THE POLICE WEREN'T AFTER ME...
THERE WAS NOTHING TO GET MAD ABOUT!
IT'S SO MUCH BETTER THAN THAT OTHER PLACE!
BUT NOW, IN THIS BODY, THERE'S NOTHING I CAN DO...
WHY DOES AN ITEM THAT MAKES YOU OLD EVEN *EXIST?*
HOLD UP! THERE IS A MAGIC ITEM THAT CAN REVERSE AGING AND MAKE ME YOUNG AGAIN...
AND I'VE GOT ONE SHOT TO GET IT!
HAAH...
HAAH...
WHAT DID YOU MEAN WHEN YOU SAID I WAS URASHIMA TAROU?
HUH ...?!
OH, YES!
HE TOOK HIS TIME, DIDN'T HE?

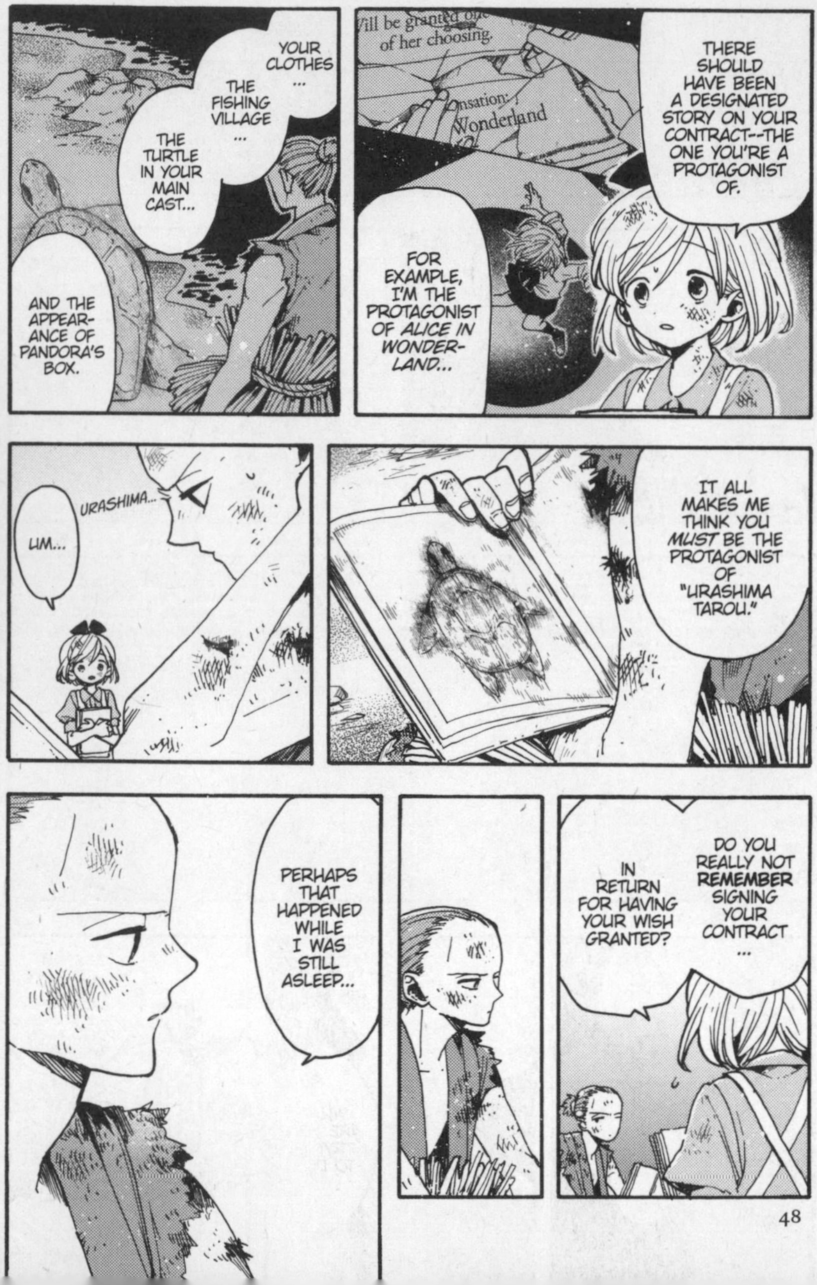

of her choosing.
Wonderland
THERE SHOULD HAVE BEEN A DESIGNATED STORY ON YOUR CONTRACT--THE ONE YOU'RE A PROTAGONIST OF.
FOR EXAMPLE, I'M THE PROTAGONIST OF *ALICE IN WONDERLAND*...
YOUR CLOTHES ...
THE FISHING VILLAGE ...
THE TURTLE IN YOUR MAIN CAST...
AND THE APPEARANCE OF PANDORA'S BOX.
IT ALL MAKES ME THINK YOU *MUST* BE THE PROTAGONIST OF "URASHIMA TAROU."
URASHIMA...
UM...
DO YOU REALLY NOT **REMEMBER** SIGNING YOUR CONTRACT ...
IN RETURN FOR HAVING YOUR WISH GRANTED?
PERHAPS THAT HAPPENED WHILE I WAS STILL ASLEEP...

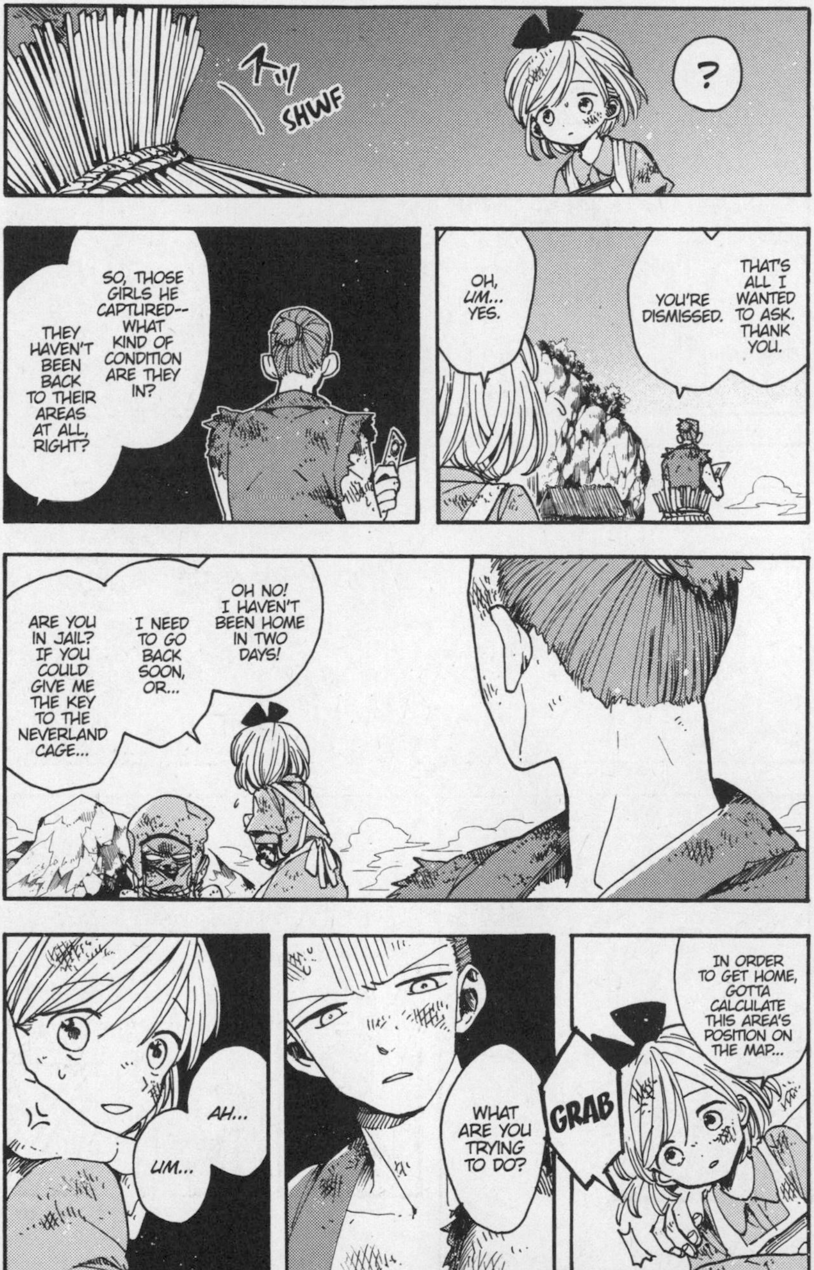
スッ
SHWF
?
THAT'S ALL I WANTED TO ASK. THANK YOU.
YOU'RE DISMISSED.
OH, UM... YES.
SO, THOSE GIRLS HE CAPTURED--WHAT KIND OF CONDITION ARE THEY IN?
THEY HAVEN'T BEEN BACK TO THEIR AREAS AT ALL, RIGHT?
OH NO! I HAVEN'T BEEN HOME IN TWO DAYS!
I NEED TO GO BACK SOON, OR...
ARE YOU IN JAIL? IF YOU COULD GIVE ME THE KEY TO THE NEVERLAND CAGE...
IN ORDER TO GET HOME, GOTTA CALCULATE THIS AREA'S POSITION ON THE MAP...
GRAB
WHAT ARE YOU TRYING TO DO?
AH...
UM...

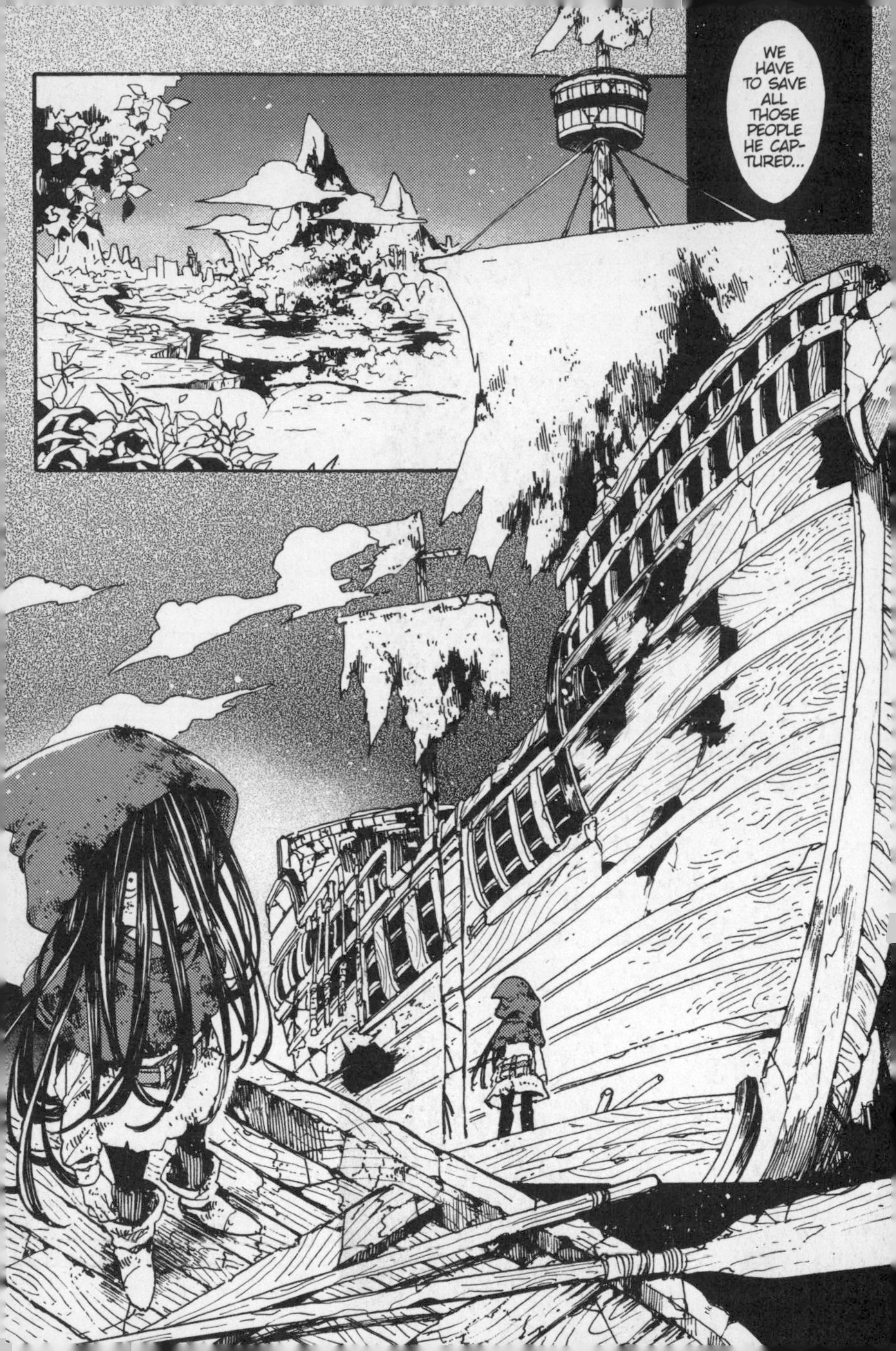
WE HAVE TO SAVE ALL THOSE PEOPLE HE CAP-TURED...

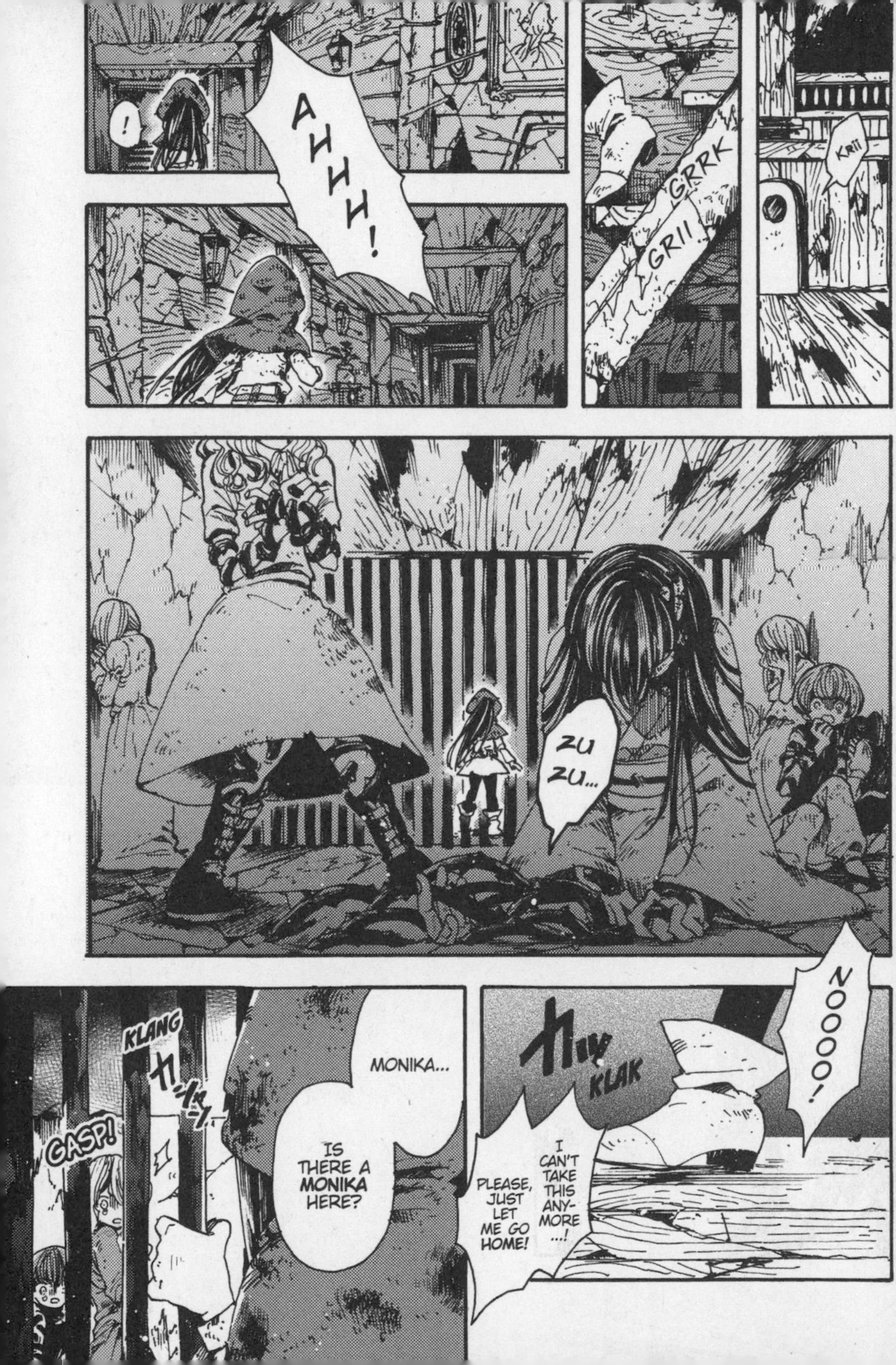
KRII
GRRK
GRII
!
AHHHH!
ZU ZU...
NOOOOO!
KLAK
I CAN'T TAKE THIS ANY-MORE ...!
PLEASE, JUST LET ME GO HOME!
MONIKA...
IS THERE A MONIKA HERE?
KLANG
GASP!

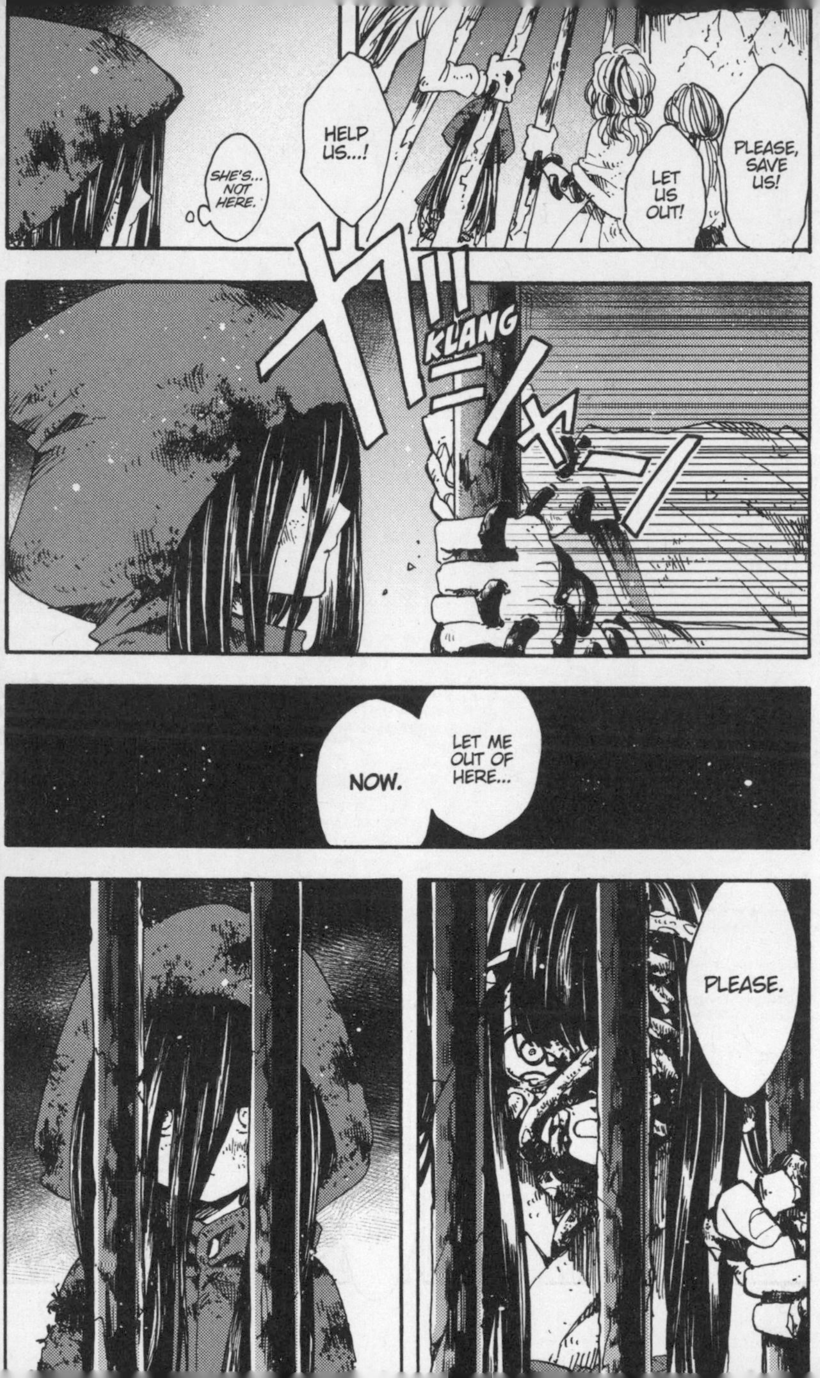
PLEASE, SAVE US!
LET US OUT!
HELP US...!
SHE'S... NOT HERE.
KLANG
LET ME OUT OF HERE...
NOW.
PLEASE.

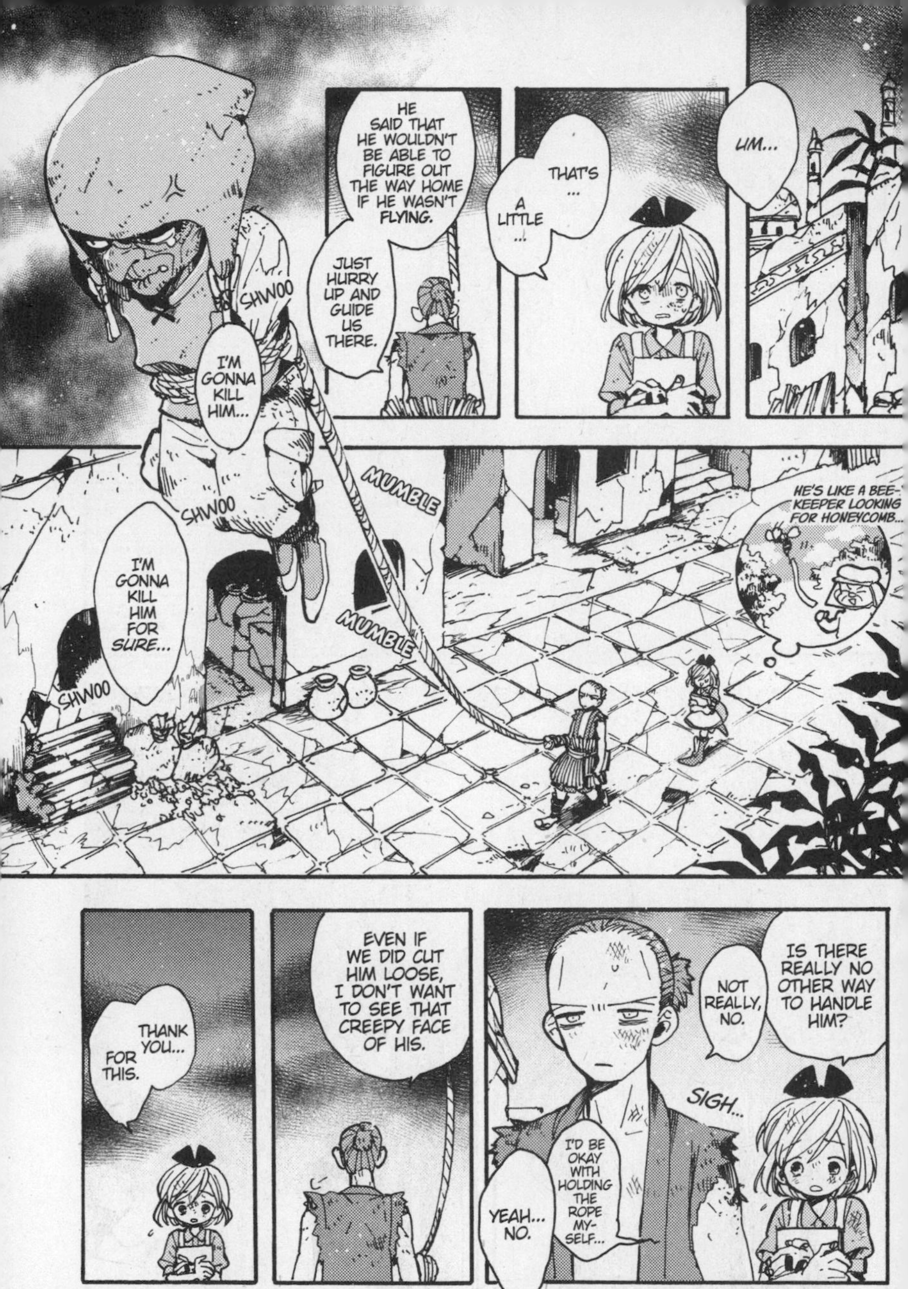
UM...
THAT'S... A LITTLE...
HE SAID THAT HE WOULDN'T BE ABLE TO FIGURE OUT THE WAY HOME IF HE WASN'T FLYING.
JUST HURRY UP AND GUIDE US THERE.
SHWOO
I'M GONNA KILL HIM...
SHWOO
HE'S LIKE A BEE-KEEPER LOOKING FOR HONEYCOMB...
MUMBLE
MUMBLE
I'M GONNA KILL HIM FOR SURE...
SHWOO
IS THERE REALLY NO OTHER WAY TO HANDLE HIM?
NOT REALLY, NO.
SIGH...
I'D BE OKAY WITH HOLDING THE ROPE MY-SELF...
YEAH... NO.
EVEN IF WE DID CUT HIM LOOSE, I DON'T WANT TO SEE THAT CREEPY FACE OF HIS.
THANK YOU... FOR THIS.

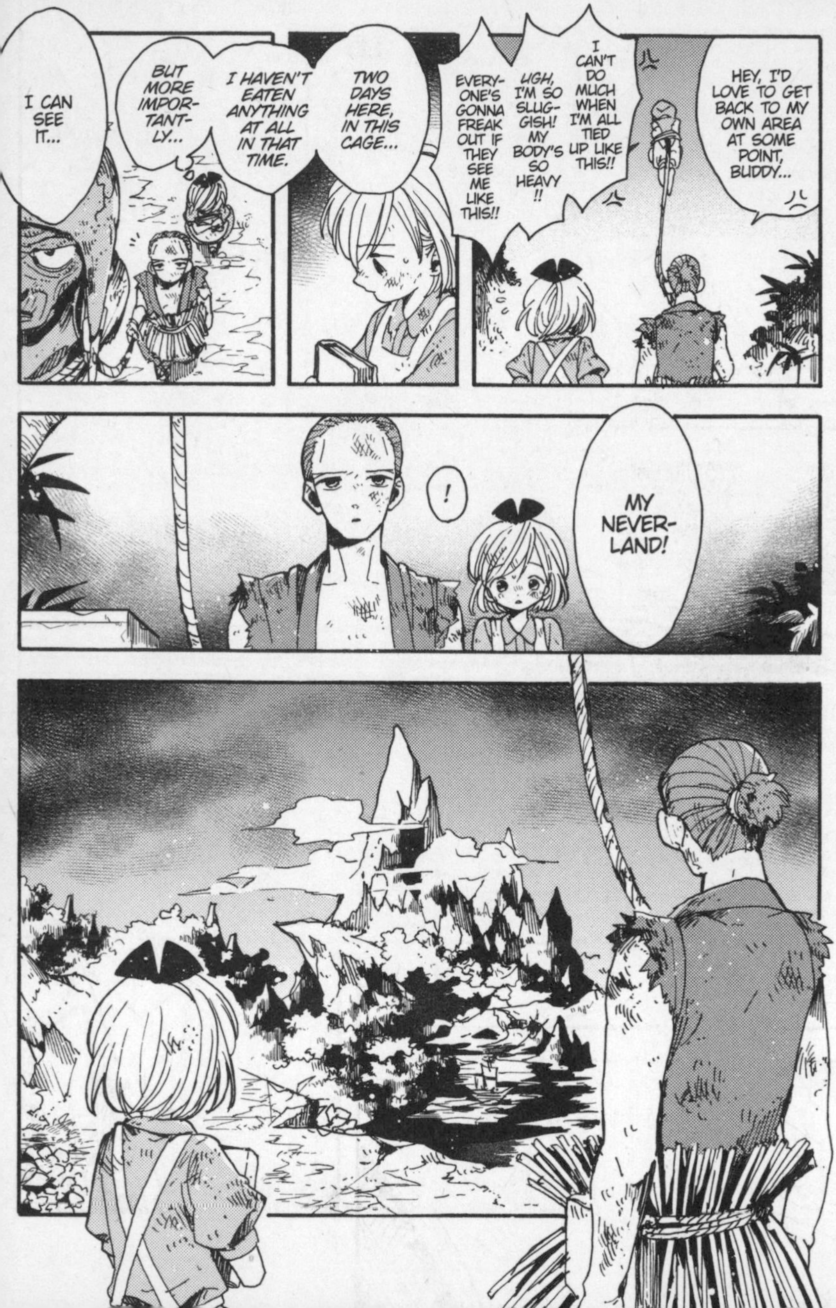
HEY, I'D LOVE TO GET BACK TO MY OWN AREA AT SOME POINT, BUDDY...
I CAN'T DO MUCH WHEN I'M ALL TIED UP LIKE THIS!!
UGH, I'M SO SLUG-GISH! MY BODY'S SO HEAVY!!
EVERY-ONE'S GONNA FREAK OUT IF THEY SEE ME LIKE THIS!!
TWO DAYS HERE, IN THIS CAGE...
I HAVEN'T EATEN ANYTHING AT ALL IN THAT TIME.
BUT MORE IMPOR-TANT-LY...
I CAN SEE IT...
MY NEVER-LAND!
!

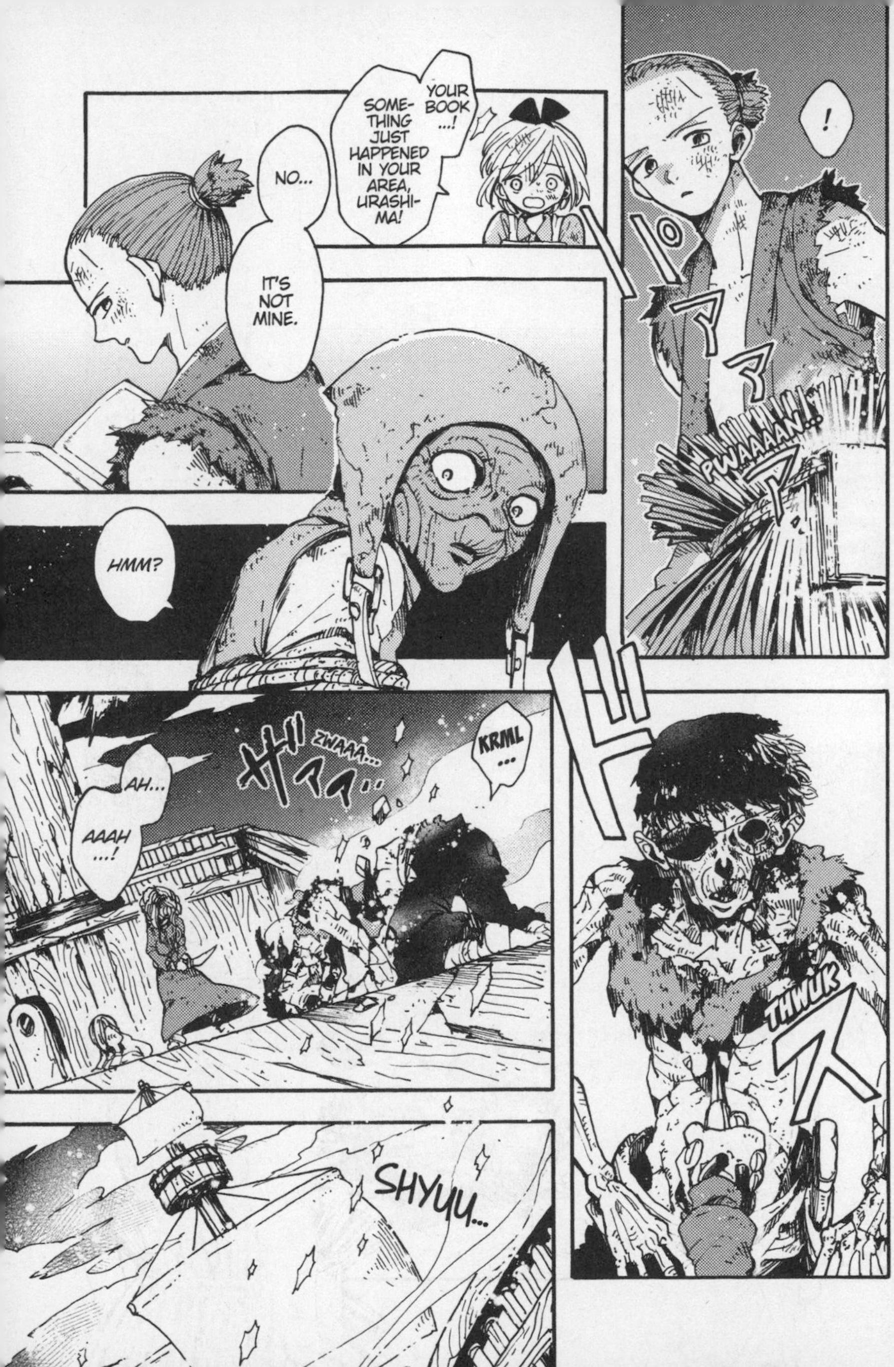

!
PWAAAAN...
YOUR BOOK...!
SOMETHING JUST HAPPENED IN YOUR AREA, URASHIMA!
NO...
IT'S NOT MINE.
HMM?
THWUK
KRML...
ZWAAA...
AH...
AAAH...!
SHYUU...

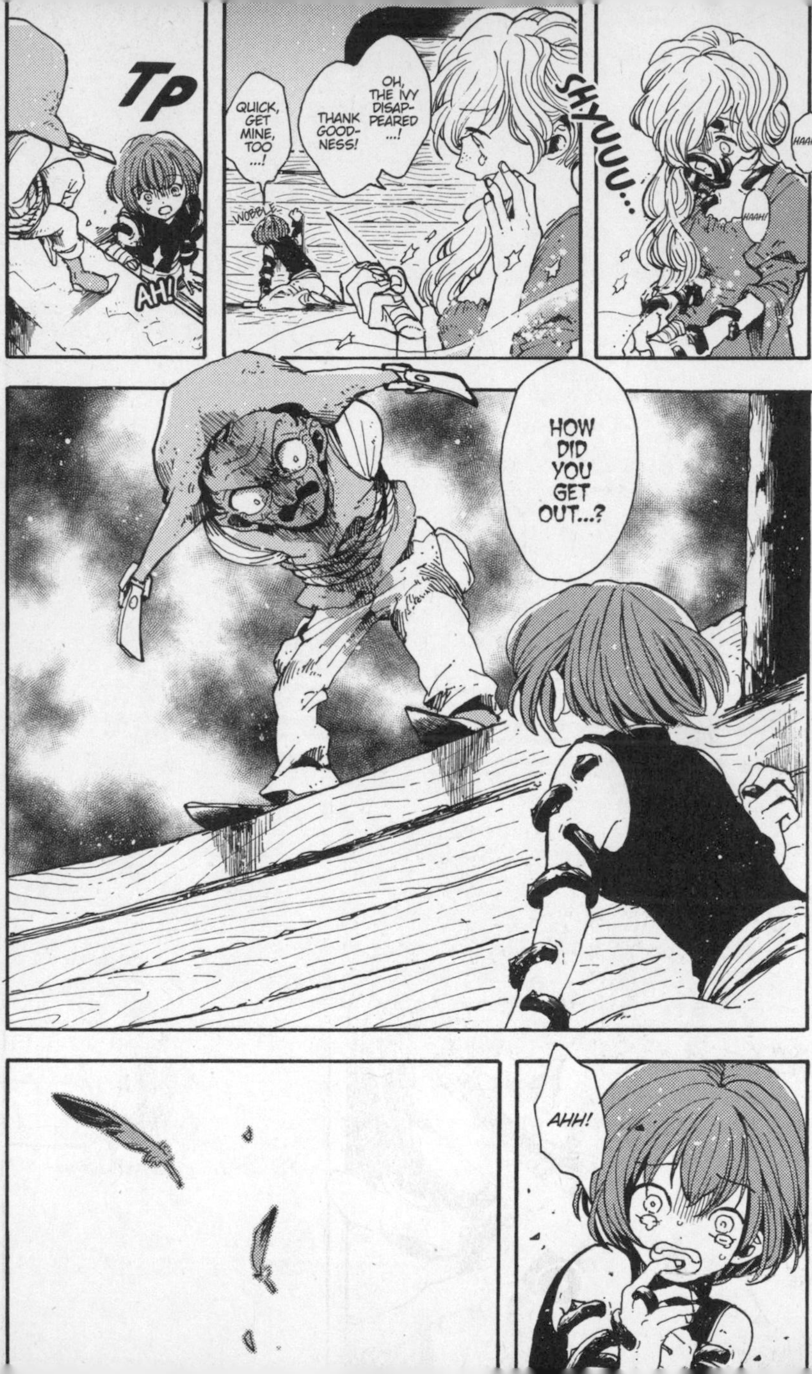
HAAH!
HAAH!
SHYUUU...
OH, THE IVY DISAPPEARED...!
THANK GOODNESS!
QUICK, GET MINE, TOO...!
WOBBLE
Tp
AH!
HOW DID YOU GET OUT...?
AHH!

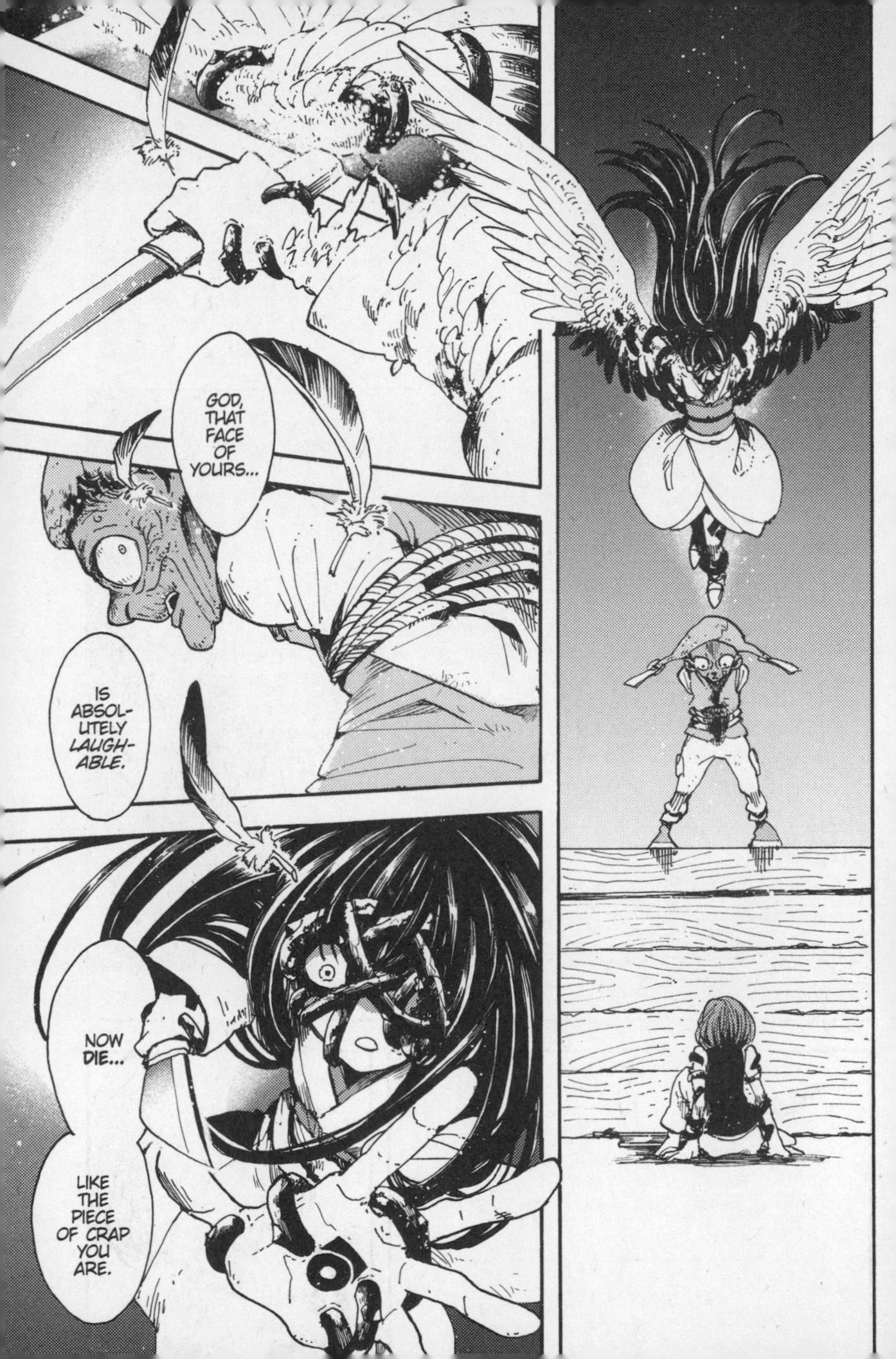
GOD, THAT FACE OF YOURS...
IS ABSOL-UTELY LAUGH-ABLE.
NOW DIE...
LIKE THE PIECE OF CRAP YOU ARE.

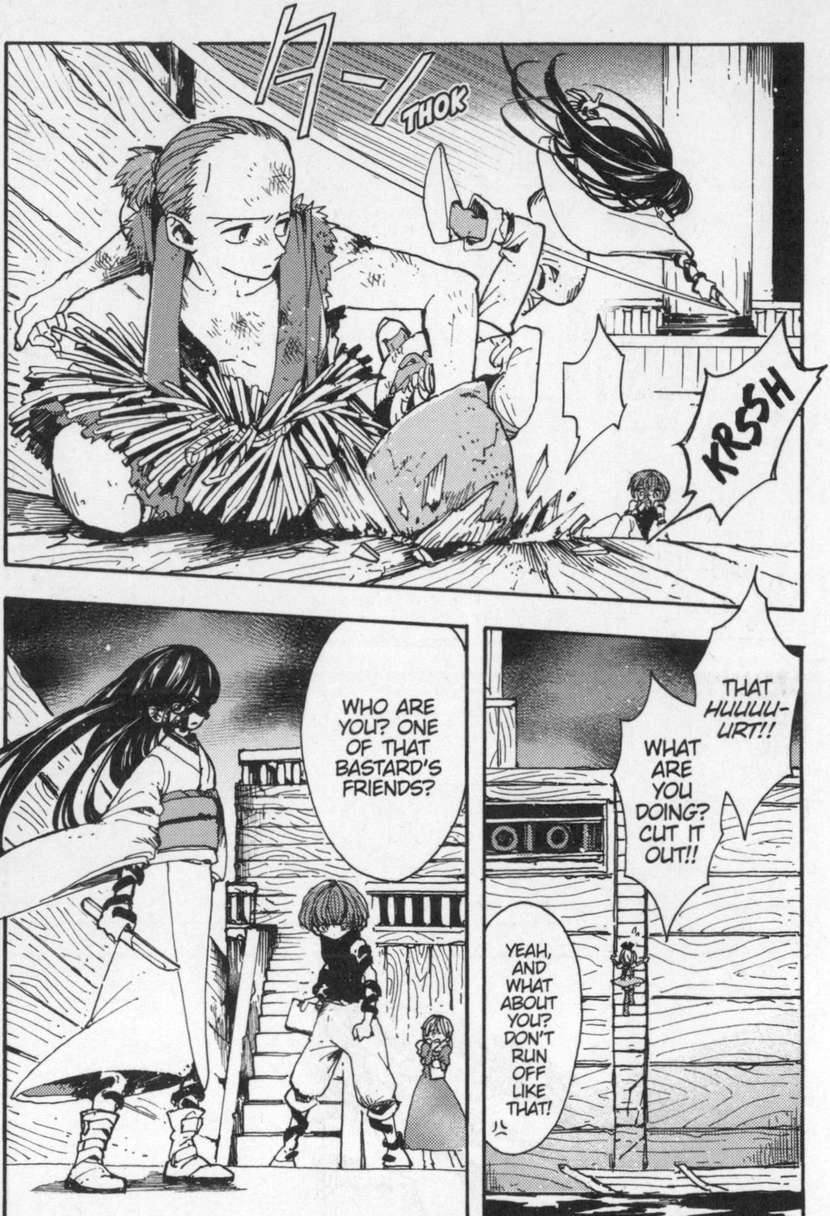
THOK
KRSSH
THAT HUUUUU-URT!!
WHAT ARE YOU DOING? CUT IT OUT!!
YEAH, AND WHAT ABOUT YOU? DON'T RUN OFF LIKE THAT!
WHO ARE YOU? ONE OF THAT BASTARD'S FRIENDS?

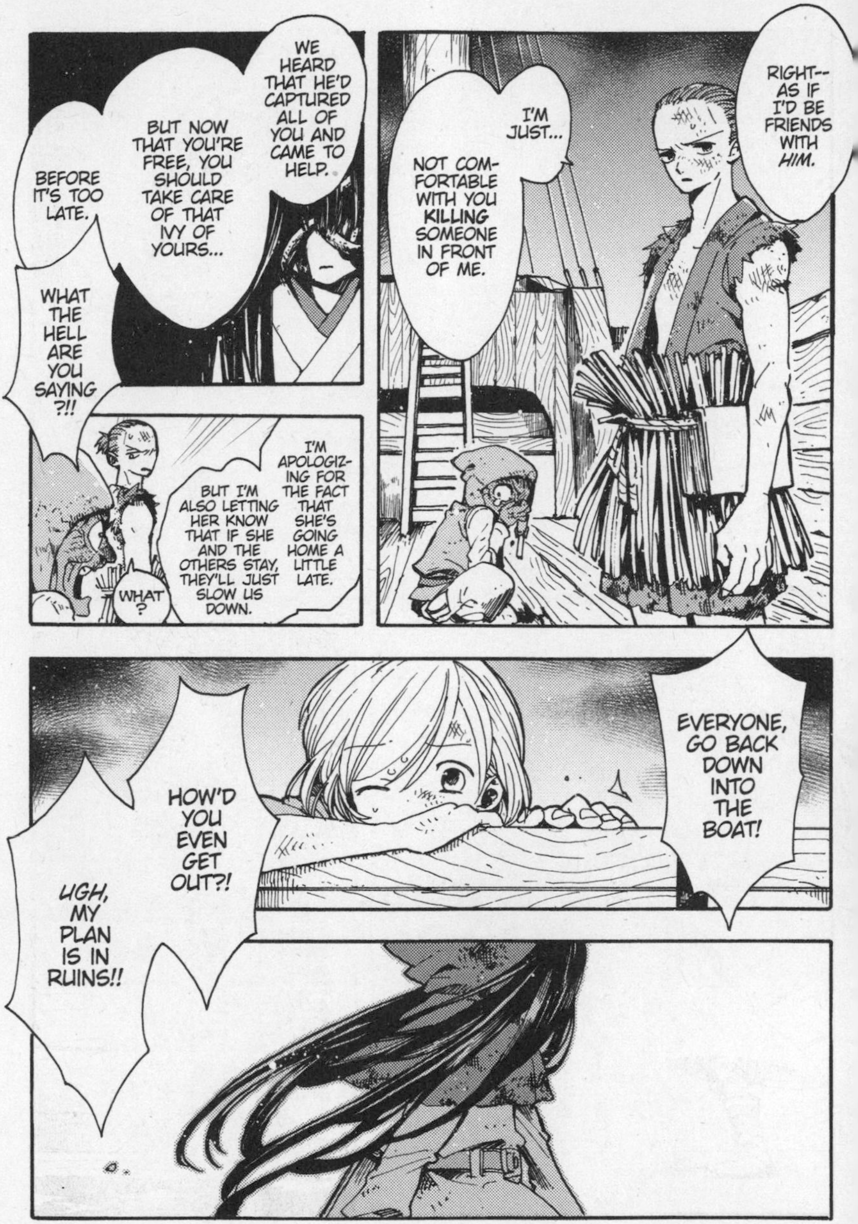
RIGHT-- AS IF I'D BE FRIENDS WITH *HIM*.
I'M JUST...
NOT COMFORTABLE WITH YOU **KILLING** SOMEONE IN FRONT OF ME.
WE HEARD THAT HE'D CAPTURED ALL OF YOU AND CAME TO HELP.
BUT NOW THAT YOU'RE FREE, YOU SHOULD TAKE CARE OF THAT IVY OF YOURS...
BEFORE IT'S TOO LATE.
WHAT THE HELL ARE YOU SAYING?!!
I'M APOLOGIZING FOR THE FACT THAT SHE'S GOING HOME A LITTLE LATE.
BUT I'M ALSO LETTING HER KNOW THAT IF SHE AND THE OTHERS STAY, THEY'LL JUST SLOW US DOWN.
WHAT?
EVERYONE, GO BACK DOWN INTO THE BOAT!
HOW'D YOU EVEN GET OUT?!
UGH, MY PLAN IS IN RUINS!!

!
AH!
FWOMP

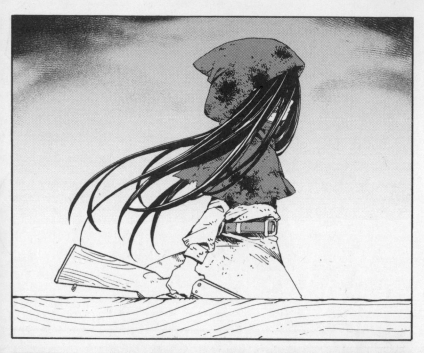

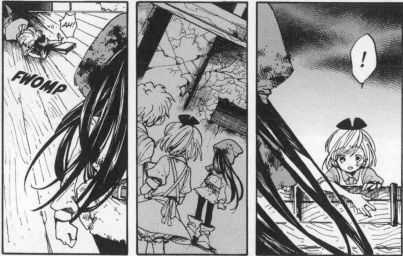

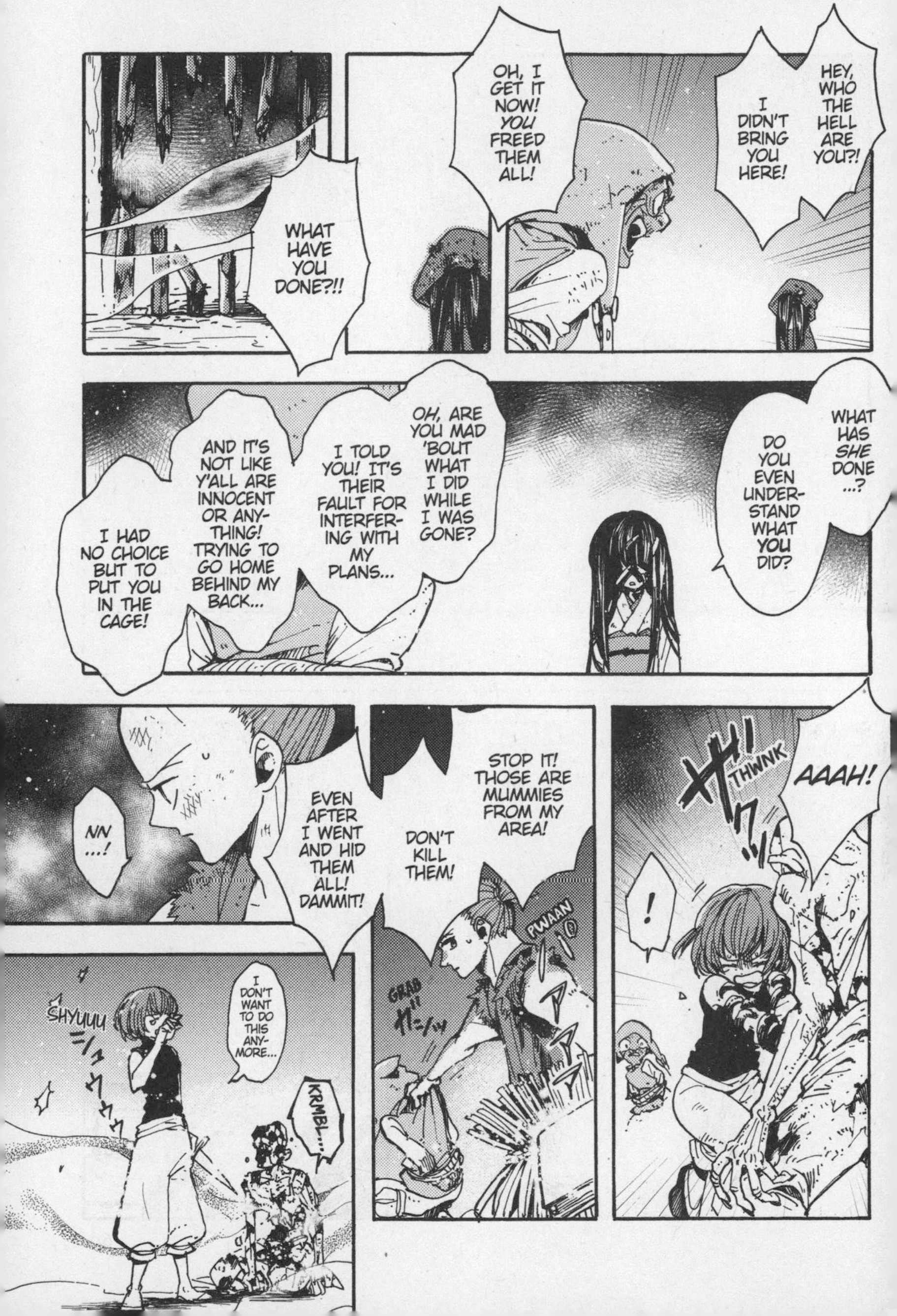
HEY, WHO THE HELL ARE YOU?!
I DIDN'T BRING YOU HERE!
OH, I GET IT NOW! YOU FREED THEM ALL!
WHAT HAVE YOU DONE?!!
WHAT HAS SHE DONE...?
DO YOU EVEN UNDERSTAND WHAT YOU DID?
OH, ARE YOU MAD 'BOUT WHAT I DID WHILE I WAS GONE?
I TOLD YOU! IT'S THEIR FAULT FOR INTERFERING WITH MY PLANS...
AND IT'S NOT LIKE Y'ALL ARE INNOCENT OR ANYTHING! TRYING TO GO HOME BEHIND MY BACK...
I HAD NO CHOICE BUT TO PUT YOU IN THE CAGE!
AAAH!
THWNK
!
STOP IT! THOSE ARE MUMMIES FROM MY AREA!
DON'T KILL THEM!
PWAAN
GRAB
EVEN AFTER I WENT AND HID THEM ALL! DAMMIT!
NN...!
SHYUUU
I DON'T WANT TO DO THIS ANYMORE...
KRMBL...

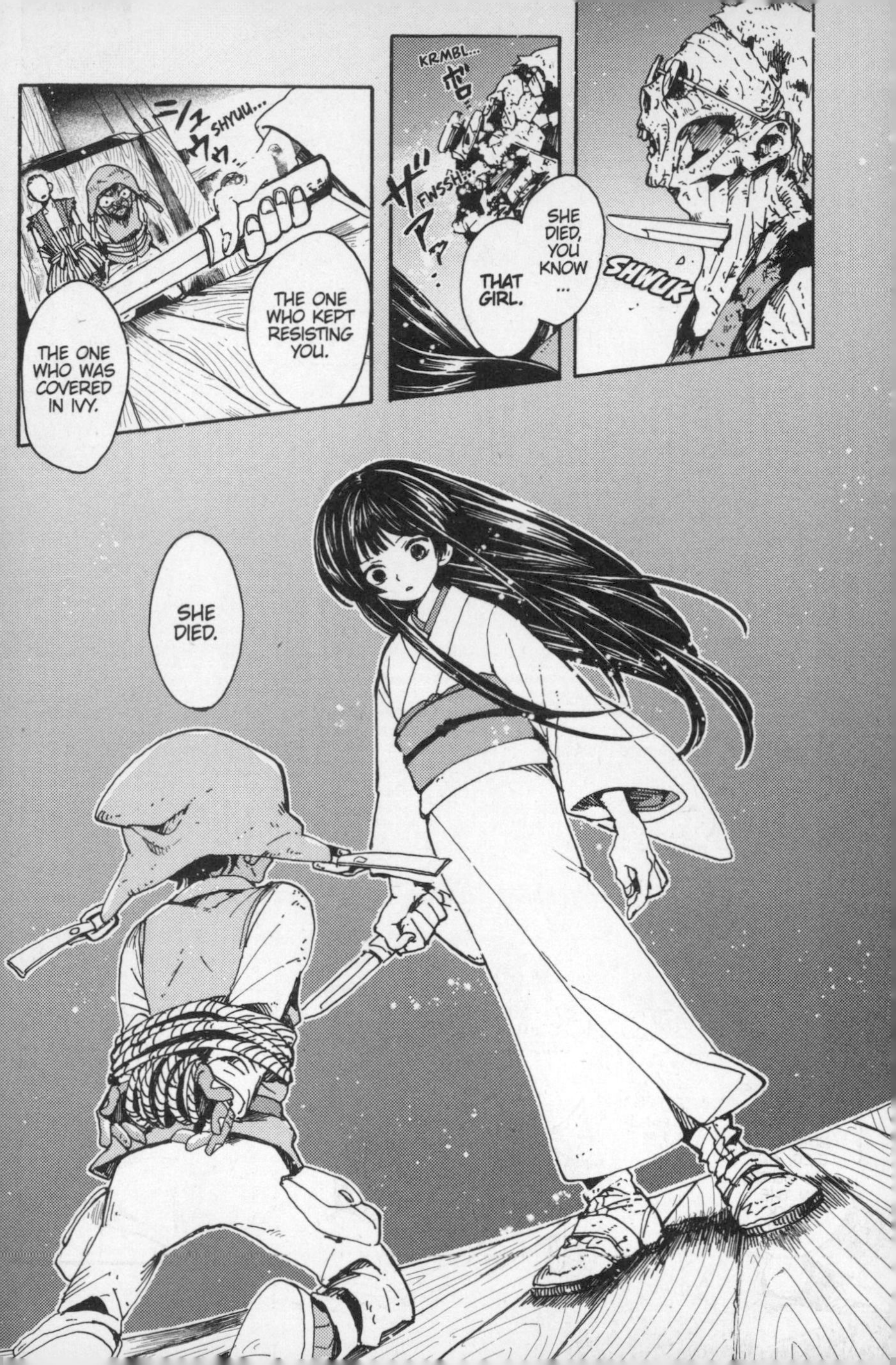
SHWUK
KRMBL...
FWSSH...
SHE DIED, YOU KNOW ...
THAT GIRL.
SHYUU...
THE ONE WHO KEPT RESISTING YOU.
THE ONE WHO WAS COVERED IN IVY.
SHE DIED.

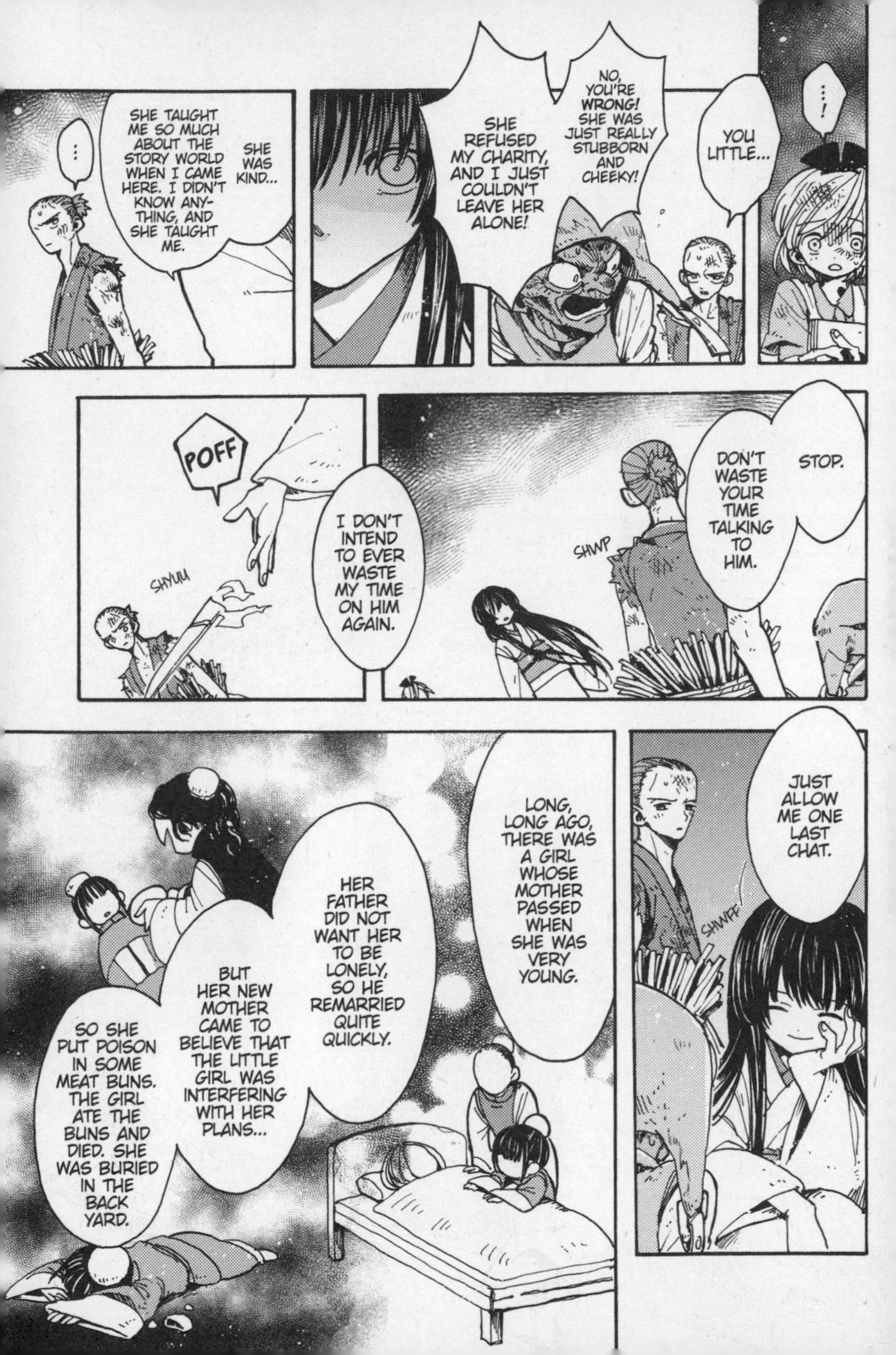
…!
YOU LITTLE...
NO, YOU'RE WRONG! SHE WAS JUST REALLY STUBBORN AND CHEEKY!
SHE REFUSED MY CHARITY, AND I JUST COULDN'T LEAVE HER ALONE!
SHE WAS KIND...
SHE TAUGHT ME SO MUCH ABOUT THE STORY WORLD WHEN I CAME HERE. I DIDN'T KNOW ANY-THING, AND SHE TAUGHT ME.
…
STOP.
DON'T WASTE YOUR TIME TALKING TO HIM.
SHWP
I DON'T INTEND TO EVER WASTE MY TIME ON HIM AGAIN.
POFF
SHYUU
JUST ALLOW ME ONE LAST CHAT.
SHWFF
LONG, LONG AGO, THERE WAS A GIRL WHOSE MOTHER PASSED WHEN SHE WAS VERY YOUNG.
HER FATHER DID NOT WANT HER TO BE LONELY, SO HE REMARRIED QUITE QUICKLY.
BUT HER NEW MOTHER CAME TO BELIEVE THAT THE LITTLE GIRL WAS INTERFERING WITH HER PLANS...
SO SHE PUT POISON IN SOME MEAT BUNS. THE GIRL ATE THE BUNS AND DIED. SHE WAS BURIED IN THE BACK YARD.

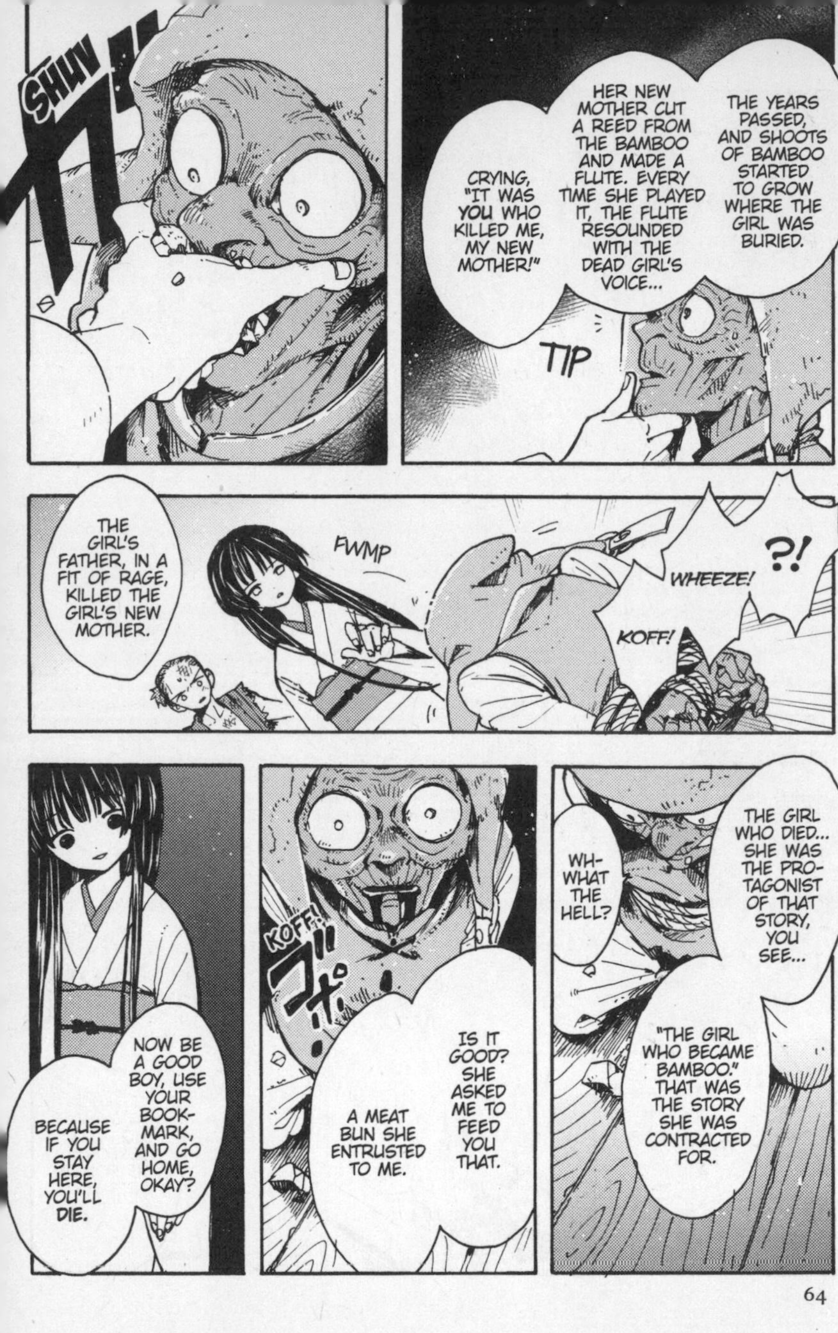
THE YEARS PASSED, AND SHOOTS OF BAMBOO STARTED TO GROW WHERE THE GIRL WAS BURIED.
HER NEW MOTHER CUT A REED FROM THE BAMBOO AND MADE A FLUTE. EVERY TIME SHE PLAYED IT, THE FLUTE RESOUNDED WITH THE DEAD GIRL'S VOICE...
CRYING, "IT WAS YOU WHO KILLED ME, MY NEW MOTHER!"
TIP
SHUV
?!
WHEEZE!
KOFF!
FWMP
THE GIRL'S FATHER, IN A FIT OF RAGE, KILLED THE GIRL'S NEW MOTHER.
THE GIRL WHO DIED... SHE WAS THE PROTAGONIST OF THAT STORY, YOU SEE...
WH-WHAT THE HELL?
"THE GIRL WHO BECAME BAMBOO." THAT WAS THE STORY SHE WAS CONTRACTED FOR.
KOFF!
IS IT GOOD? SHE ASKED ME TO FEED YOU THAT.
A MEAT BUN SHE ENTRUSTED TO ME.
NOW BE A GOOD BOY, USE YOUR BOOKMARK, AND GO HOME, OKAY?
BECAUSE IF YOU STAY HERE, YOU'LL DIE.

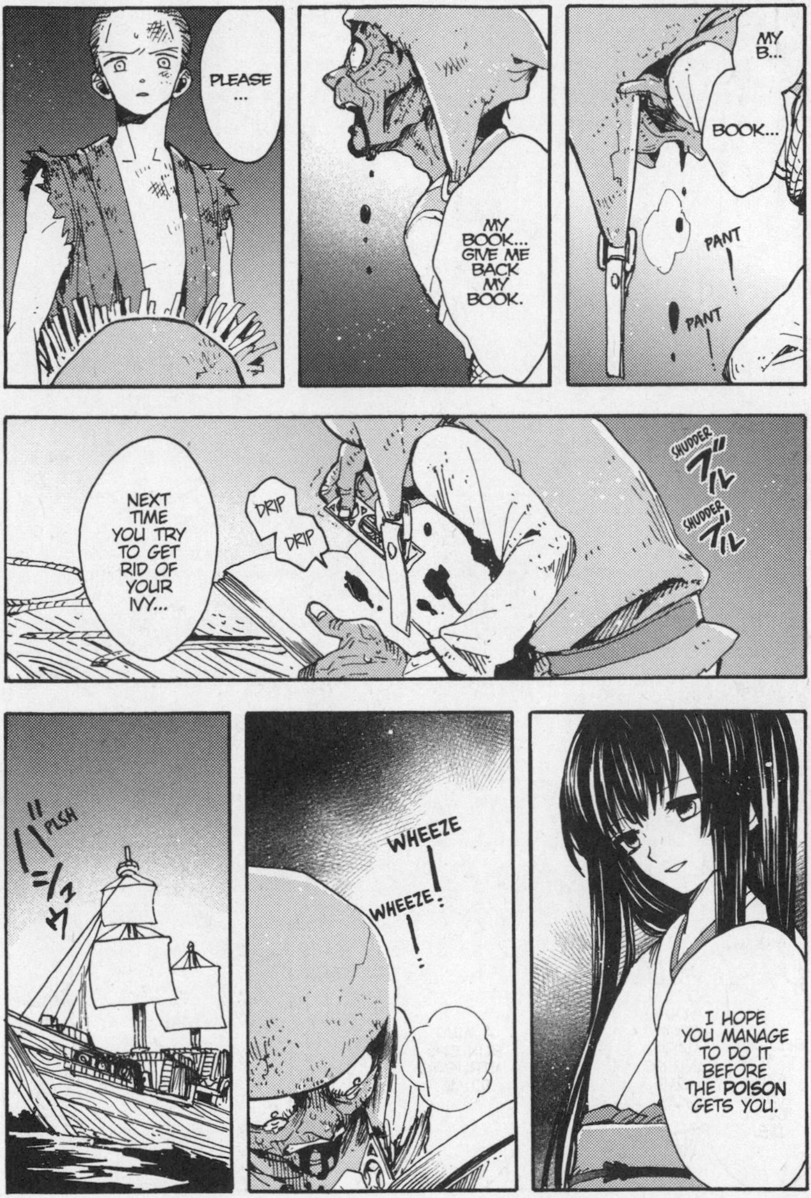
MY B...
BOOK...
PANT
PANT
MY BOOK... GIVE ME BACK MY BOOK.
PLEASE ...
SHUDDER ブル
SHUDDER ブル
DRIP
DRIP
NEXT TIME YOU TRY TO GET RID OF YOUR IVY...
I HOPE YOU MANAGE TO DO IT BEFORE THE POISON GETS YOU.
WHEEZE
WHEEZE
PLSH

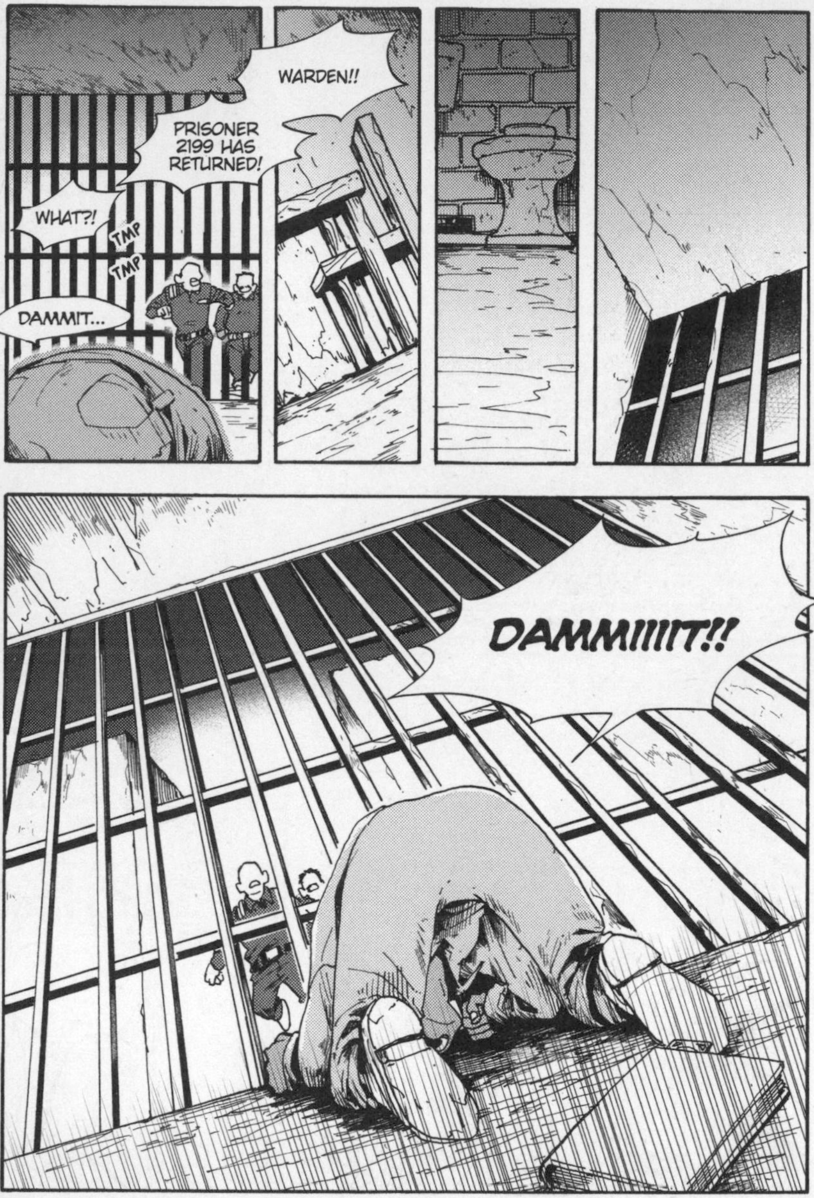
WARDEN!!
PRISONER 2199 HAS RETURNED!
WHAT?!
TMP
TMP
DAMMIT...
DAMMIIIIT!!

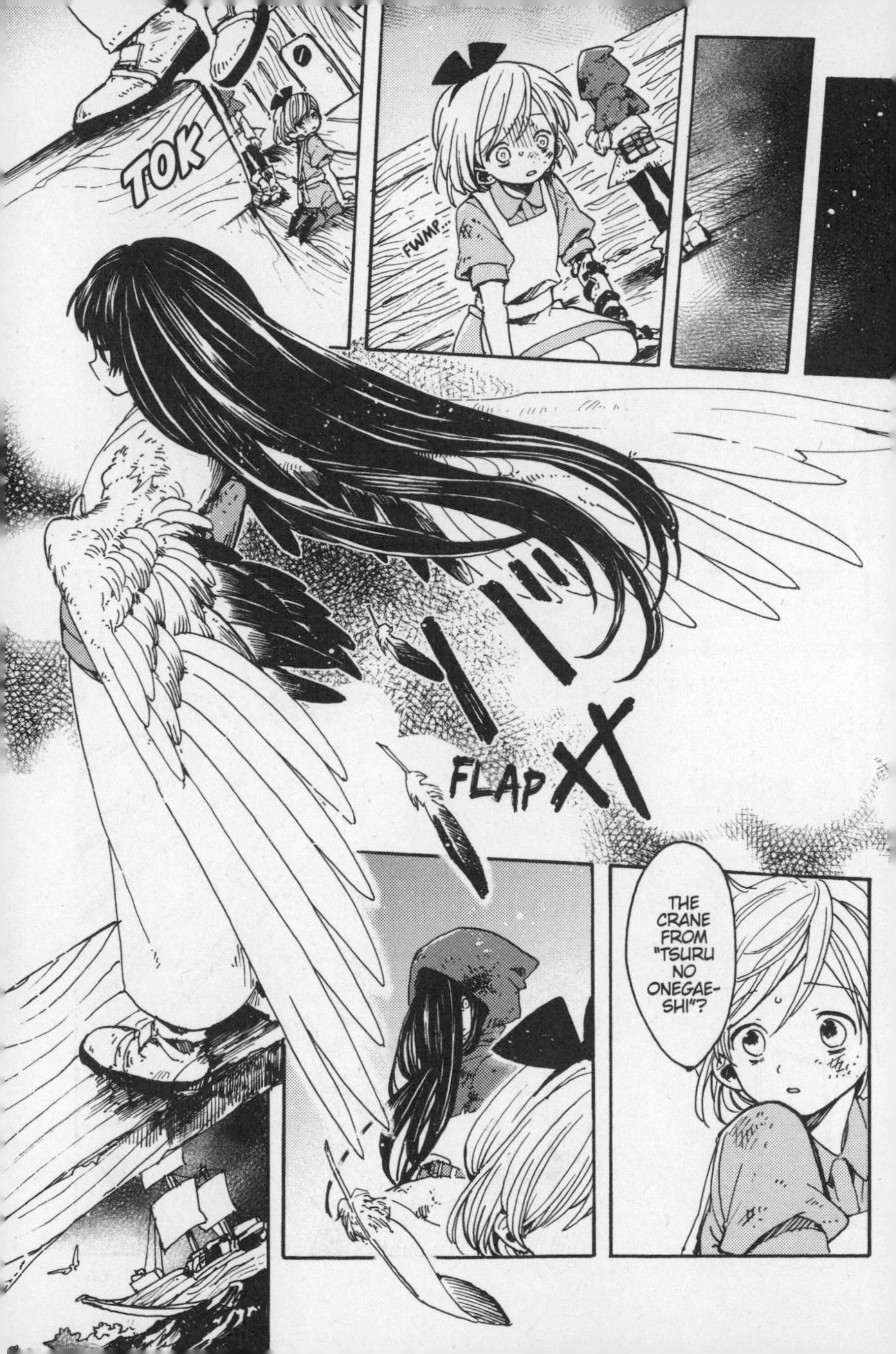
TOK
FWMP...
FLAP
THE CRANE FROM "TSURU NO ONEGAE-SHI"?

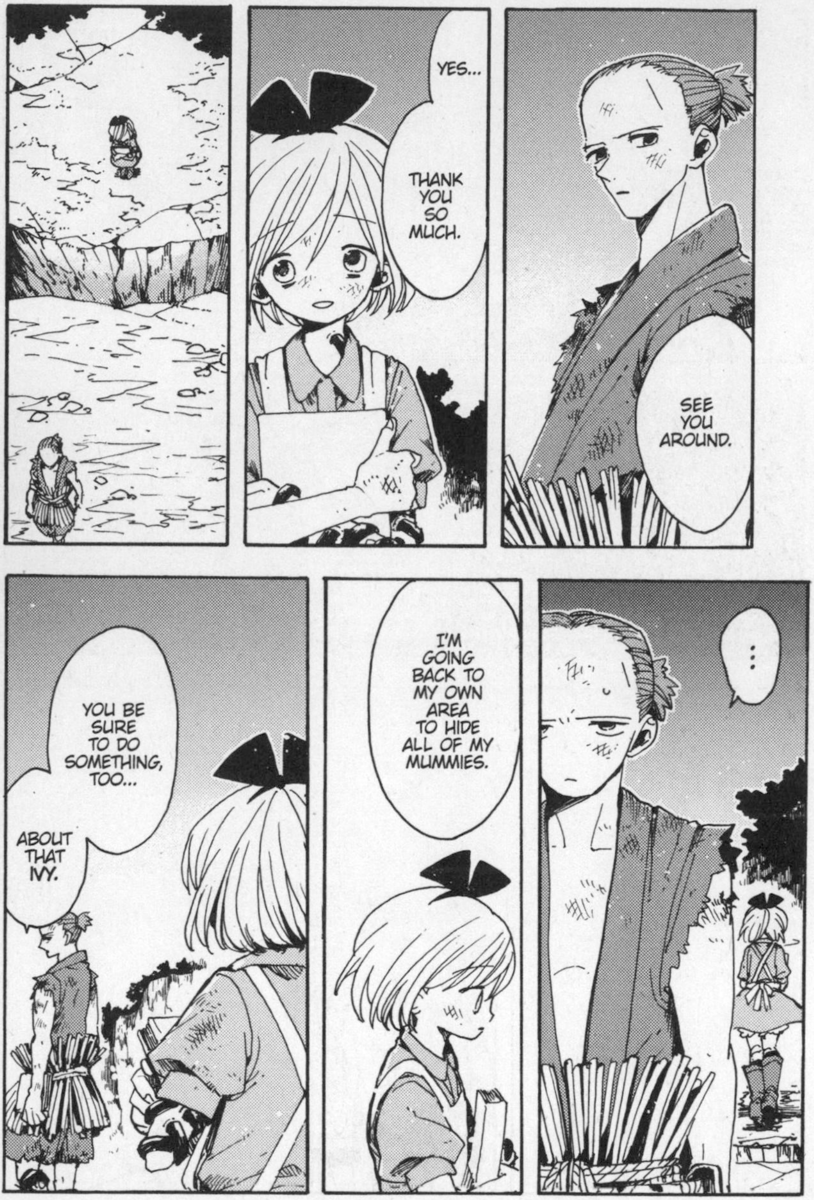
SEE YOU AROUND.
YES...
THANK YOU SO MUCH.
...
I'M GOING BACK TO MY OWN AREA TO HIDE ALL OF MY MUMMIES.
YOU BE SURE TO DO SOMETHING, TOO...
ABOUT THAT IVY.

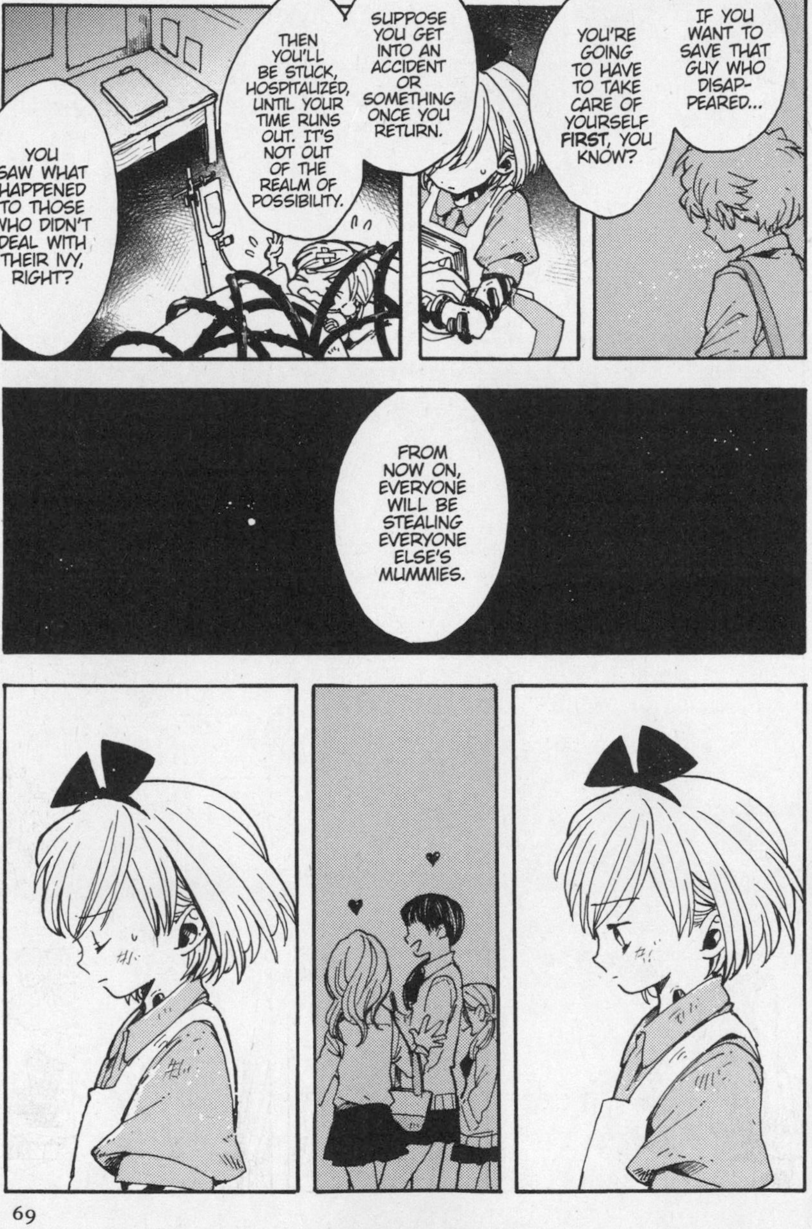
IF YOU WANT TO SAVE THAT GUY WHO DISAP-PEARED...
YOU'RE GOING TO HAVE TO TAKE CARE OF YOURSELF FIRST, YOU KNOW?
SUPPOSE YOU GET INTO AN ACCIDENT OR SOMETHING ONCE YOU RETURN.
THEN YOU'LL BE STUCK, HOSPITALIZED, UNTIL YOUR TIME RUNS OUT. IT'S NOT OUT OF THE REALM OF POSSIBILITY.
YOU SAW WHAT HAPPENED TO THOSE WHO DIDN'T DEAL WITH THEIR IVY, RIGHT?
FROM NOW ON, EVERYONE WILL BE STEALING EVERYONE ELSE'S MUMMIES.

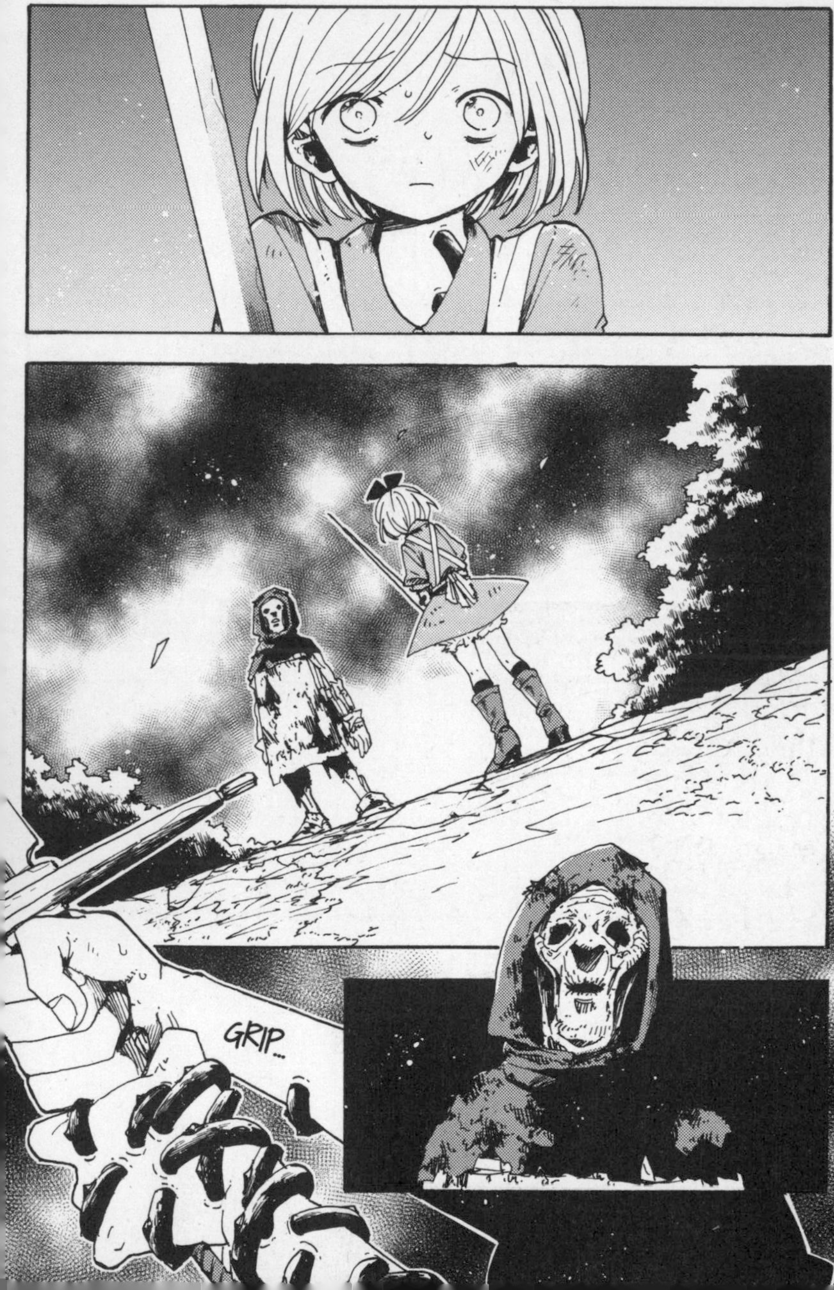
GRIP...

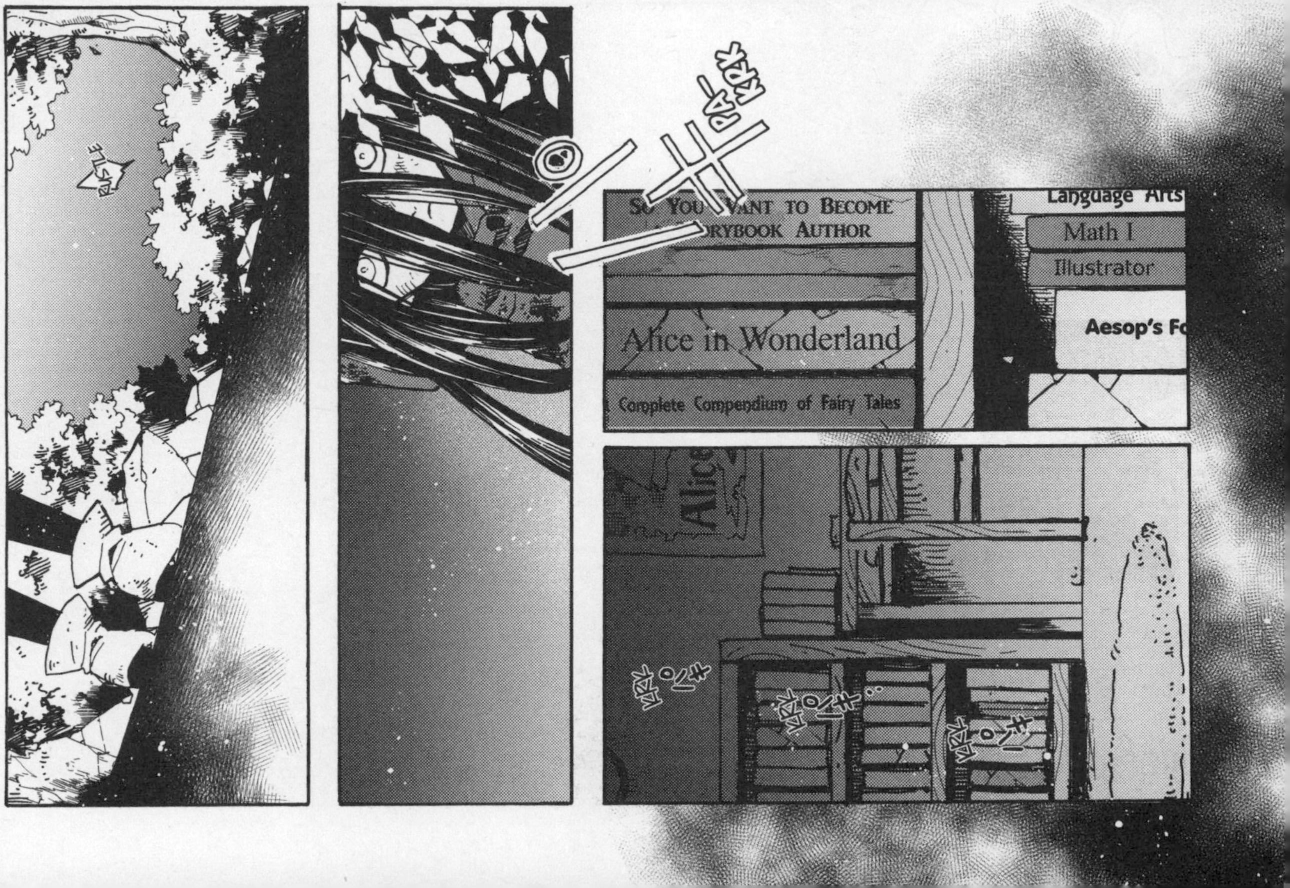
Language Arts
Math I
Illustrator
Aesop's Fa
So You Want to Become a Storybook Author
Alice in Wonderland
Complete Compendium of Fairy Tales
PA-KRK
Alice
KRK
KRK
KRK
RUSTLE

FAIRY
TALE
BATTLE
ROYALE

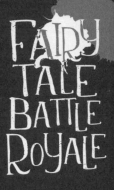

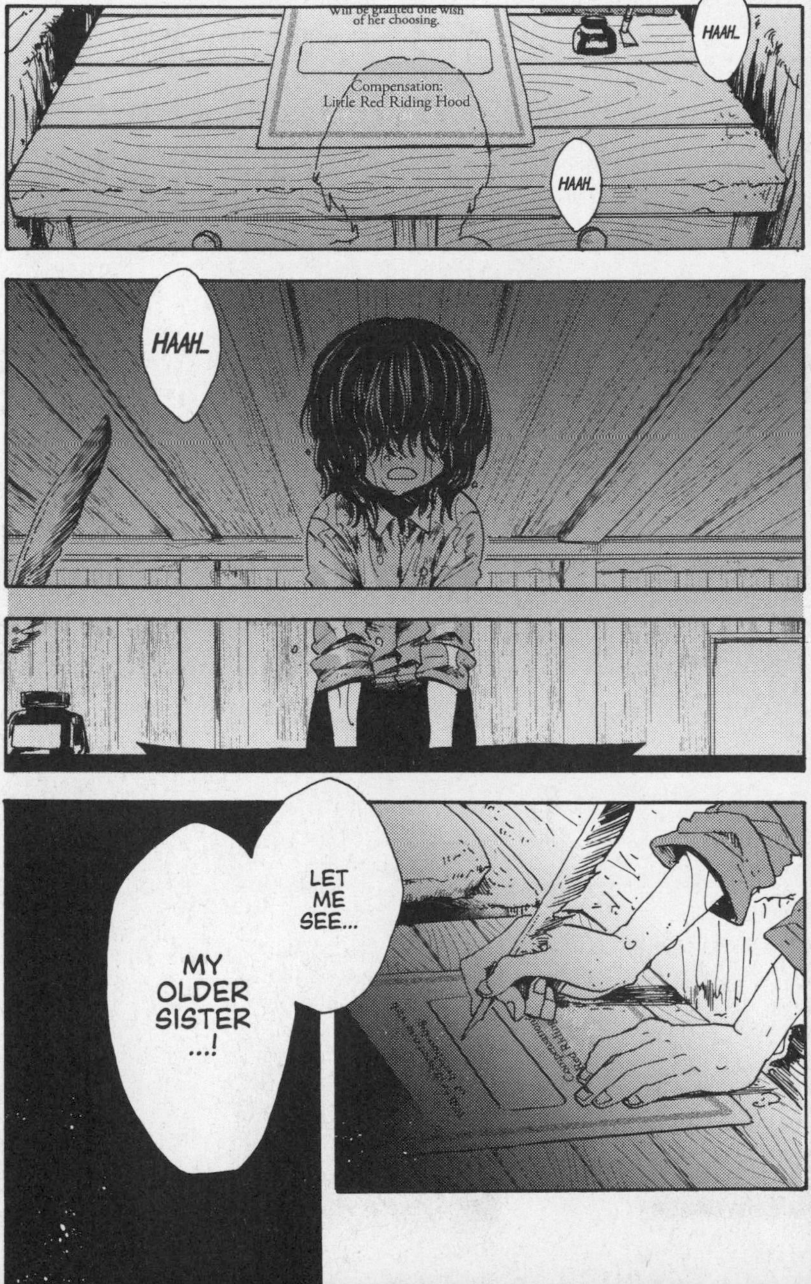
HAAH_
Will be granted one wish
of her choosing.
Compensation:
Little Red Riding Hood
HAAH_
HAAH_
LET ME SEE...
MY OLDER SISTER ...!

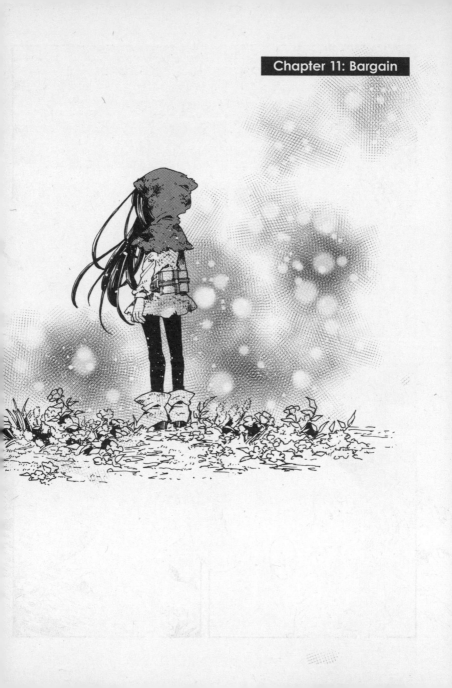

Chapter 11: Bargain

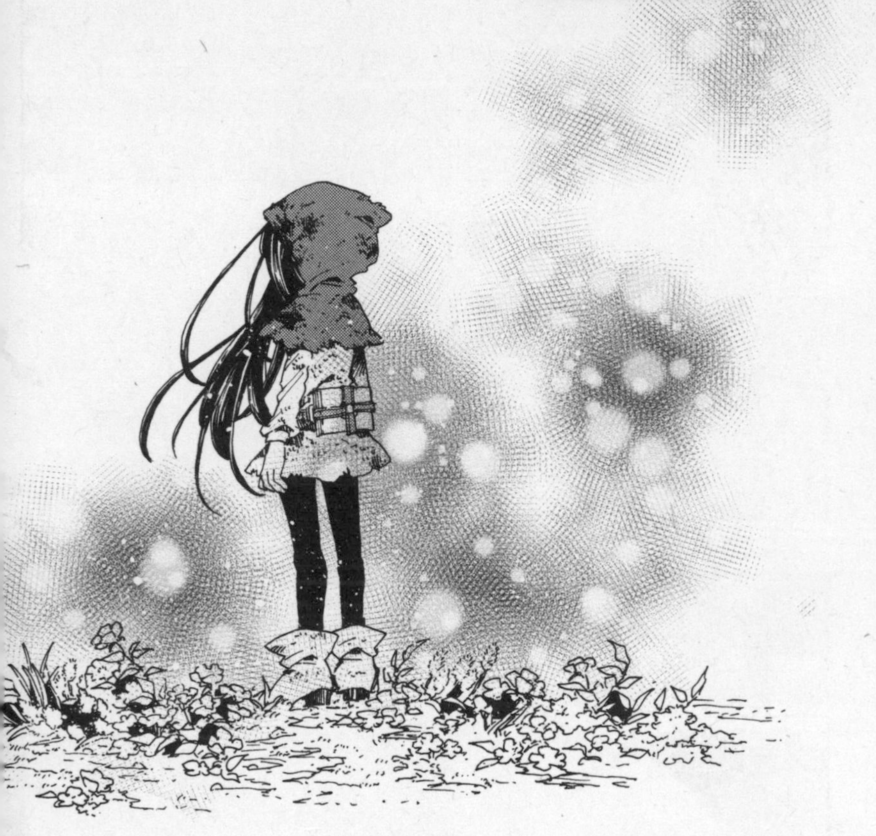

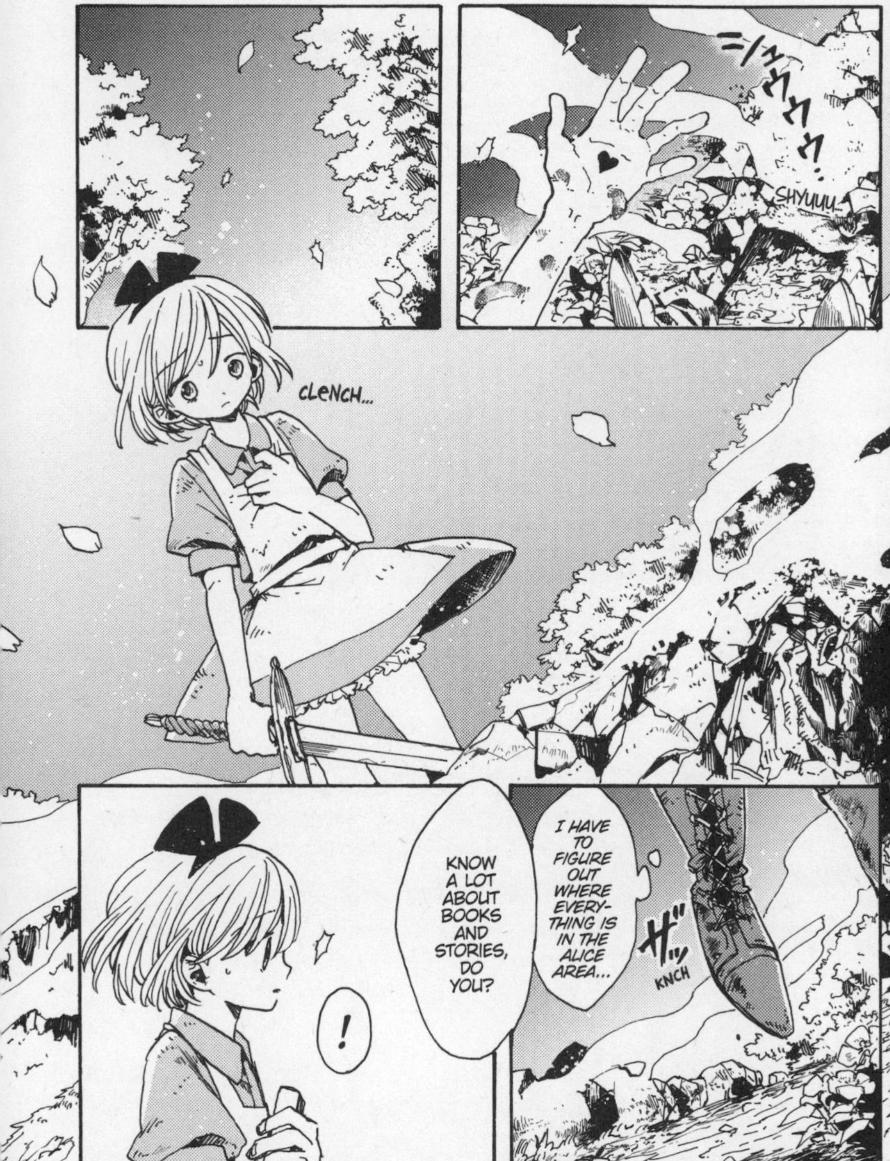
SHYUUU...
CLENCH...
I HAVE TO FIGURE OUT WHERE EVERYTHING IS IN THE ALICE AREA...
KNCH
KNOW A LOT ABOUT BOOKS AND STORIES, DO YOU?
!

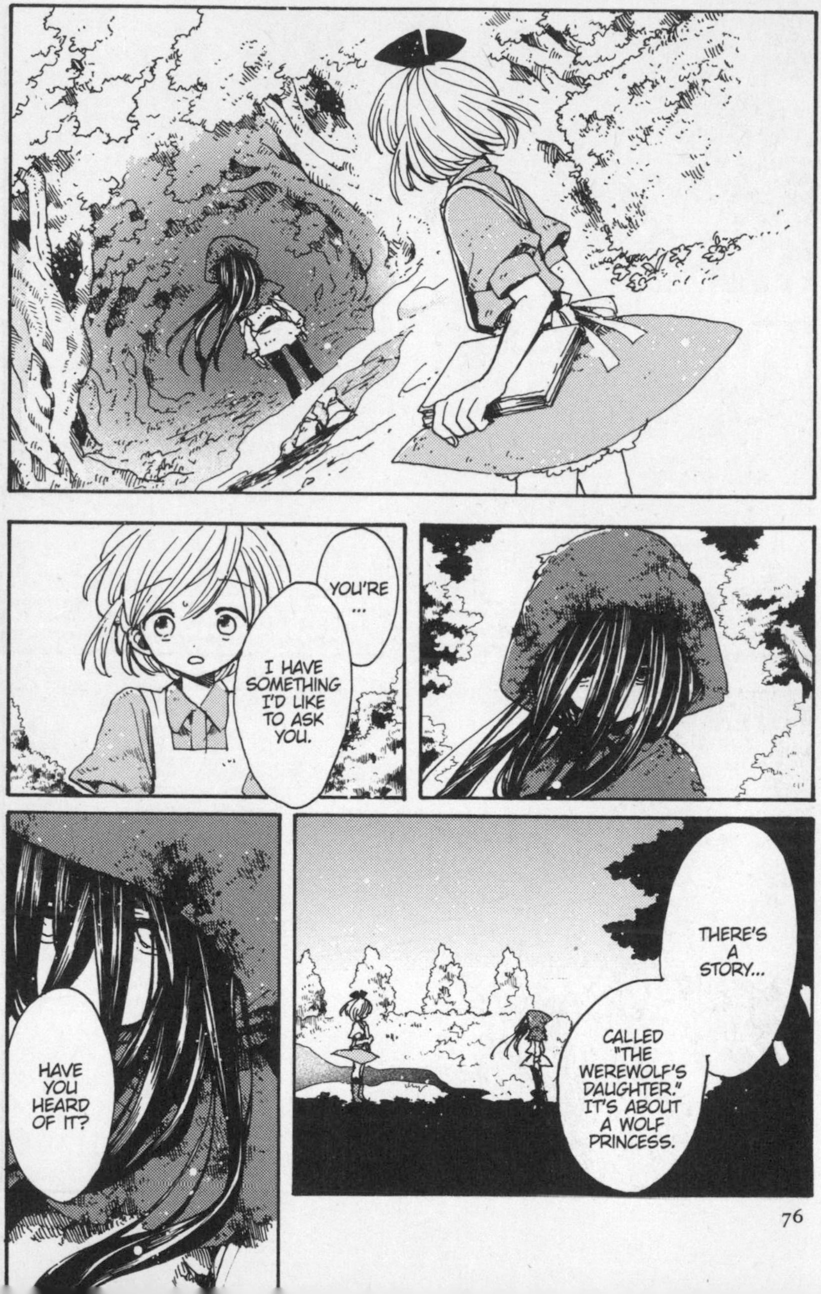
YOU'RE ...
I HAVE SOMETHING I'D LIKE TO ASK YOU.
THERE'S A STORY...
CALLED "THE WEREWOLF'S DAUGHTER." IT'S ABOUT A WOLF PRINCESS.
HAVE YOU HEARD OF IT?

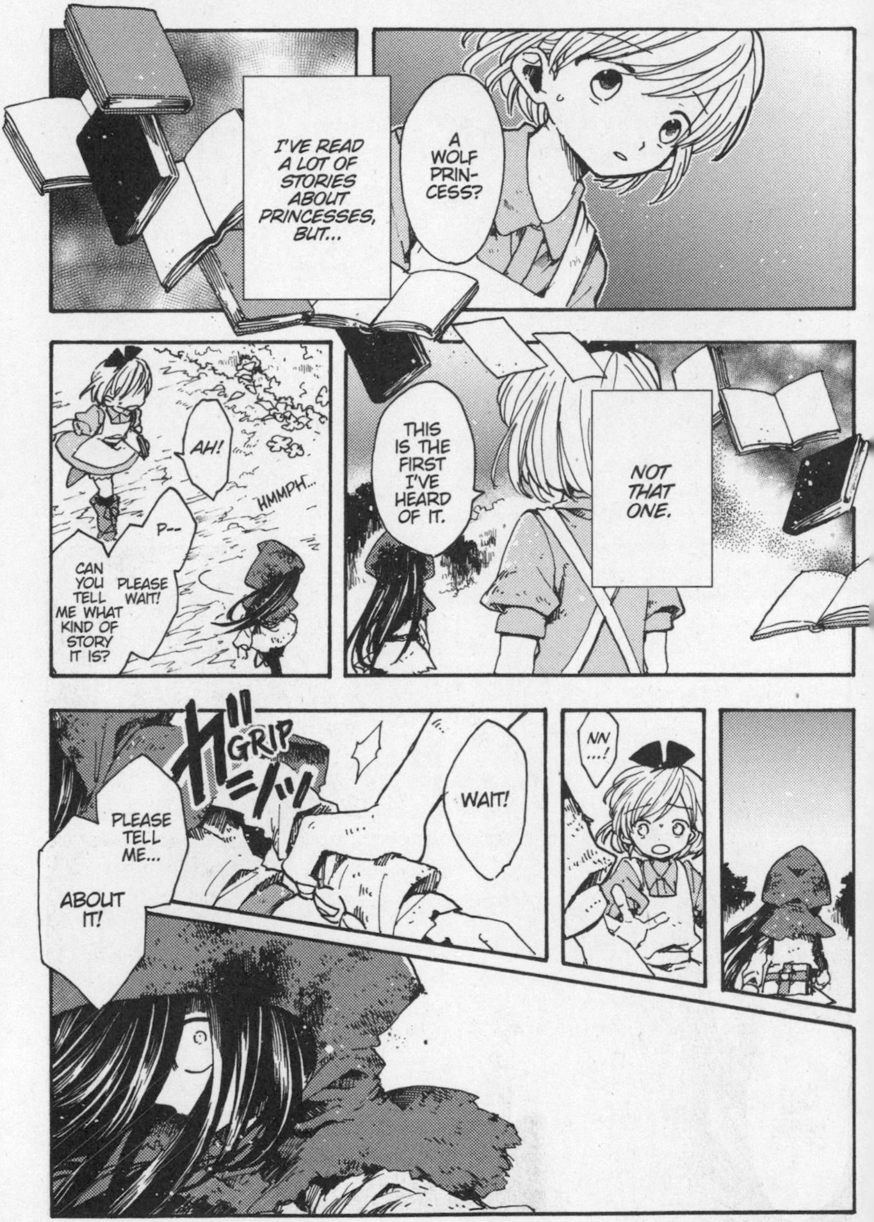
A WOLF PRIN-CESS?
I'VE READ A LOT OF STORIES ABOUT PRINCESSES, BUT...
NOT THAT ONE.
THIS IS THE FIRST I'VE HEARD OF IT.
AH!
HMMPH...
P--
PLEASE WAIT!
CAN YOU TELL ME WHAT KIND OF STORY IT IS?
NN ...!
WAIT!
GRIP
PLEASE TELL ME...
ABOUT IT!

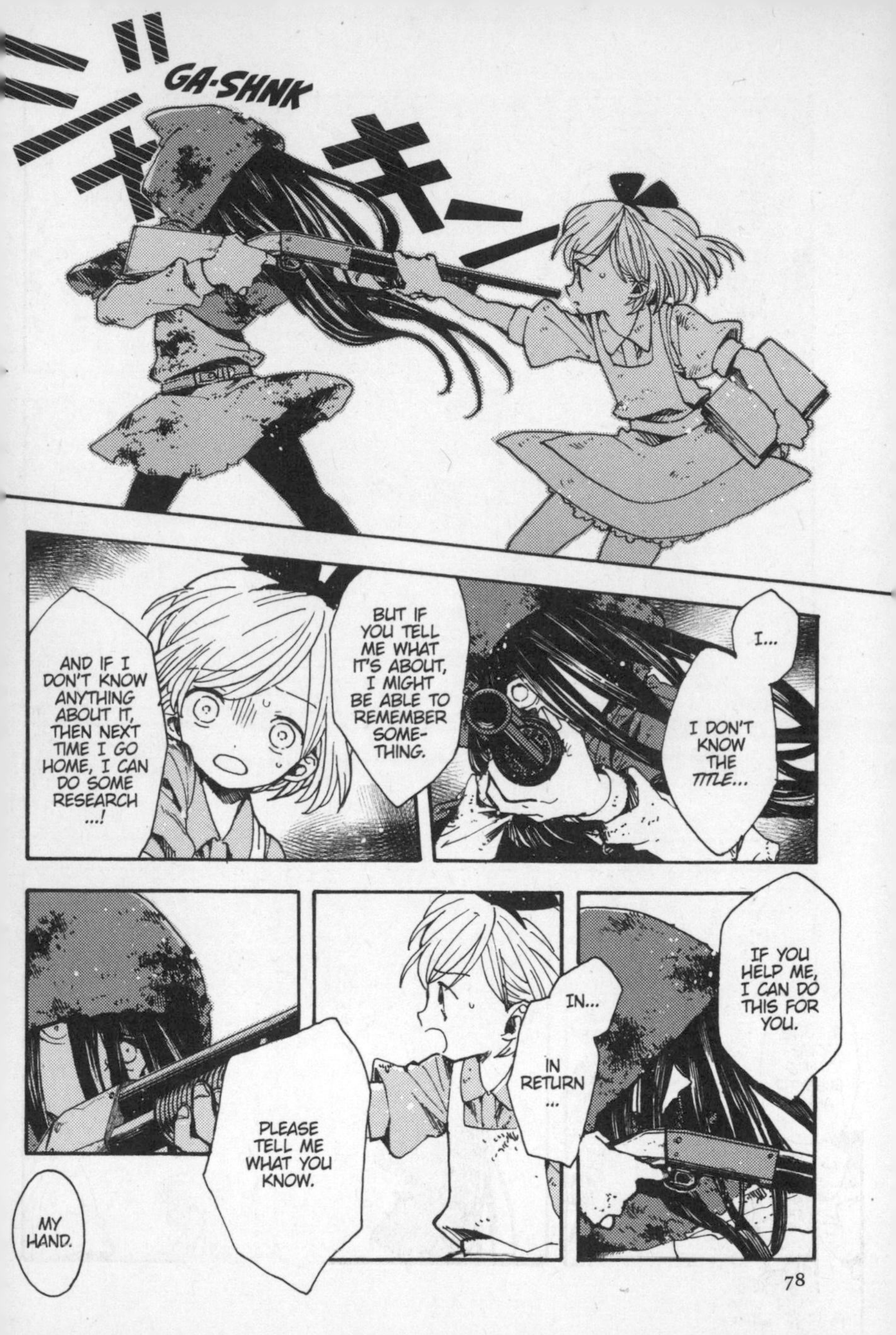
GA-SHNK
I...
I DON'T KNOW THE TITLE...
BUT IF YOU TELL ME WHAT IT'S ABOUT, I MIGHT BE ABLE TO REMEMBER SOME-THING.
AND IF I DON'T KNOW ANYTHING ABOUT IT, THEN NEXT TIME I GO HOME, I CAN DO SOME RESEARCH ...!
IF YOU HELP ME, I CAN DO THIS FOR YOU.
IN...
IN RETURN ...
PLEASE TELL ME WHAT YOU KNOW.
MY HAND.

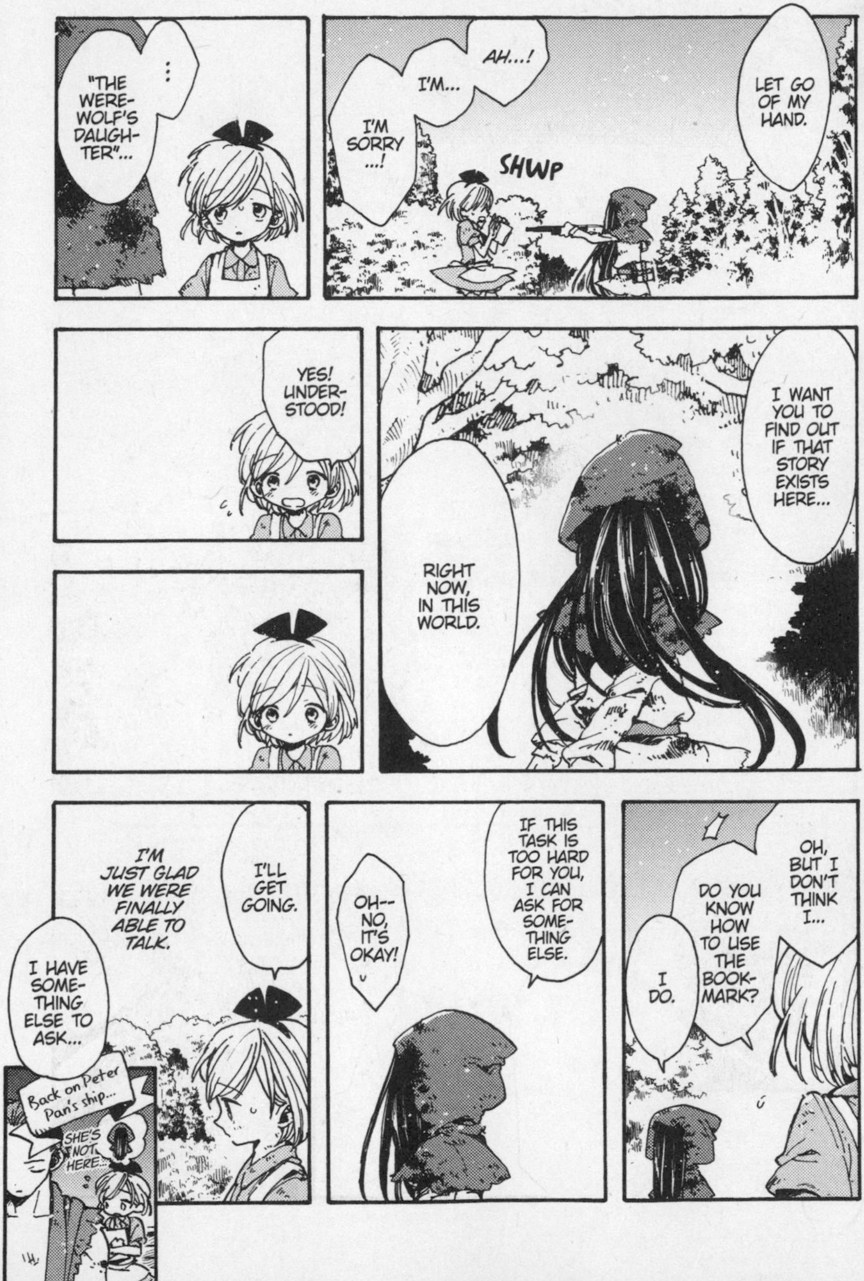
LET GO OF MY HAND.
SHWP
AH...!
I'M...
I'M SORRY ...!
...
"THE WERE-WOLF'S DAUGH-TER"...
I WANT YOU TO FIND OUT IF THAT STORY EXISTS HERE...
RIGHT NOW, IN THIS WORLD.
YES! UNDER-STOOD!
OH, BUT I DON'T THINK I...
DO YOU KNOW HOW TO USE THE BOOK-MARK?
I DO.
IF THIS TASK IS TOO HARD FOR YOU, I CAN ASK FOR SOME-THING ELSE.
OH-- NO, IT'S OKAY!
I'LL GET GOING.
I'M JUST GLAD WE WERE FINALLY ABLE TO TALK.
I HAVE SOME-THING ELSE TO ASK...
Back on Peter Pan's ship...
SHE'S NOT HERE...

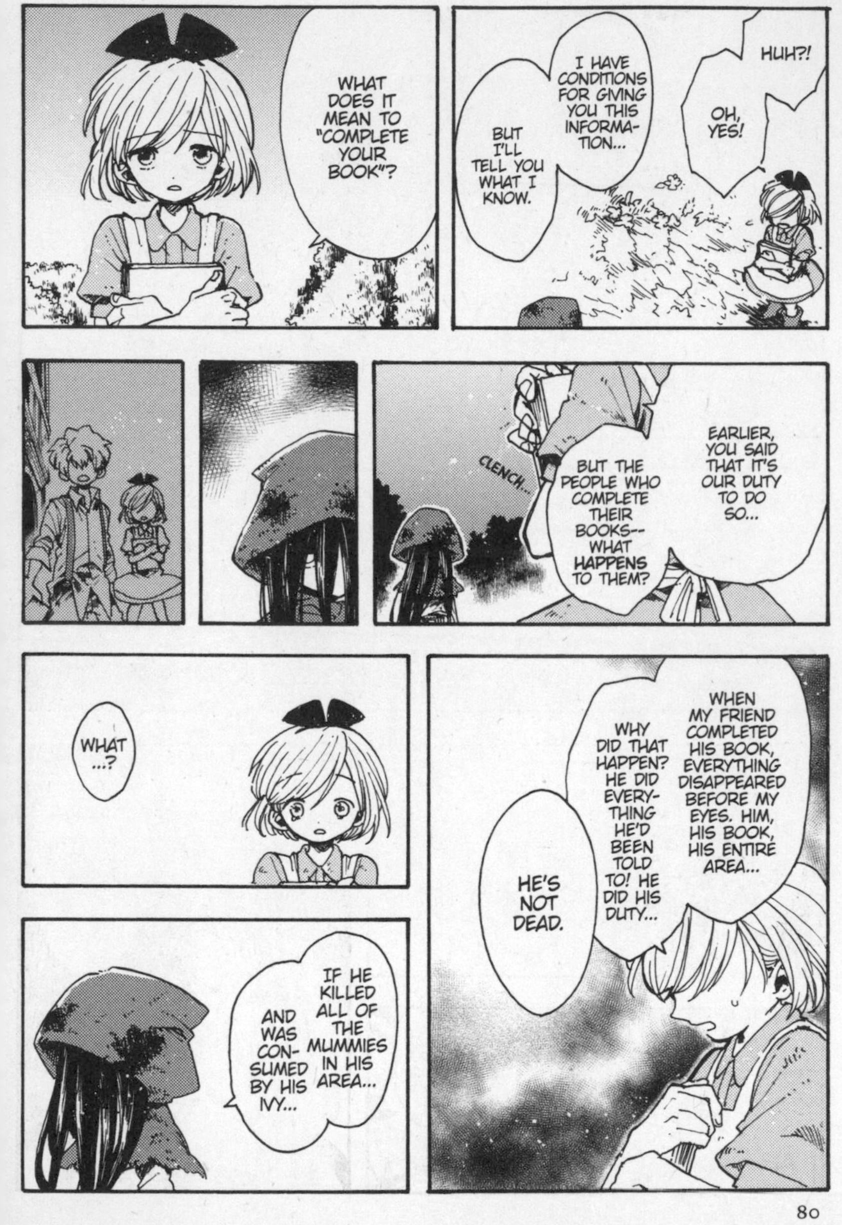

HUH?!
OH, YES!
I HAVE CONDITIONS FOR GIVING YOU THIS INFORMATION...
BUT I'LL TELL YOU WHAT I KNOW.
WHAT DOES IT MEAN TO "COMPLETE YOUR BOOK"?
EARLIER, YOU SAID THAT IT'S OUR DUTY TO DO SO...
CLENCH...
BUT THE PEOPLE WHO COMPLETE THEIR BOOKS-- WHAT HAPPENS TO THEM?
WHEN MY FRIEND COMPLETED HIS BOOK, EVERYTHING DISAPPEARED BEFORE MY EYES. HIM, HIS BOOK, HIS ENTIRE AREA...
WHY DID THAT HAPPEN? HE DID EVERYTHING HE'D BEEN TOLD TO! HE DID HIS DUTY...
HE'S NOT DEAD.
WHAT ...?
IF HE KILLED ALL OF THE MUMMIES IN HIS AREA...
AND WAS CONSUMED BY HIS IVY...

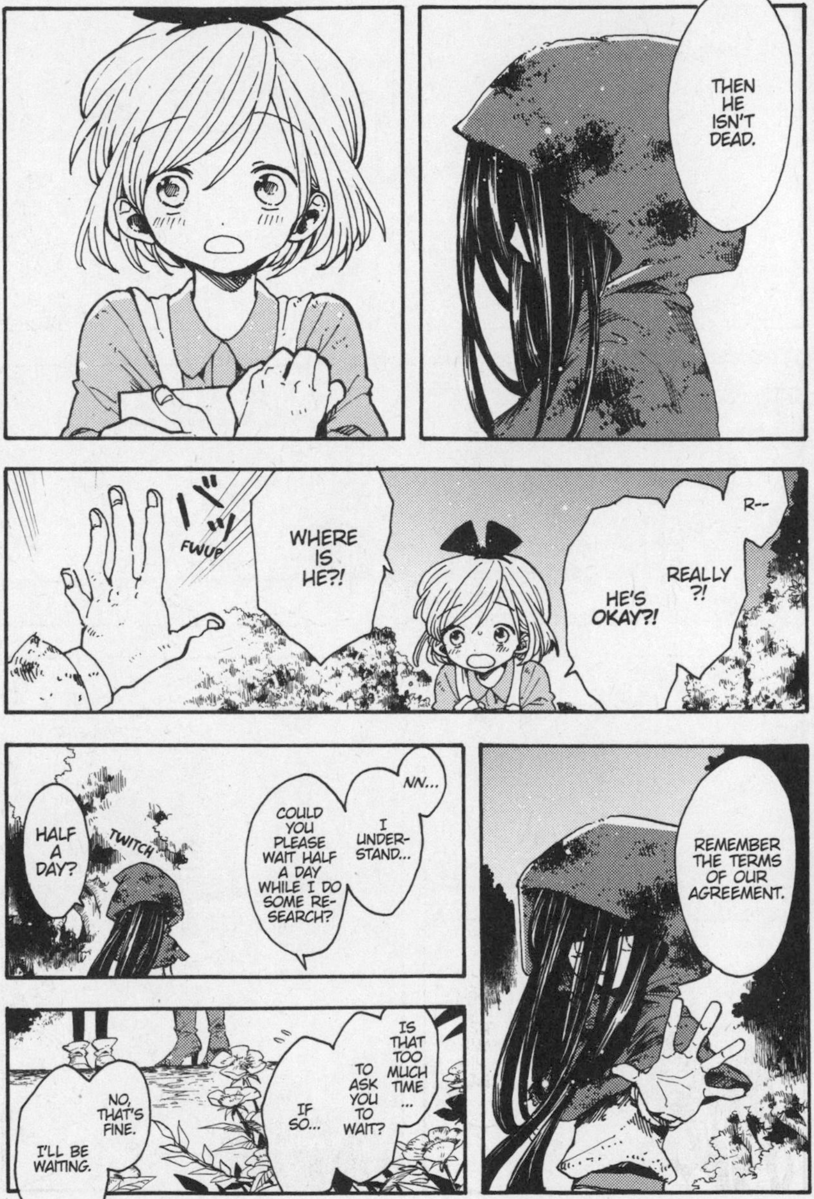
THEN HE ISN'T DEAD.
R--
REALLY?!
HE'S OKAY?!
WHERE IS HE?!
FWUP
REMEMBER THE TERMS OF OUR AGREEMENT.
NN... I UNDERSTAND...
COULD YOU PLEASE WAIT HALF A DAY WHILE I DO SOME RESEARCH?
TWITCH
HALF A DAY?
IS THAT TOO MUCH TIME...
TO ASK YOU TO WAIT?
IF SO...
NO, THAT'S FINE.
I'LL BE WAITING.

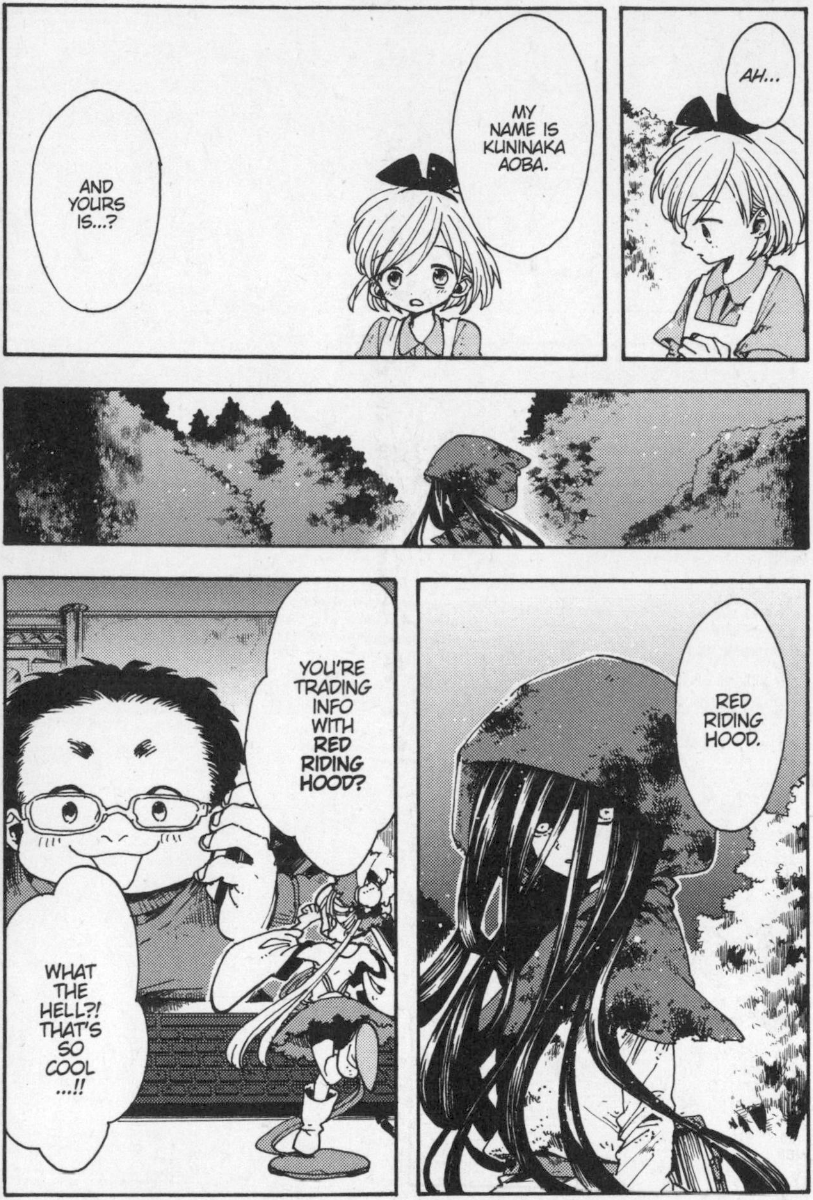
AH...
MY NAME IS KUNINAKA AOBA.
AND YOURS IS...?
RED RIDING HOOD.
YOU'RE TRADING INFO WITH RED RIDING HOOD?
WHAT THE HELL?! THAT'S SO COOL ...!!

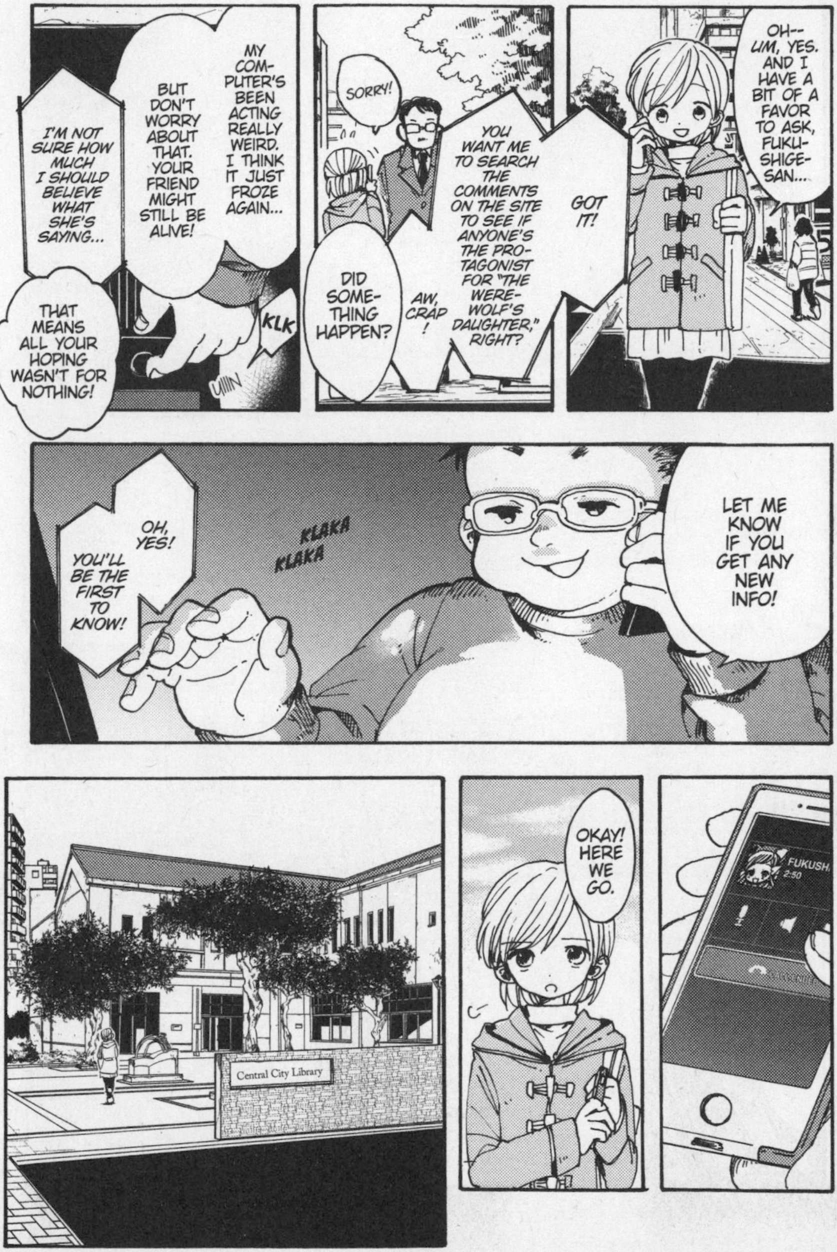
OH-- UM, YES. AND I HAVE A BIT OF A FAVOR TO ASK, FUKU-SHIGE-SAN...
GOT IT!
YOU WANT ME TO SEARCH THE COMMENTS ON THE SITE TO SEE IF ANYONE'S THE PRO-TAGONIST FOR "THE WERE-WOLF'S DAUGHTER," RIGHT?
SORRY!
AW, CRAP!
DID SOME-THING HAPPEN?
MY COM-PUTER'S BEEN ACTING REALLY WEIRD. I THINK IT JUST FROZE AGAIN...
BUT DON'T WORRY ABOUT THAT. YOUR FRIEND MIGHT STILL BE ALIVE!
KLK
I'M NOT SURE HOW MUCH I SHOULD BELIEVE WHAT SHE'S SAYING...
THAT MEANS ALL YOUR HOPING WASN'T FOR NOTHING!
LET ME KNOW IF YOU GET ANY NEW INFO!
KLAKA KLAKA
OH, YES! YOU'LL BE THE FIRST TO KNOW!
2:50
OKAY! HERE WE GO.
Central City Library

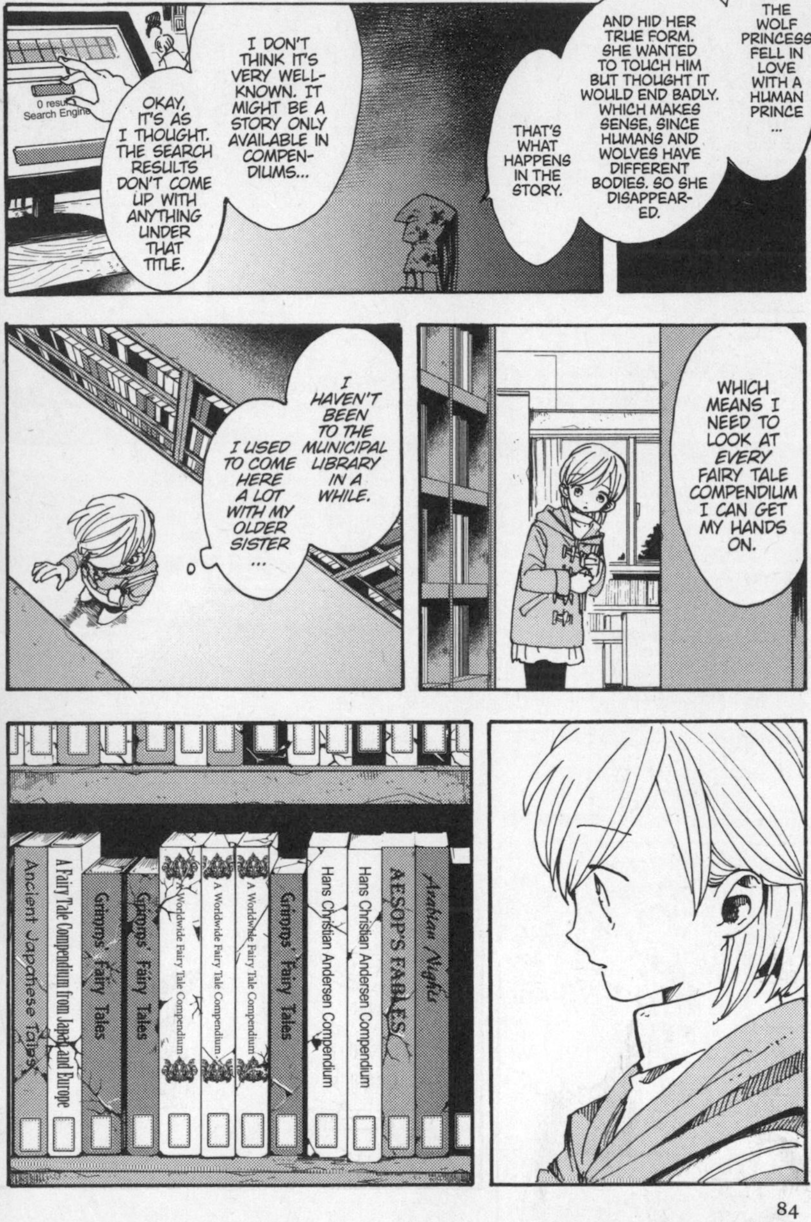
THE WOLF PRINCESS FELL IN LOVE WITH A HUMAN PRINCE ...
AND HID HER TRUE FORM. SHE WANTED TO TOUCH HIM BUT THOUGHT IT WOULD END BADLY. WHICH MAKES SENSE, SINCE HUMANS AND WOLVES HAVE DIFFERENT BODIES. SO SHE DISAPPEARED.
THAT'S WHAT HAPPENS IN THE STORY.
I DON'T THINK IT'S VERY WELL-KNOWN. IT MIGHT BE A STORY ONLY AVAILABLE IN COMPENDIUMS...
Search Engine
OKAY, IT'S AS I THOUGHT. THE SEARCH RESULTS DON'T COME UP WITH ANYTHING UNDER THAT TITLE.
WHICH MEANS I NEED TO LOOK AT *EVERY* FAIRY TALE COMPENDIUM I CAN GET MY HANDS ON.
I HAVEN'T BEEN TO THE MUNICIPAL LIBRARY IN A WHILE.
I USED TO COME HERE A LOT WITH MY OLDER SISTER ...
Ancient Japanese Tales
A Fairy Tale Compendium from Japan and Europe
Grimms' Fairy Tales
Grimms' Fairy Tales
A Worldwide Fairy Tale Compendium
A Worldwide Fairy Tale Compendium
A Worldwide Fairy Tale Compendium
Grimms' Fairy Tales
Hans Christian Andersen Compendium
Hans Christian Andersen Compendium
AESOP'S FABLES
Arabian Nights

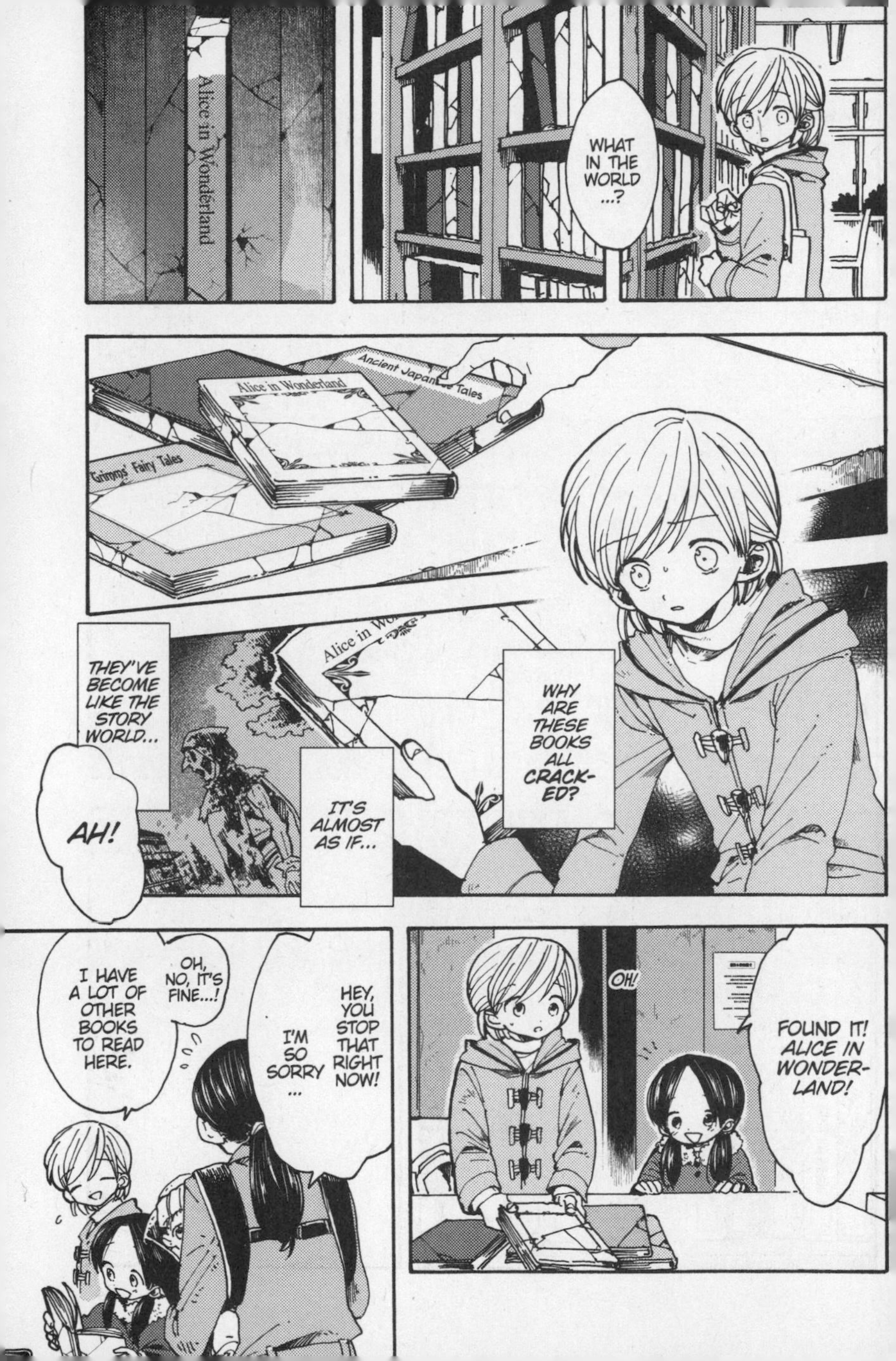

WHAT IN THE WORLD ...?
Alice in Wonderland
Alice in Wonderland
Grimms' Fairy Tales
WHY ARE THESE BOOKS ALL CRACKED?
IT'S ALMOST AS IF...
THEY'VE BECOME LIKE THE STORY WORLD...
AH!
FOUND IT! ALICE IN WONDERLAND!
OH!
HEY, YOU STOP THAT RIGHT NOW!
I'M SO SORRY ...
OH, NO, IT'S FINE...!
I HAVE A LOT OF OTHER BOOKS TO READ HERE.

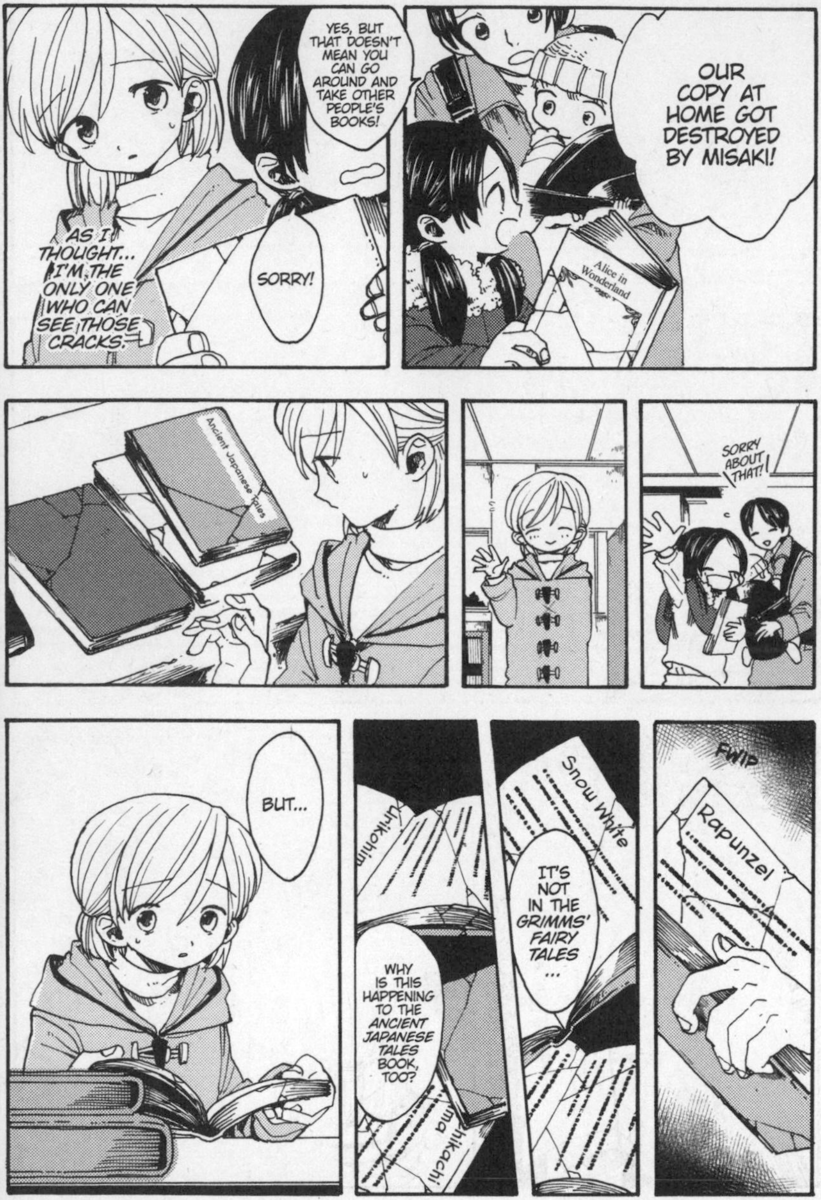
OUR COPY AT HOME GOT DESTROYED BY MISAKI!
Alice in Wonderland
YES, BUT THAT DOESN'T MEAN YOU CAN GO AROUND AND TAKE OTHER PEOPLE'S BOOKS!
SORRY!
AS I THOUGHT... I'M THE ONLY ONE WHO CAN SEE THOSE CRACKS.
SORRY ABOUT THAT!
Ancient Japanese Tales
FWIP
Rapunzel
Snow White
IT'S NOT IN THE GRIMMS' FAIRY TALES...
WHY IS THIS HAPPENING TO THE ANCIENT JAPANESE TALES BOOK, TOO?
BUT...

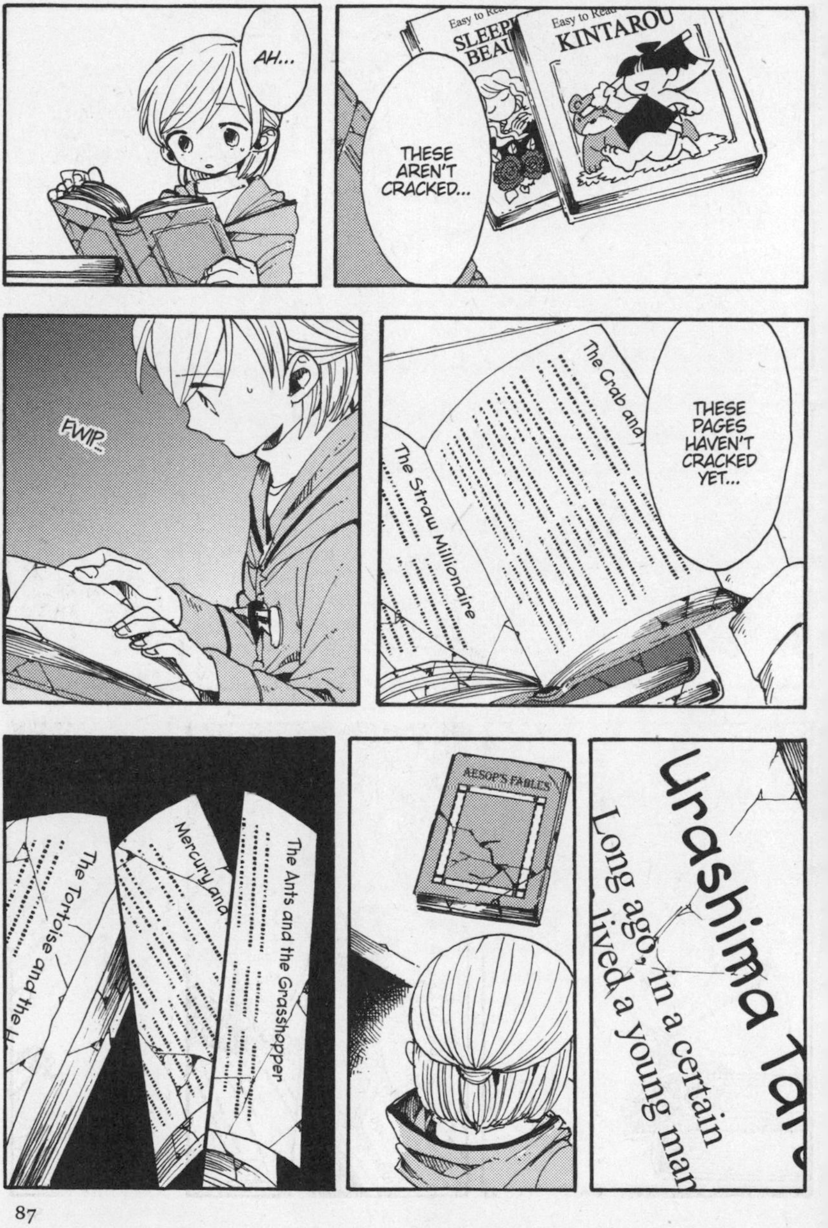
Easy to Read
SLEEP
BEAU
Easy to Read
KINTAROU
THESE AREN'T CRACKED...
AH...
The Crab and
The Straw Millionaire
THESE PAGES HAVEN'T CRACKED YET...
FWIP..
Urashima Ta
Long ago, in a certain
lived a young man
AESOP'S FABLES
The Ants and the Grasshopper
Mercury and
The Tortoise and the H

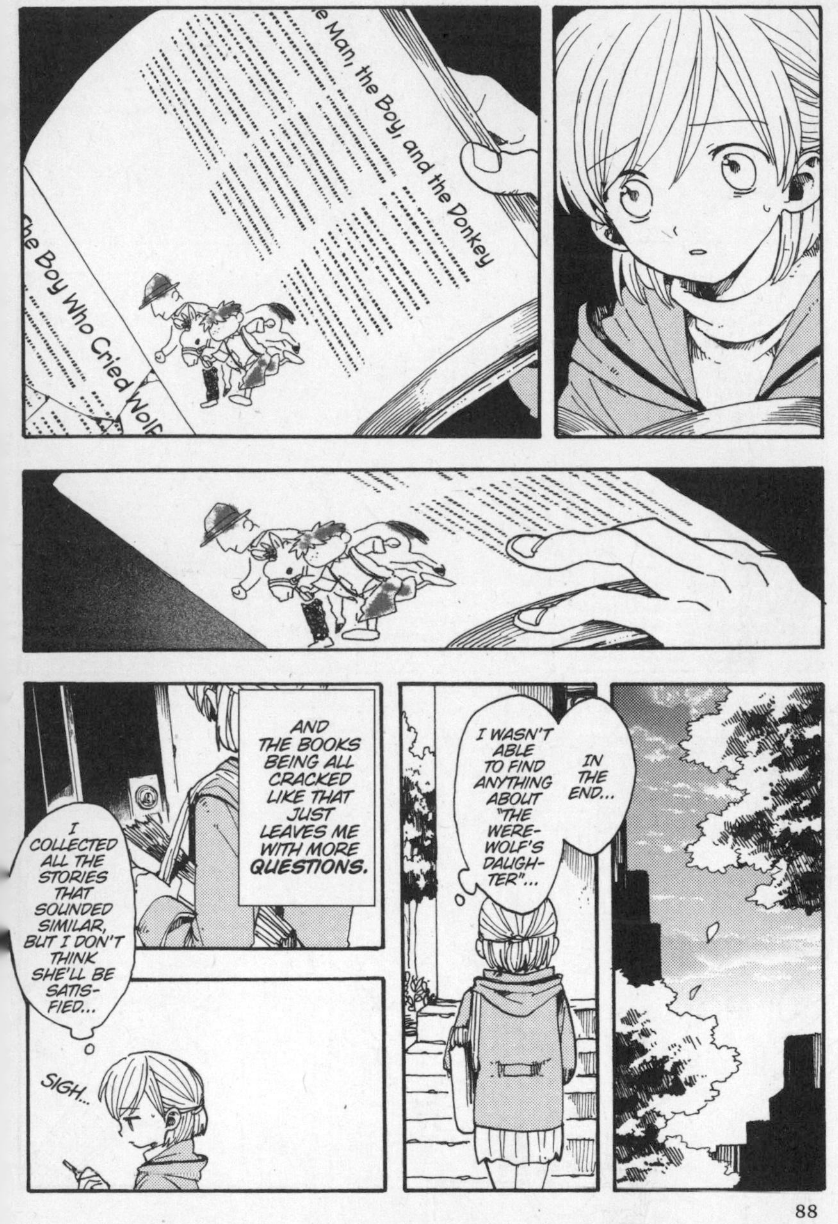
e Man, the Boy, and the Donkey
The Boy Who Cried Wolf
IN THE END...
I WASN'T ABLE TO FIND ANYTHING ABOUT "THE WERE-WOLF'S DAUGHTER"...
I COLLECTED ALL THE STORIES THAT SOUNDED SIMILAR, BUT I DON'T THINK SHE'LL BE SATIS-FIED...
AND THE BOOKS BEING ALL CRACKED LIKE THAT JUST LEAVES ME WITH MORE **QUESTIONS.**
SIGH...

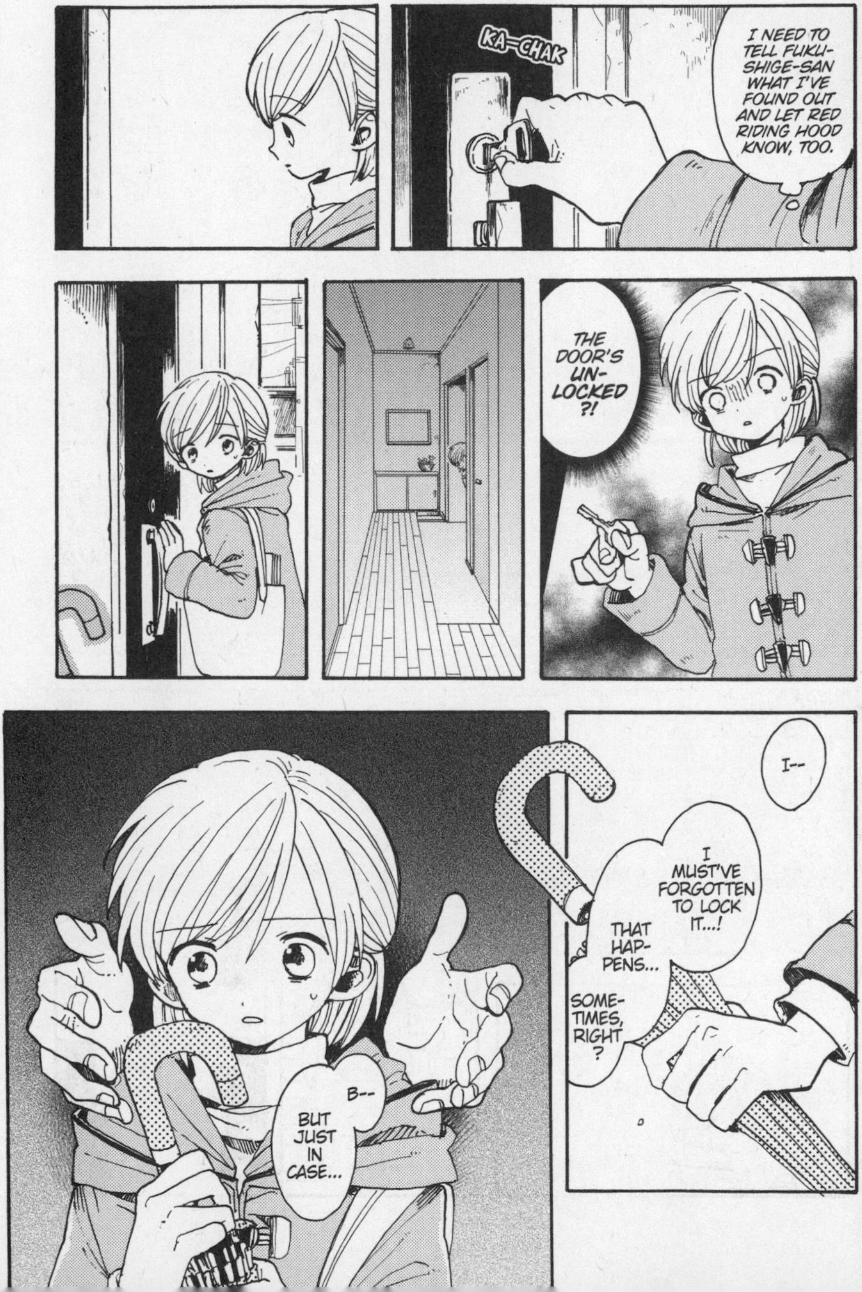
KA-CHAK
I NEED TO TELL FUKU-SHIGE-SAN WHAT I'VE FOUND OUT AND LET RED RIDING HOOD KNOW, TOO.
THE DOOR'S UN-LOCKED ?!
I--
I MUST'VE FORGOTTEN TO LOCK IT...!
THAT HAP-PENS...
SOME-TIMES, RIGHT ?
B--
BUT JUST IN CASE...

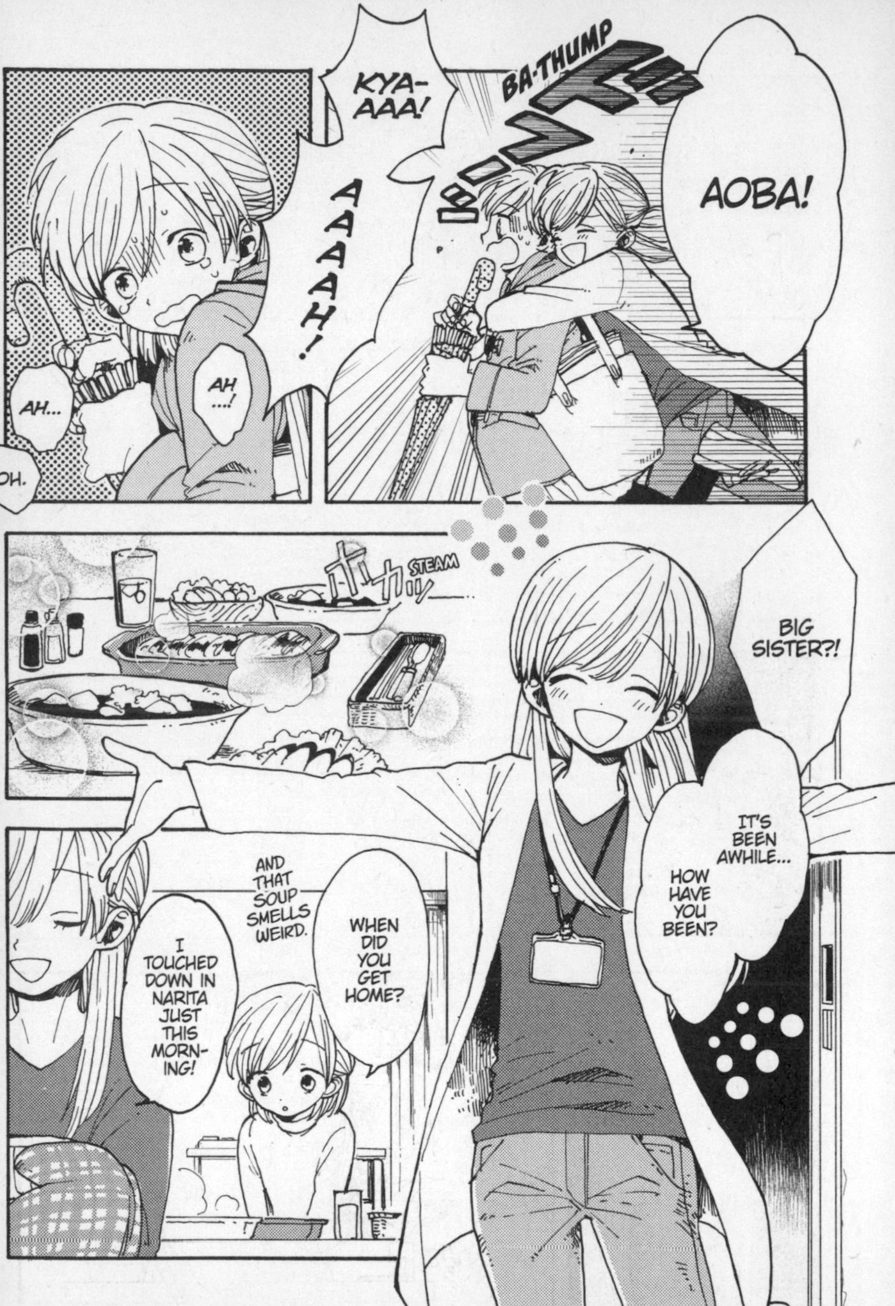
AOBA!
BA-THUMP
KYA-AAA!
AAAAAH!
AH ...!
AH...
OH.
BIG SISTER?!
STEAM
IT'S BEEN AWHILE...
HOW HAVE YOU BEEN?
WHEN DID YOU GET HOME?
I TOUCHED DOWN IN NARITA JUST THIS MORN-ING!
AND THAT SOUP SMELLS WEIRD.

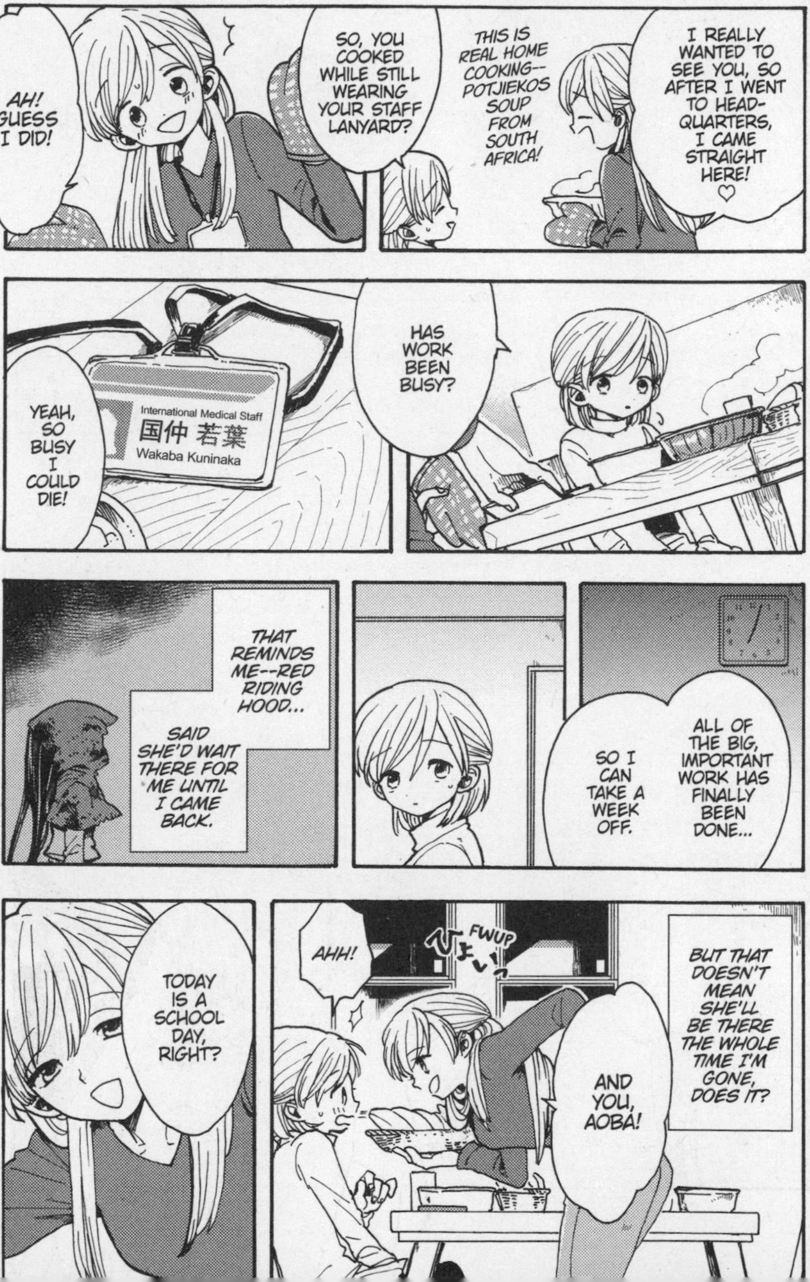
I REALLY WANTED TO SEE YOU, SO AFTER I WENT TO HEAD-QUARTERS, I CAME STRAIGHT HERE! ♡
THIS IS REAL HOME COOKING-- POTJIEKOS SOUP FROM SOUTH AFRICA!
SO, YOU COOKED WHILE STILL WEARING YOUR STAFF LANYARD?
AH! GUESS I DID!
HAS WORK BEEN BUSY?
International Medical Staff
国仲 若葉
Wakaba Kuninaka
YEAH, SO BUSY I COULD DIE!
ALL OF THE BIG, IMPORTANT WORK HAS FINALLY BEEN DONE...
SO I CAN TAKE A WEEK OFF.
THAT REMINDS ME--RED RIDING HOOD...
SAID SHE'D WAIT THERE FOR ME UNTIL I CAME BACK.
BUT THAT DOESN'T MEAN SHE'LL BE THERE THE WHOLE TIME I'M GONE, DOES IT?
AND YOU, AOBA!
ひょいっ
FWUP
AHH!
TODAY IS A SCHOOL DAY, RIGHT?

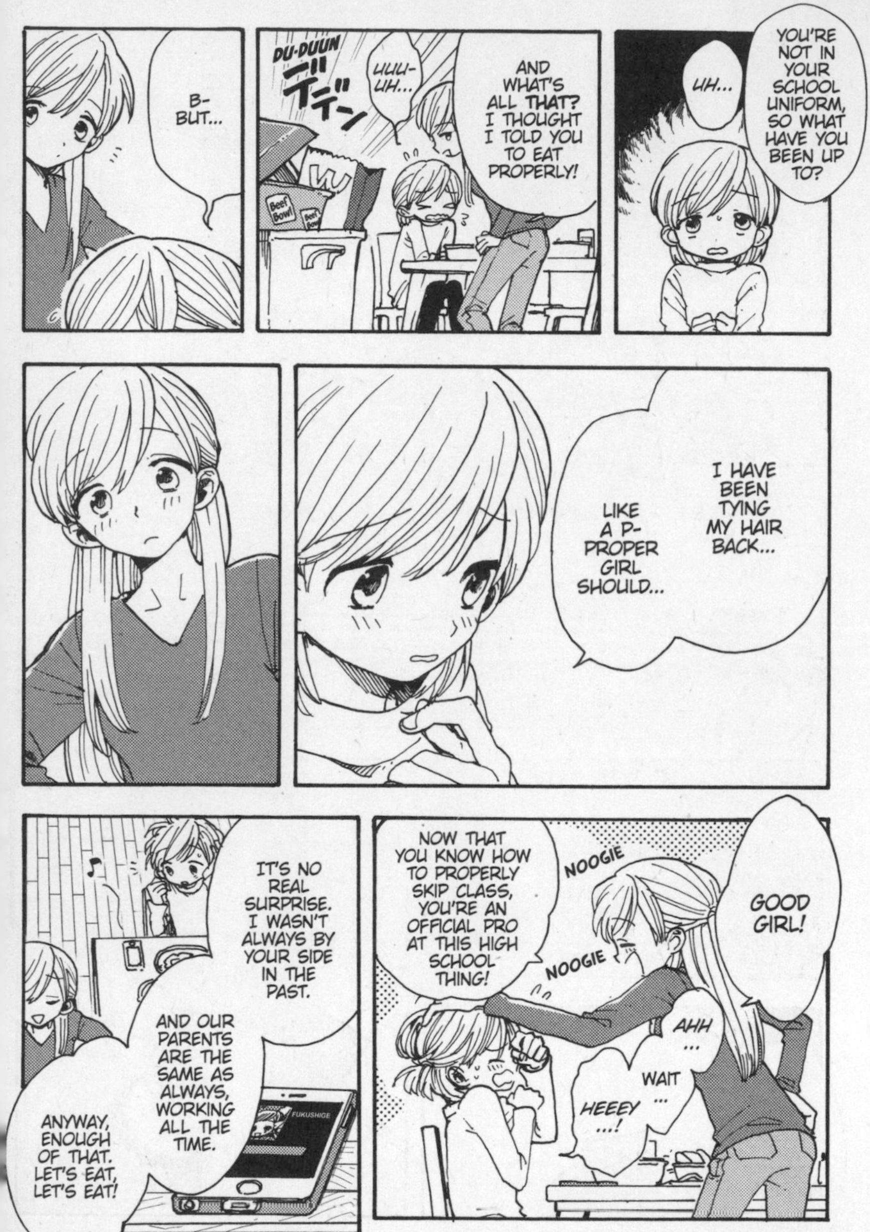

YOU'RE NOT IN YOUR SCHOOL UNIFORM, SO WHAT HAVE YOU BEEN UP TO?
UH...
AND WHAT'S ALL THAT? I THOUGHT I TOLD YOU TO EAT PROPERLY!
UUU-UH...
DU-DUUN
デデン
Beef Bowl!
Beef Bowl
B-BUT...
I HAVE BEEN TYING MY HAIR BACK...
LIKE A P-PROPER GIRL SHOULD...
GOOD GIRL!
NOW THAT YOU KNOW HOW TO PROPERLY SKIP CLASS, YOU'RE AN OFFICIAL PRO AT THIS HIGH SCHOOL THING!
NOOGIE
NOOGIE
AHH ...
WAIT ...
HEEEY ...!
IT'S NO REAL SURPRISE. I WASN'T ALWAYS BY YOUR SIDE IN THE PAST.
AND OUR PARENTS ARE THE SAME AS ALWAYS, WORKING ALL THE TIME.
FUKUSHIGE
ANYWAY, ENOUGH OF THAT. LET'S EAT, LET'S EAT!

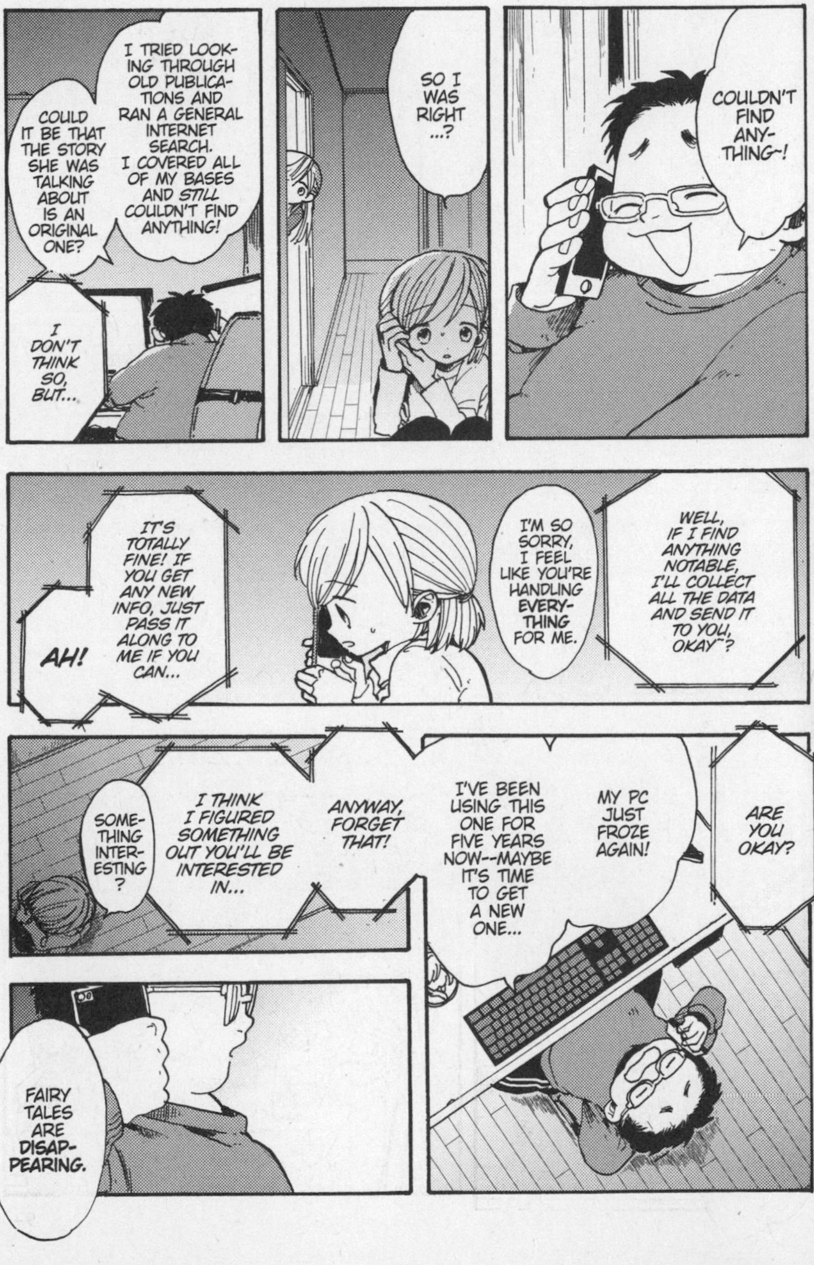
COULDN'T FIND ANY-THING~!
SO I WAS RIGHT ...?
I TRIED LOOK-ING THROUGH OLD PUBLICA-TIONS AND RAN A GENERAL INTERNET SEARCH. I COVERED ALL OF MY BASES AND STILL COULDN'T FIND ANYTHING!
COULD IT BE THAT THE STORY SHE WAS TALKING ABOUT IS AN ORIGINAL ONE?
I DON'T THINK SO, BUT...
WELL, IF I FIND ANYTHING NOTABLE, I'LL COLLECT ALL THE DATA AND SEND IT TO YOU, OKAY~?
I'M SO SORRY, I FEEL LIKE YOU'RE HANDLING EVERY-THING FOR ME.
IT'S TOTALLY FINE! IF YOU GET ANY NEW INFO, JUST PASS IT ALONG TO ME IF YOU CAN...
AH!
ARE YOU OKAY?
MY PC JUST FROZE AGAIN!
I'VE BEEN USING THIS ONE FOR FIVE YEARS NOW--MAYBE IT'S TIME TO GET A NEW ONE...
ANYWAY, FORGET THAT!
I THINK I FIGURED SOMETHING OUT YOU'LL BE INTERESTED IN...
SOME-THING INTER-ESTING ?
FAIRY TALES ARE DISAP-PEARING.

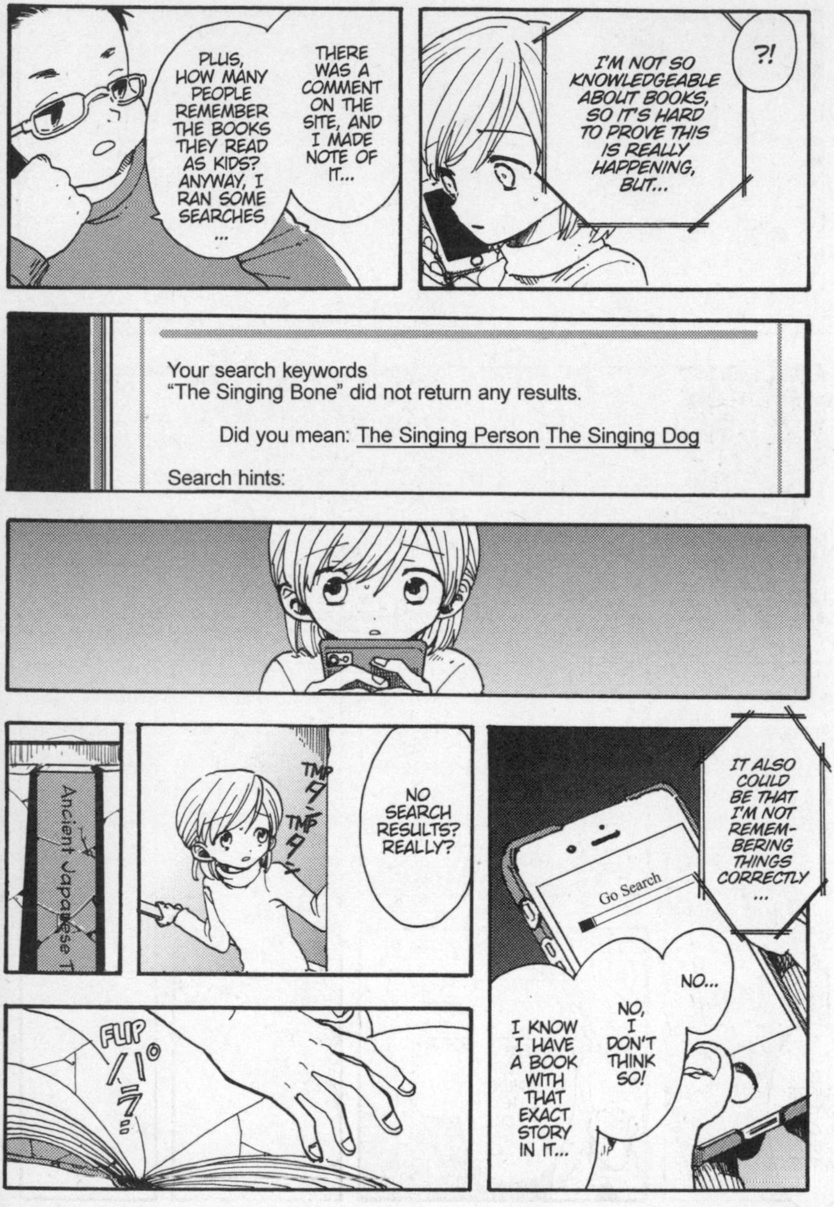
?!
I'M NOT SO KNOWLEDGEABLE ABOUT BOOKS, SO IT'S HARD TO PROVE THIS IS REALLY HAPPENING, BUT...
THERE WAS A COMMENT ON THE SITE, AND I MADE NOTE OF IT...
PLUS, HOW MANY PEOPLE REMEMBER THE BOOKS THEY READ AS KIDS? ANYWAY, I RAN SOME SEARCHES ...
Your search keywords
"The Singing Bone" did not return any results.
Did you mean: The Singing Person The Singing Dog
Search hints:
IT ALSO COULD BE THAT I'M NOT REMEMBERING THINGS CORRECTLY ...
Go Search
NO...
NO, I DON'T THINK SO!
I KNOW I HAVE A BOOK WITH THAT EXACT STORY IN IT...
NO SEARCH RESULTS? REALLY?
TMP
TMP
Ancient Japanese
FLIP

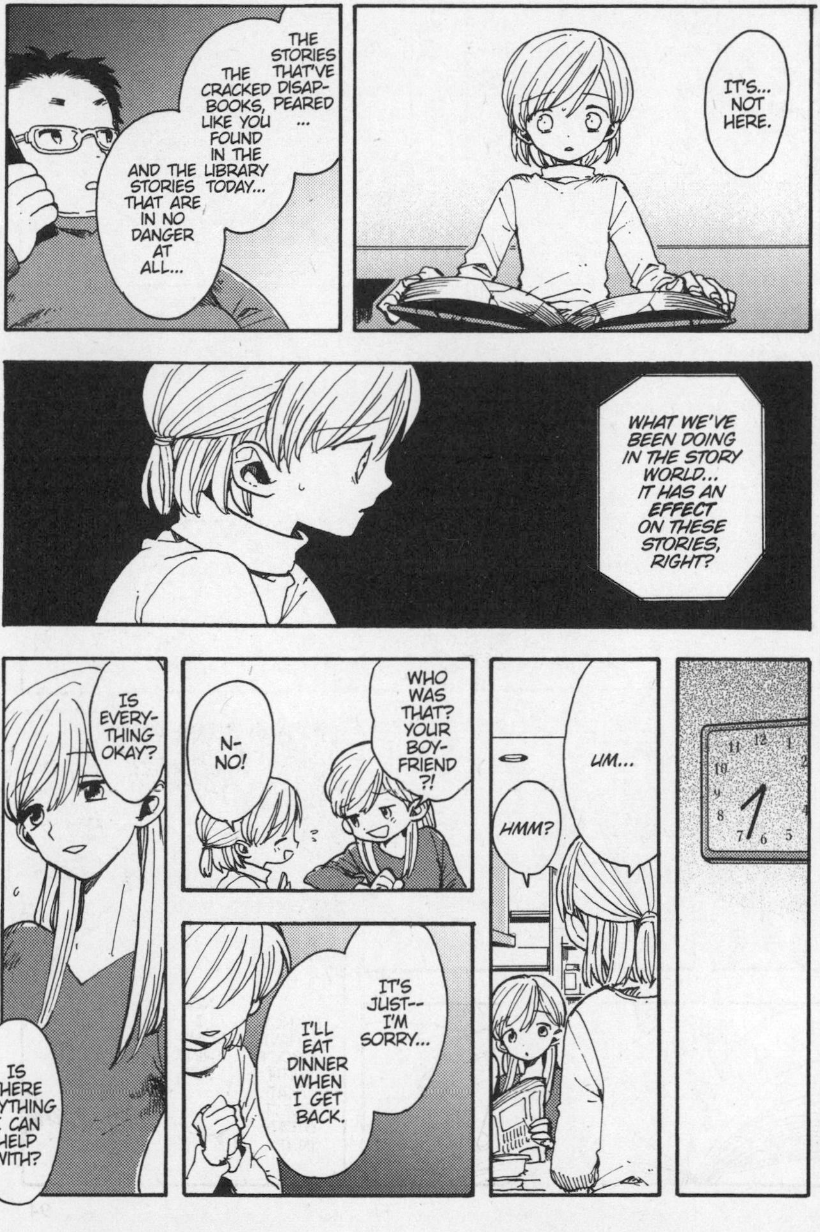
IT'S... NOT HERE.
THE STORIES THAT'VE DISAPPEARED...
THE CRACKED BOOKS, LIKE YOU FOUND IN THE LIBRARY TODAY...
AND THE STORIES THAT ARE IN NO DANGER AT ALL...
WHAT WE'VE BEEN DOING IN THE STORY WORLD... IT HAS AN EFFECT ON THESE STORIES, RIGHT?
UM...
HMM?
WHO WAS THAT? YOUR BOYFRIEND?!
N-NO!
IT'S JUST-- I'M SORRY...
I'LL EAT DINNER WHEN I GET BACK.
IS EVERYTHING OKAY?
IS THERE ANYTHING I CAN HELP WITH?

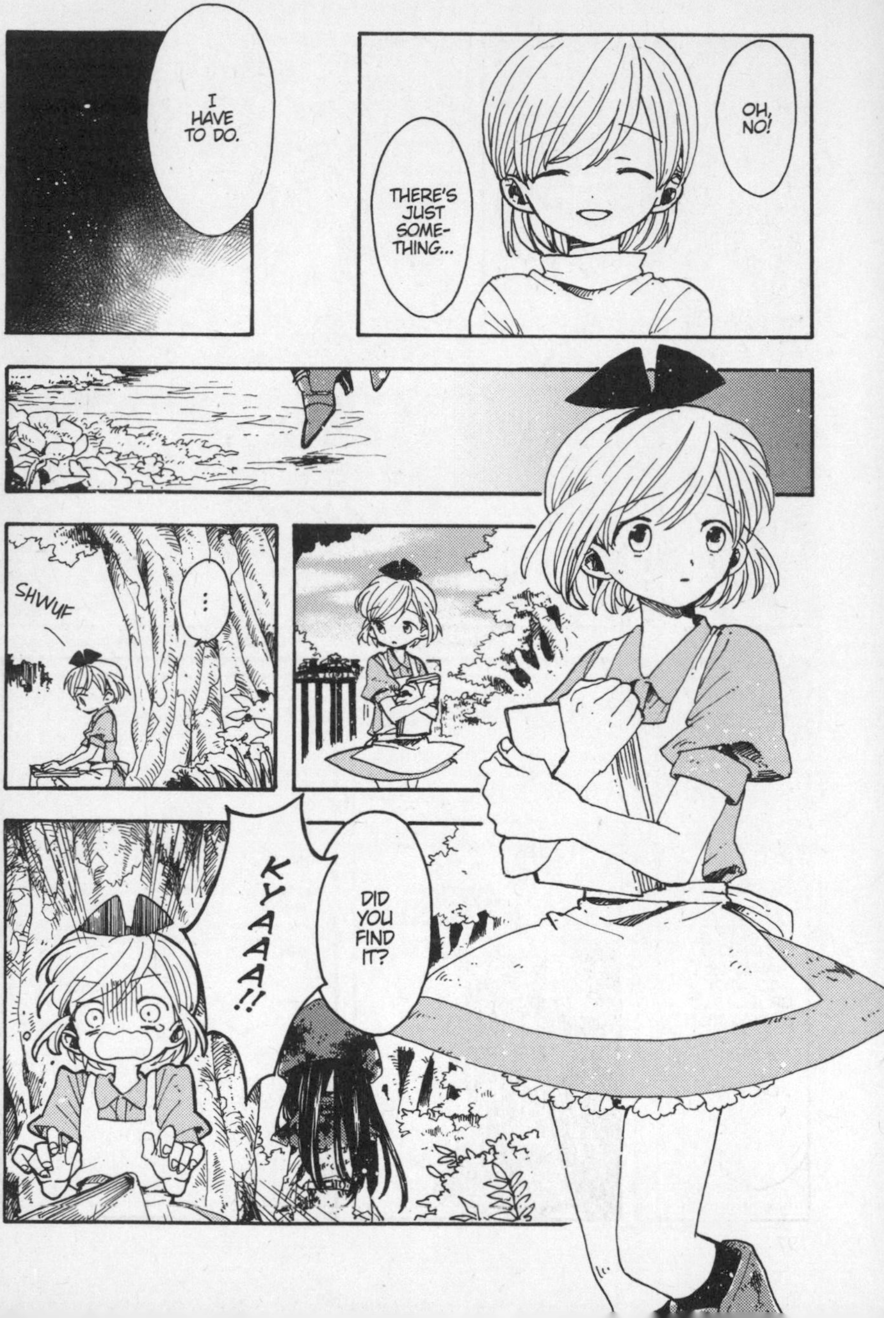
OH, NO!
THERE'S JUST SOMETHING...
I HAVE TO DO.
...
SHWUF
DID YOU FIND IT?
KYAAAA!!

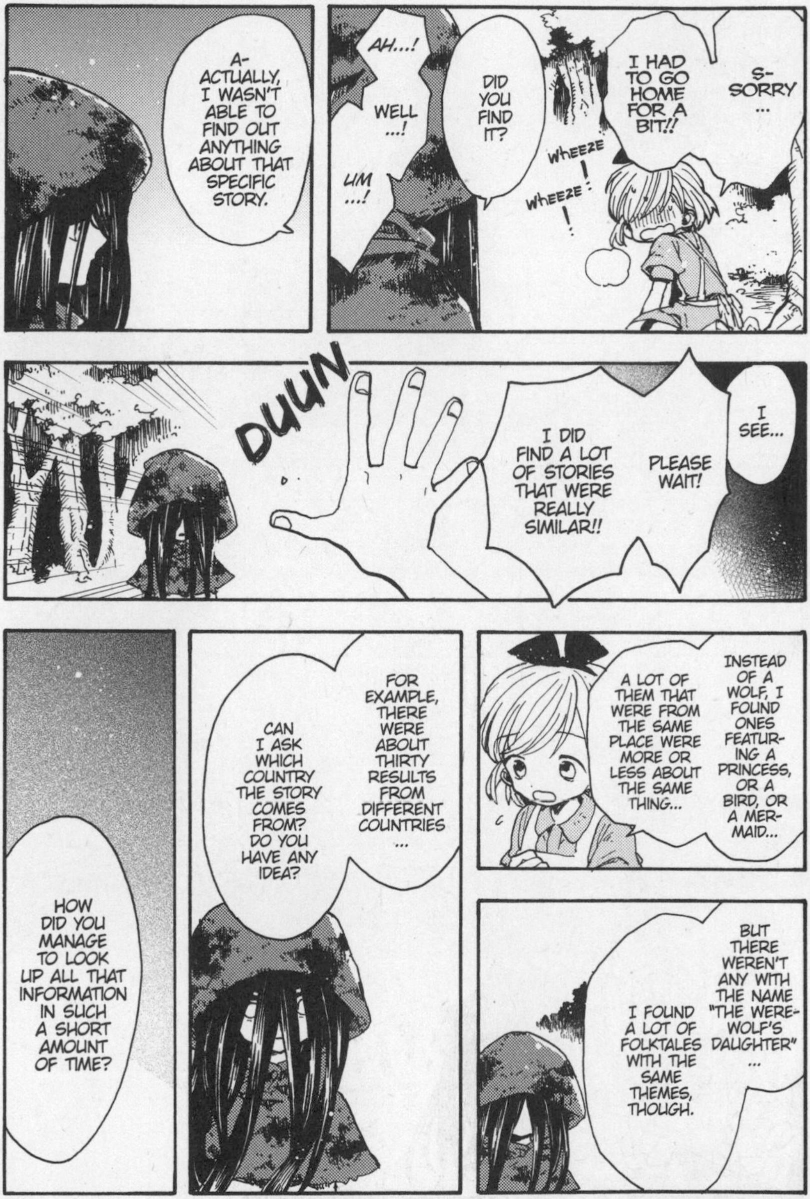
S-SORRY...
I HAD TO GO HOME FOR A BIT!!
Wheeze! Wheeze!
DID YOU FIND IT?
AH...! WELL...! UM...!
A-ACTUALLY, I WASN'T ABLE TO FIND OUT ANYTHING ABOUT THAT SPECIFIC STORY.
I SEE...
PLEASE WAIT!
I DID FIND A LOT OF STORIES THAT WERE REALLY SIMILAR!!
DUUN
INSTEAD OF A WOLF, I FOUND ONES FEATURING A PRINCESS, OR A BIRD, OR A MERMAID...
A LOT OF THEM THAT WERE FROM THE SAME PLACE WERE MORE OR LESS ABOUT THE SAME THING...
BUT THERE WEREN'T ANY WITH THE NAME "THE WEREWOLF'S DAUGHTER"...
I FOUND A LOT OF FOLKTALES WITH THE SAME THEMES, THOUGH.
FOR EXAMPLE, THERE WERE ABOUT THIRTY RESULTS FROM DIFFERENT COUNTRIES...
CAN I ASK WHICH COUNTRY THE STORY COMES FROM? DO YOU HAVE ANY IDEA?
HOW DID YOU MANAGE TO LOOK UP ALL THAT INFORMATION IN SUCH A SHORT AMOUNT OF TIME?

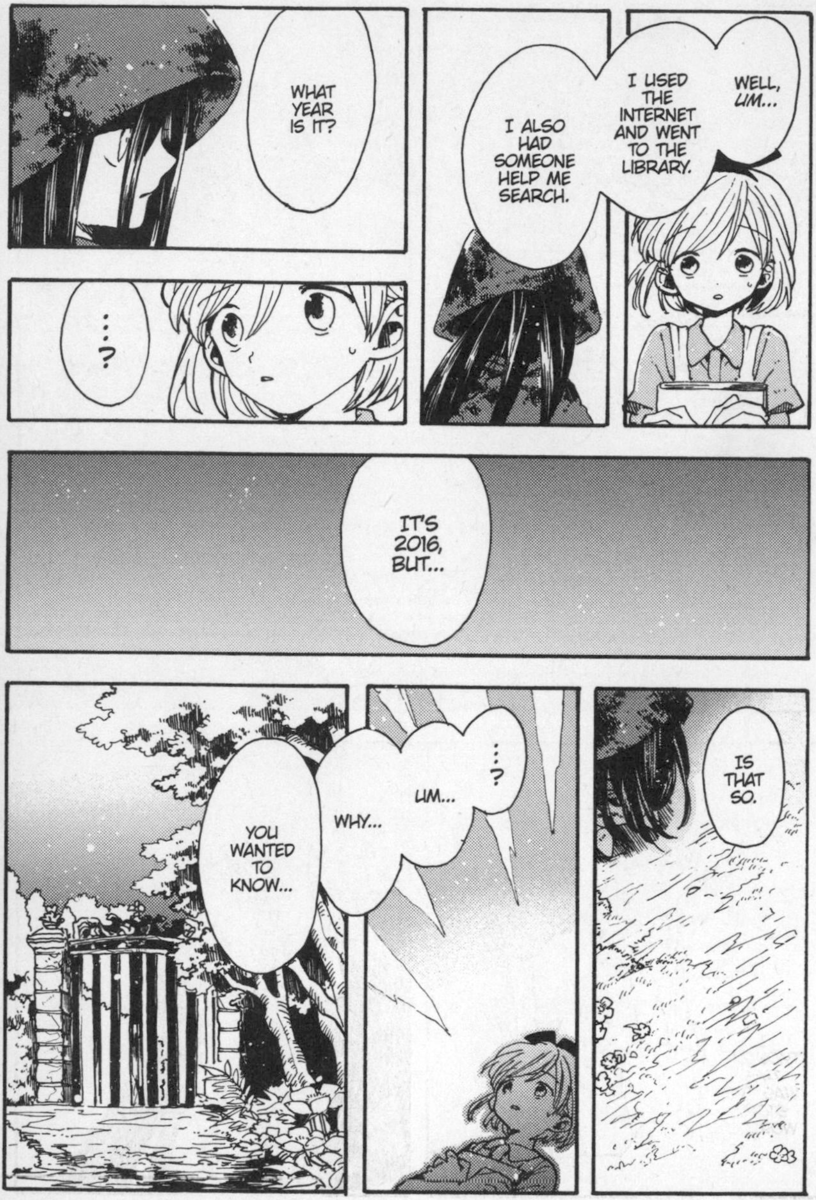
WELL, UM...
I USED THE INTERNET AND WENT TO THE LIBRARY.
I ALSO HAD SOMEONE HELP ME SEARCH.
WHAT YEAR IS IT?
...?
IT'S 2016, BUT...
IS THAT SO.
...?
UM...
WHY...
YOU WANTED TO KNOW...

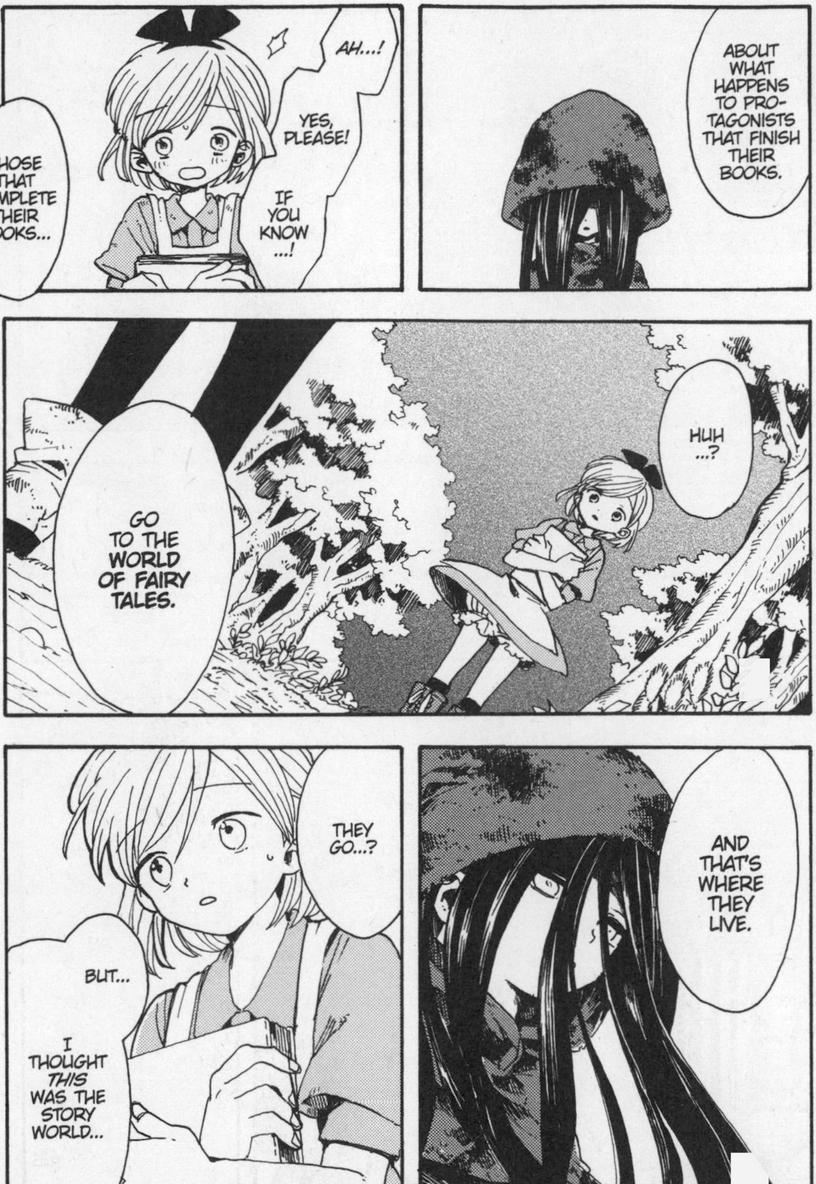
ABOUT WHAT HAPPENS TO PRO-TAGONISTS THAT FINISH THEIR BOOKS.
AH...!
YES, PLEASE!
IF YOU KNOW ...!
THOSE THAT COMPLETE THEIR BOOKS...
HUH ...?
GO TO THE WORLD OF FAIRY TALES.
AND THAT'S WHERE THEY LIVE.
THEY GO...?
BUT...
I THOUGHT *THIS* WAS THE STORY WORLD...

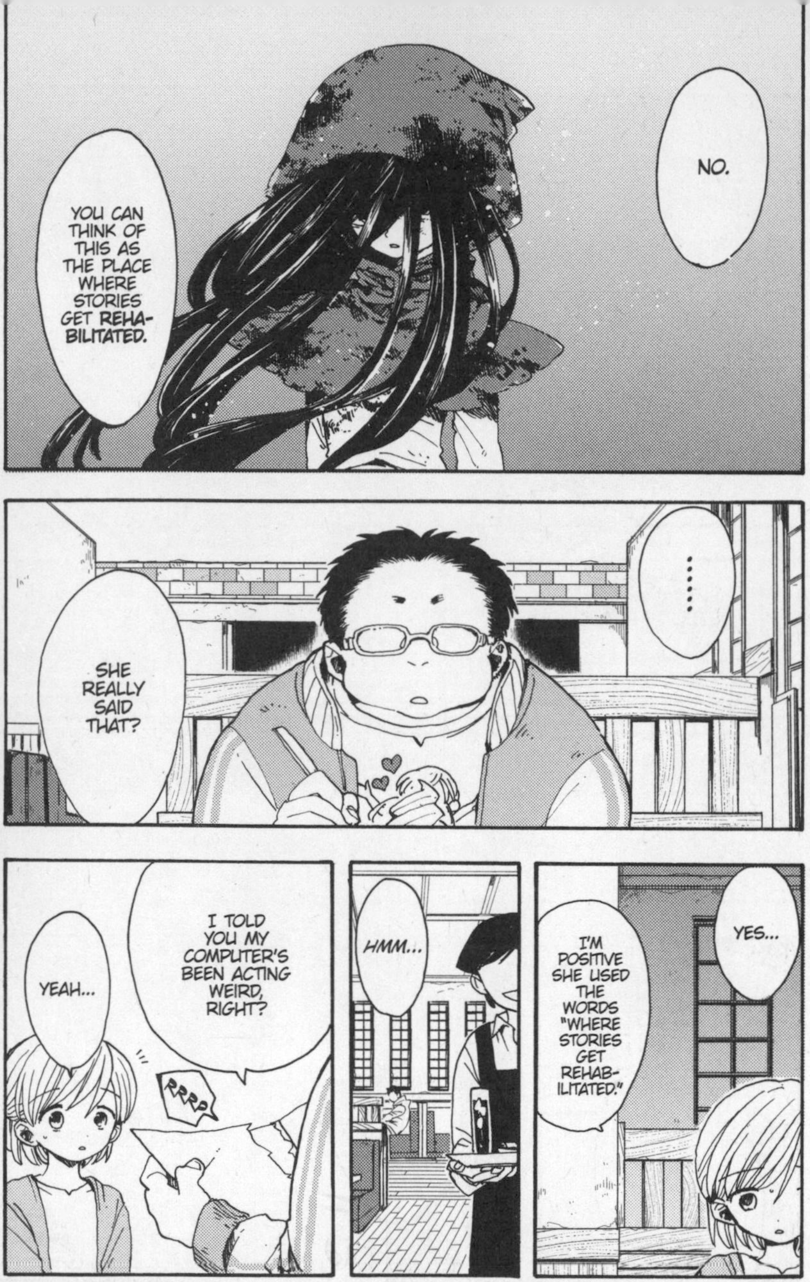
NO.
YOU CAN THINK OF THIS AS THE PLACE WHERE STORIES GET REHA-BILITATED.
......
SHE REALLY SAID THAT?
YES...
I'M POSITIVE SHE USED THE WORDS "WHERE STORIES GET REHAB-ILITATED."
HMM...
I TOLD YOU MY COMPUTER'S BEEN ACTING WEIRD, RIGHT?
YEAH...
RRRP

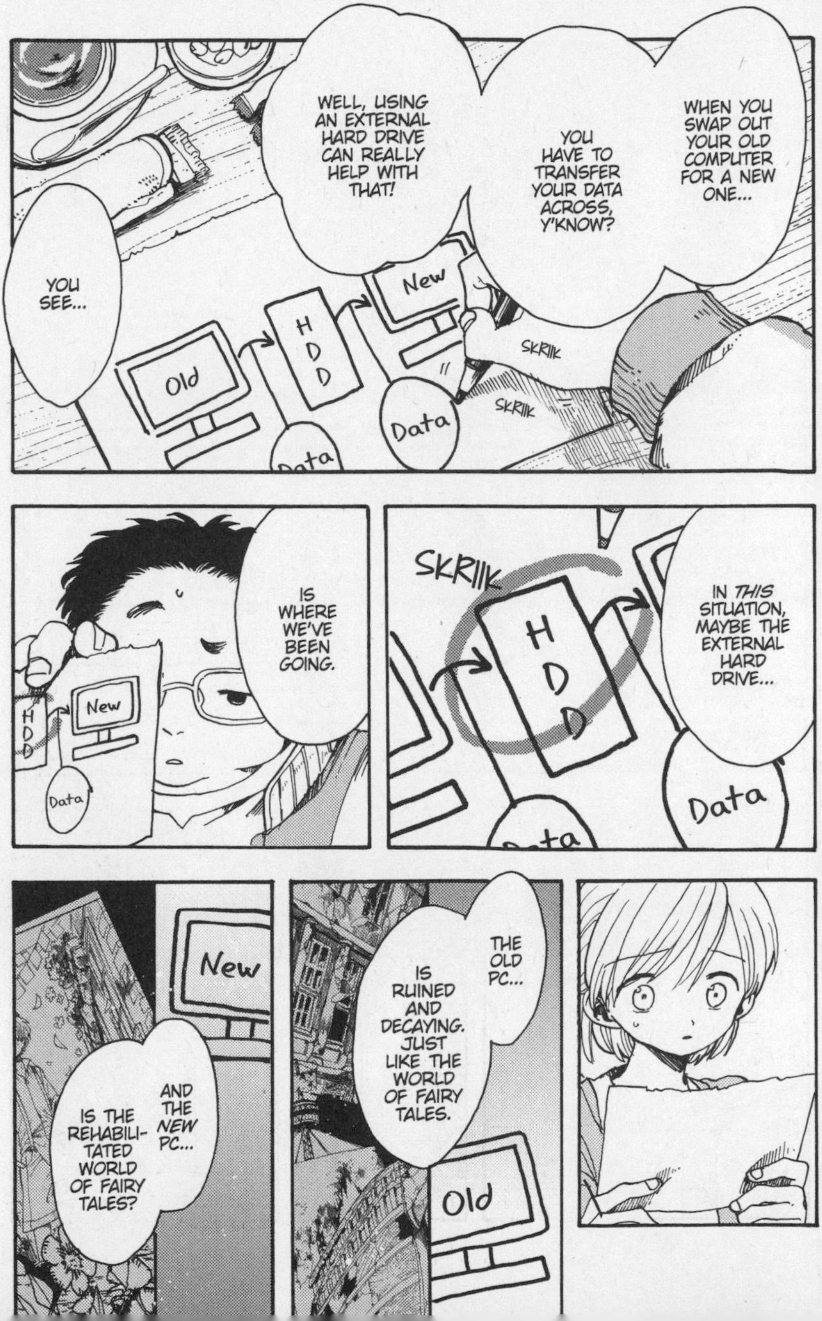
WHEN YOU SWAP OUT YOUR OLD COMPUTER FOR A NEW ONE...
YOU HAVE TO TRANSFER YOUR DATA ACROSS, Y'KNOW?
WELL, USING AN EXTERNAL HARD DRIVE CAN REALLY HELP WITH THAT!
YOU SEE...
New
HDD
Old
Data
Data
SKRIIK
SKRIIK
SKRIIK
IN *THIS* SITUATION, MAYBE THE EXTERNAL HARD DRIVE...
HDD
Data
IS WHERE WE'VE BEEN GOING.
HDD
New
Data
THE OLD PC...
IS RUINED AND DECAYING. JUST LIKE THE WORLD OF FAIRY TALES.
Old
New
AND THE *NEW* PC...
IS THE REHABILITATED WORLD OF FAIRY TALES?

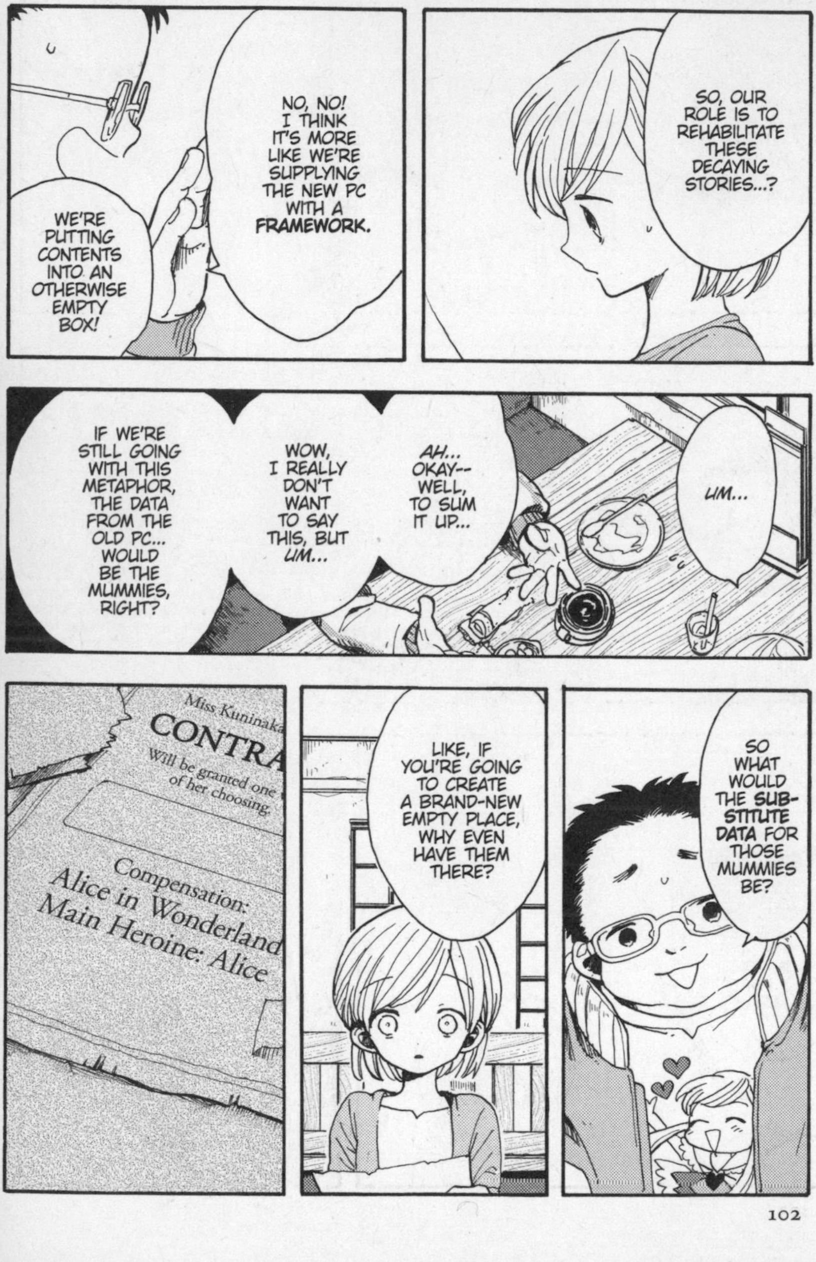
SO, OUR ROLE IS TO REHABILITATE THESE DECAYING STORIES...?
NO, NO! I THINK IT'S MORE LIKE WE'RE SUPPLYING THE NEW PC WITH A FRAMEWORK.
WE'RE PUTTING CONTENTS INTO AN OTHERWISE EMPTY BOX!
UM...
AH... OKAY-- WELL, TO SUM IT UP...
WOW, I REALLY DON'T WANT TO SAY THIS, BUT UM...
IF WE'RE STILL GOING WITH THIS METAPHOR, THE DATA FROM THE OLD PC... WOULD BE THE MUMMIES, RIGHT?
SO WHAT WOULD THE SUB-STITUTE DATA FOR THOSE MUMMIES BE?
LIKE, IF YOU'RE GOING TO CREATE A BRAND-NEW EMPTY PLACE, WHY EVEN HAVE THEM THERE?
Miss Kuninaka
CONTRA
Will be granted one
of her choosing.
Compensation:
Alice in Wonderland
Main Heroine: Alice

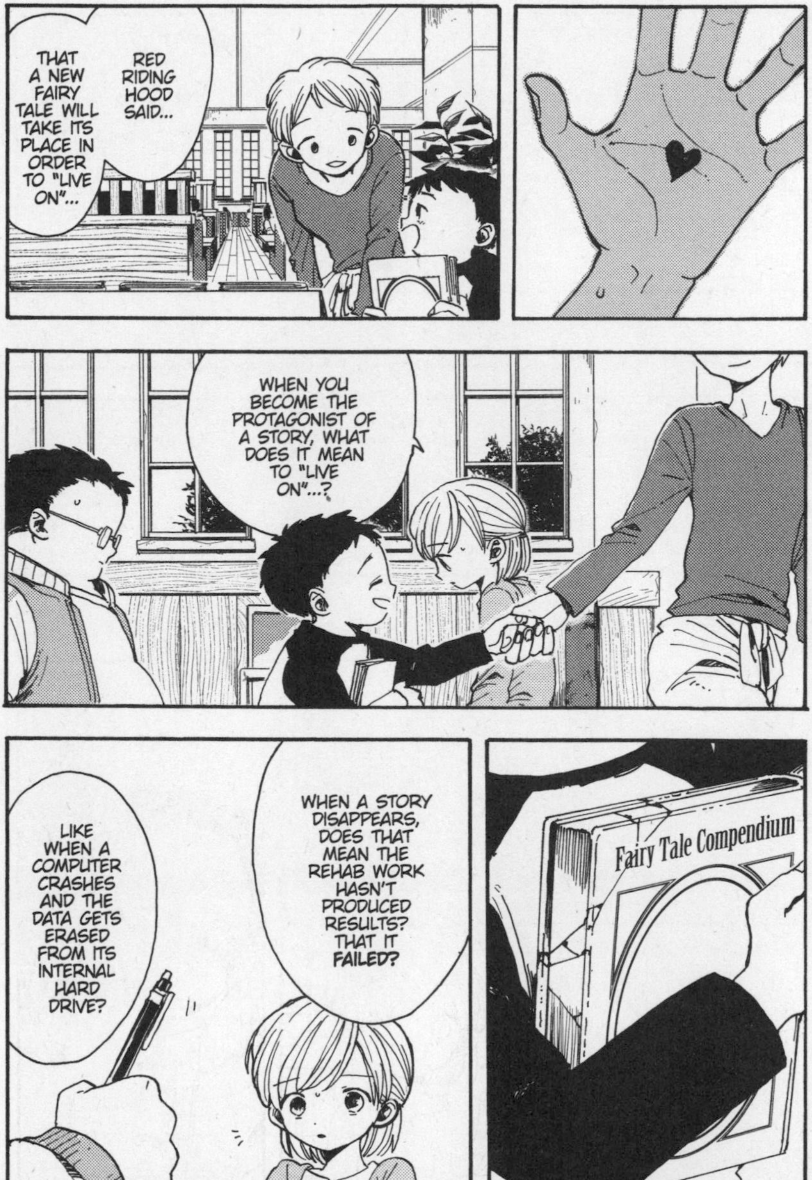
RED RIDING HOOD SAID...
THAT A NEW FAIRY TALE WILL TAKE ITS PLACE IN ORDER TO "LIVE ON"...
WHEN YOU BECOME THE PROTAGONIST OF A STORY, WHAT DOES IT MEAN TO "LIVE ON"...?
Fairy Tale Compendium
WHEN A STORY DISAPPEARS, DOES THAT MEAN THE REHAB WORK HASN'T PRODUCED RESULTS? THAT IT **FAILED?**
LIKE WHEN A COMPUTER CRASHES AND THE DATA GETS ERASED FROM ITS INTERNAL HARD DRIVE?

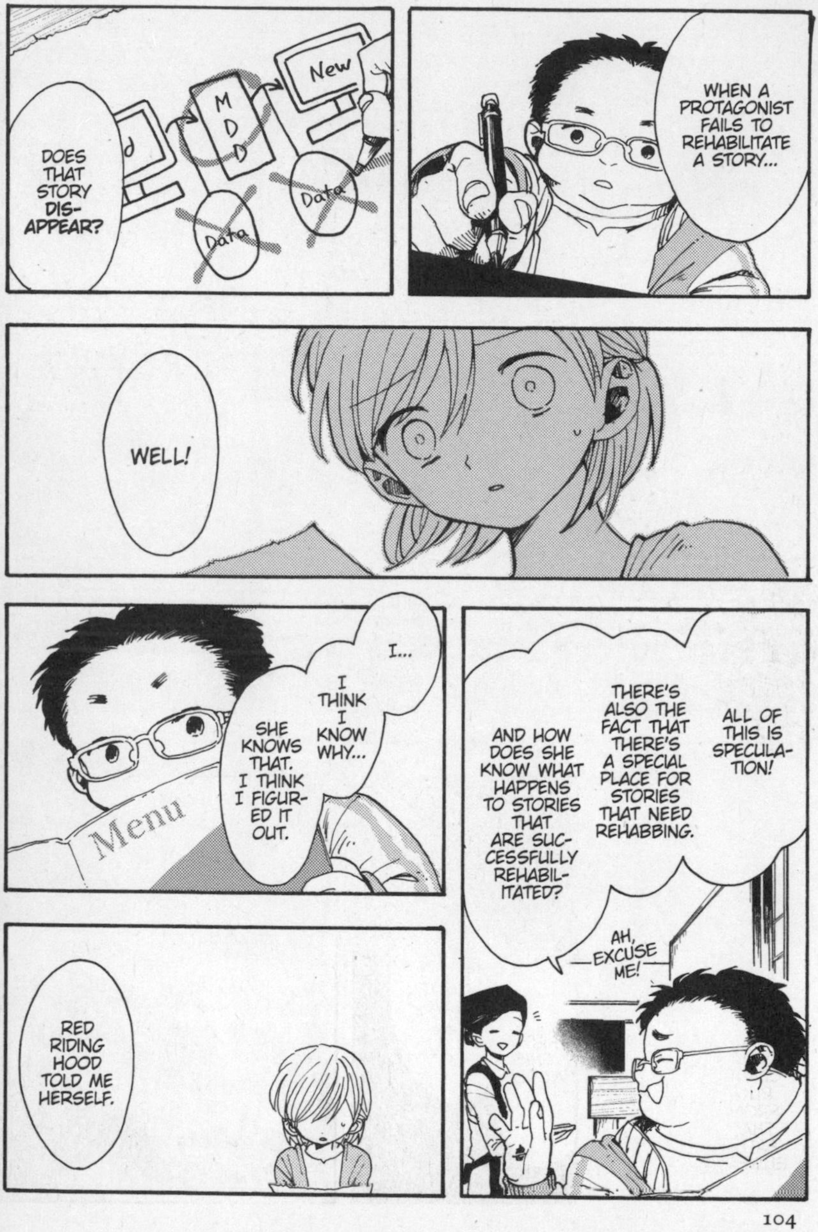
WHEN A PROTAGONIST FAILS TO REHABILITATE A STORY...
New
MDD
Data
Data
DOES THAT STORY DIS-APPEAR?
WELL!
ALL OF THIS IS SPECULATION!
THERE'S ALSO THE FACT THAT THERE'S A SPECIAL PLACE FOR STORIES THAT NEED REHABBING.
AND HOW DOES SHE KNOW WHAT HAPPENS TO STORIES THAT ARE SUCCESSFULLY REHABILITATED?
AH, EXCUSE ME!
I...
I THINK I KNOW WHY...
SHE KNOWS THAT. I THINK I FIGURED IT OUT.
Menu
RED RIDING HOOD TOLD ME HERSELF.

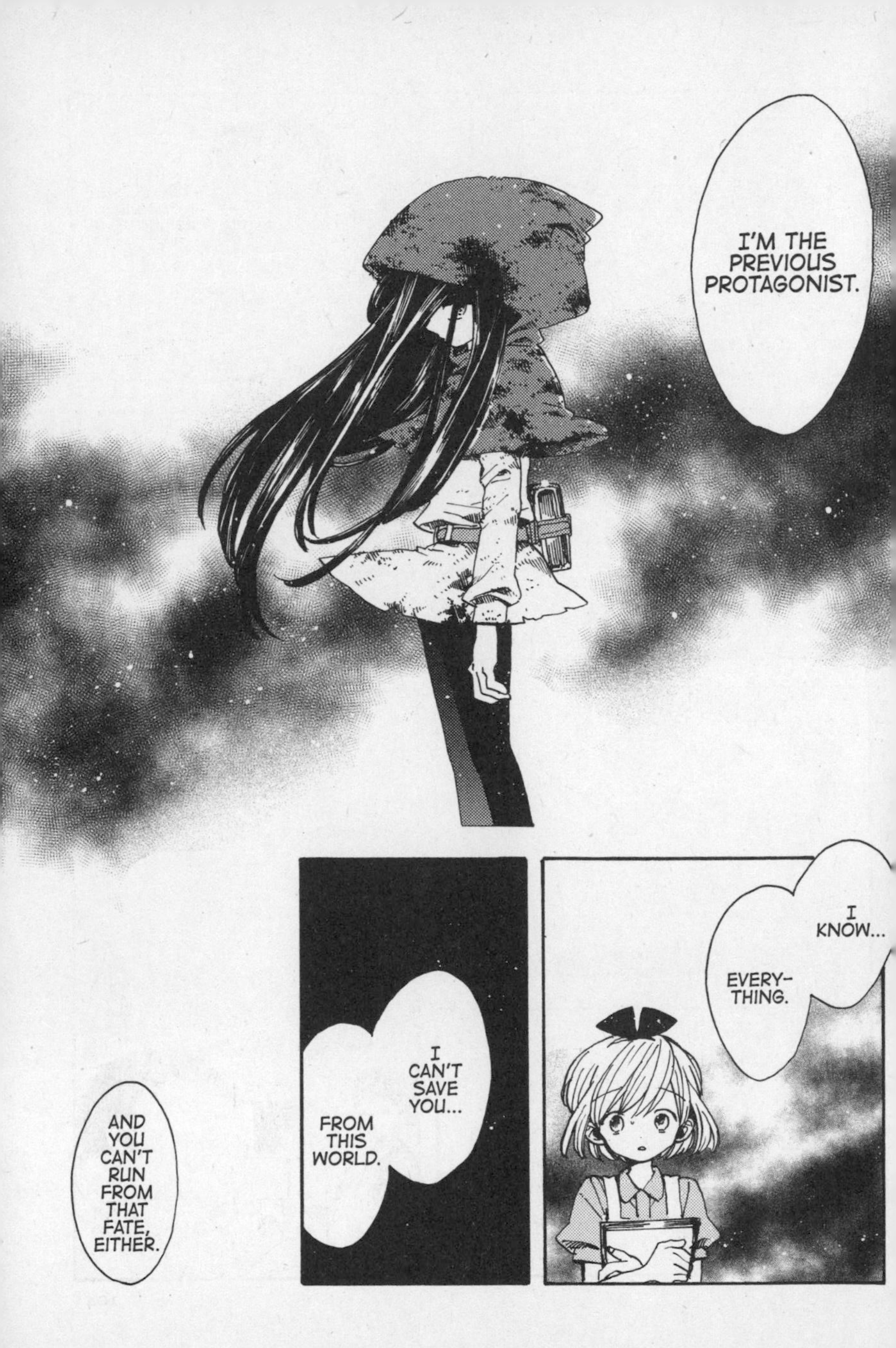
I'M THE PREVIOUS PROTAGONIST.
I KNOW...
EVERY-THING.
I CAN'T SAVE YOU...
FROM THIS WORLD.
AND YOU CAN'T RUN FROM THAT FATE, EITHER.

FAIRY
TALE
BATTLE
ROYALE

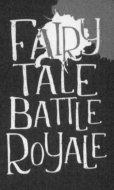

Chapter 12: Item

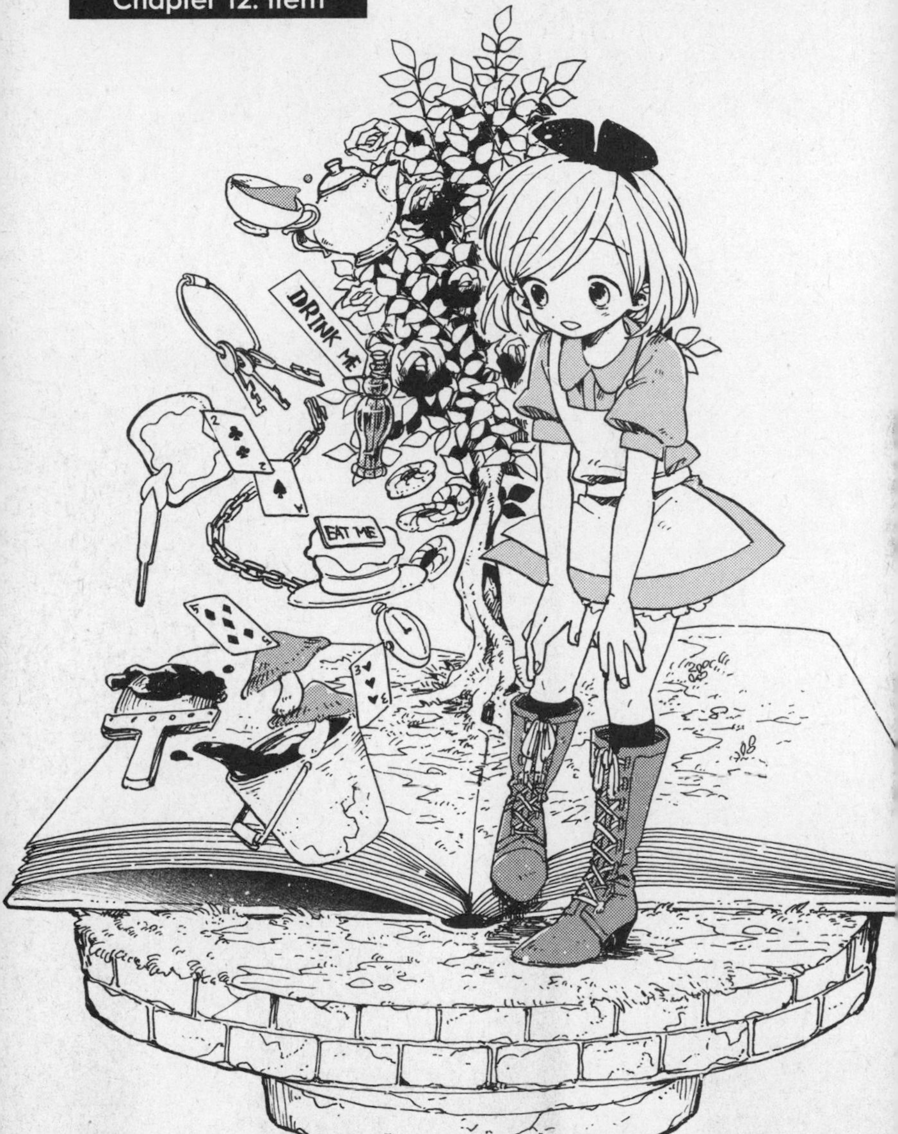
DRINK ME
EAT ME

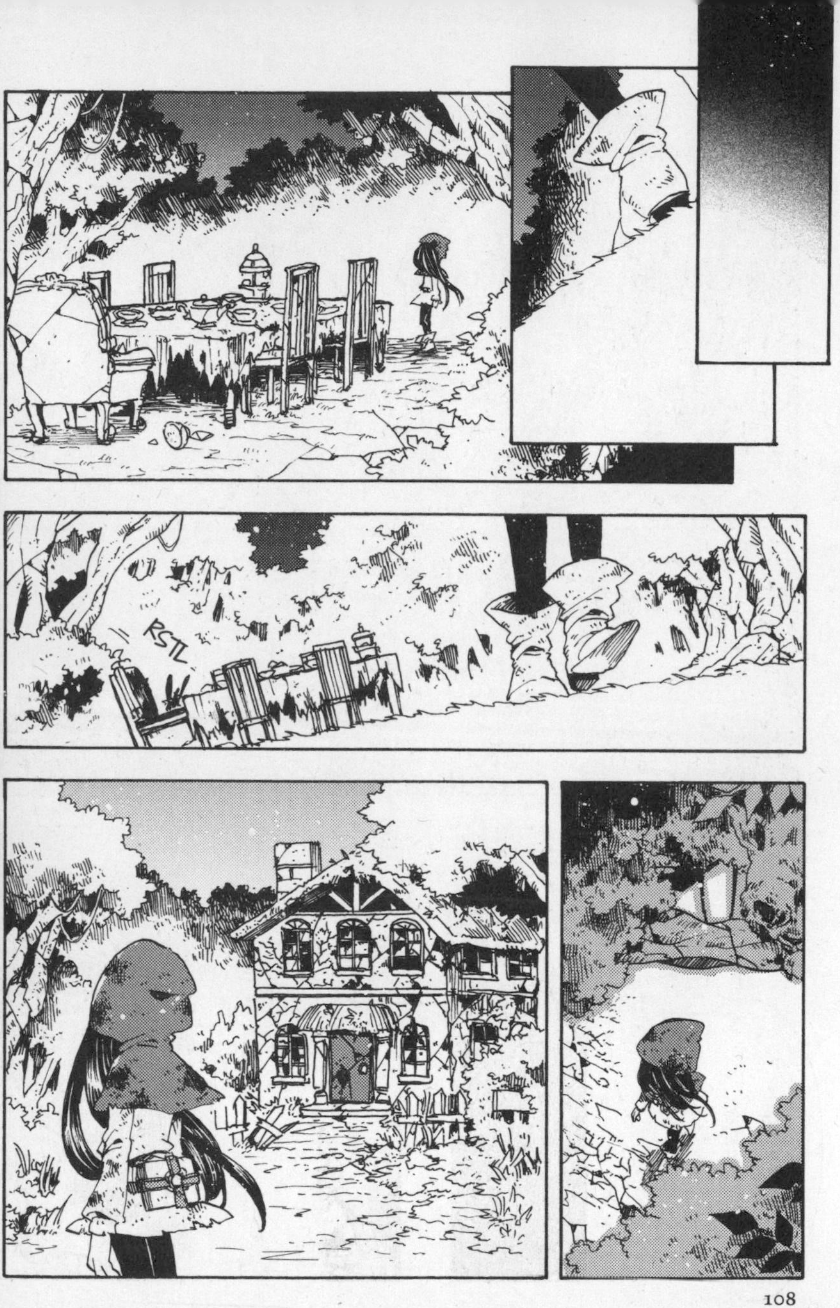
RSTL

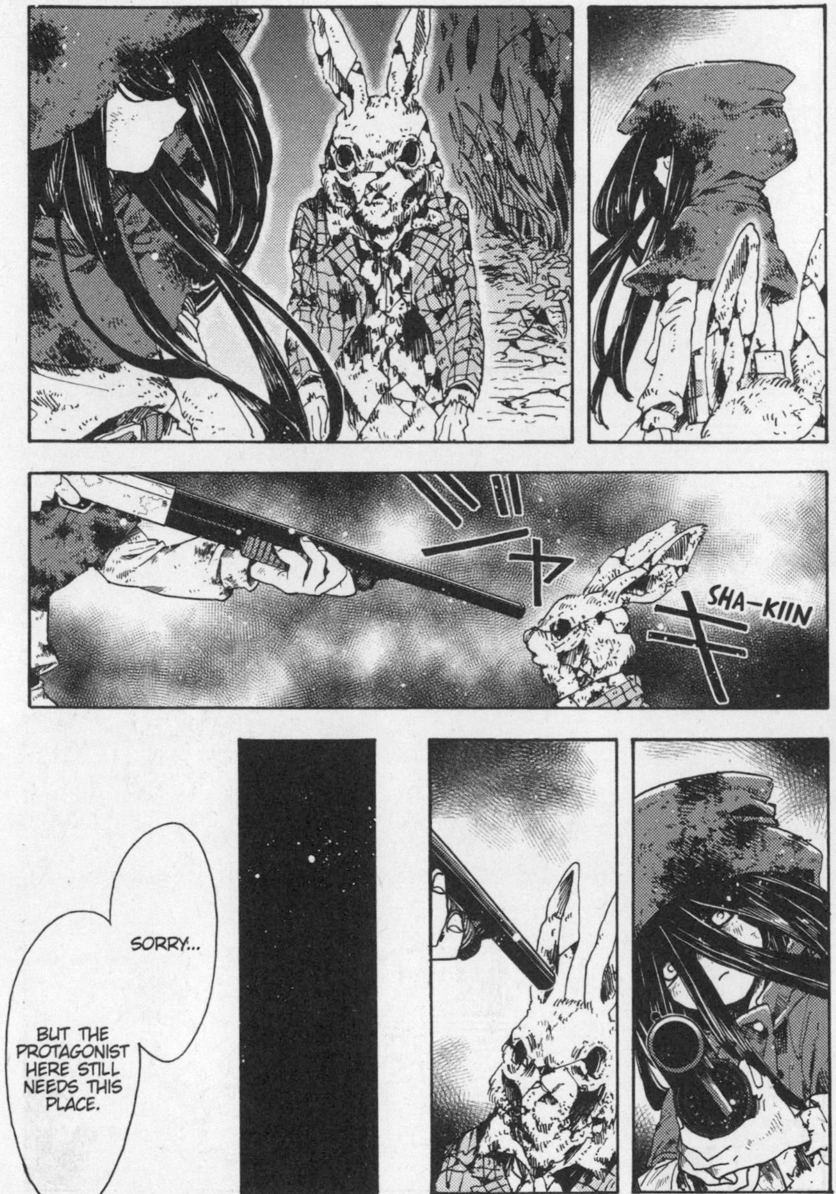
ジャキ
SHA-KIIN
SORRY...
BUT THE PROTAGONIST HERE STILL NEEDS THIS PLACE.

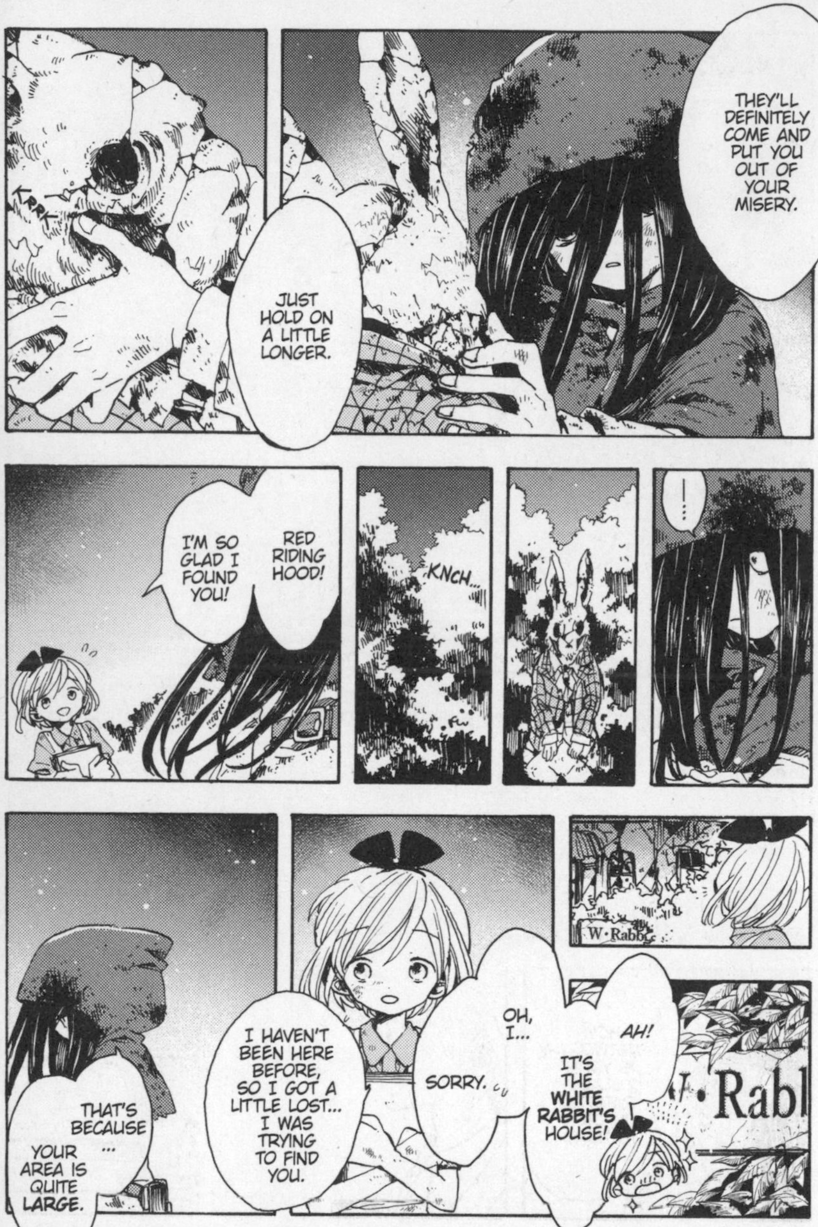
THEY'LL DEFINITELY COME AND PUT YOU OUT OF YOUR MISERY.
JUST HOLD ON A LITTLE LONGER.
KRRK
!...
KNCH...
RED RIDING HOOD!
I'M SO GLAD I FOUND YOU!
W·Rabb
AH!
IT'S THE WHITE RABBIT'S HOUSE!
W·Rabl
OH, I...
SORRY.
I HAVEN'T BEEN HERE BEFORE, SO I GOT A LITTLE LOST... I WAS TRYING TO FIND YOU.
THAT'S BECAUSE...
YOUR AREA IS QUITE LARGE.

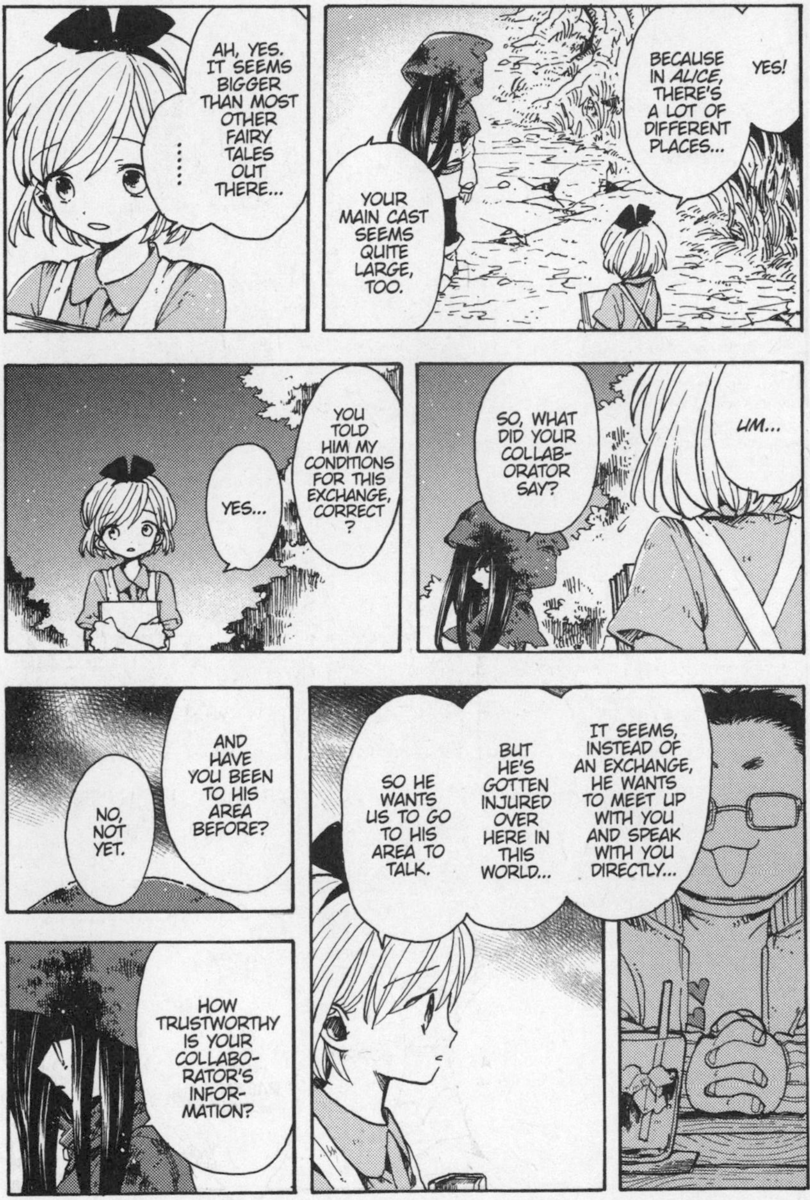
YES!
BECAUSE IN *ALICE*, THERE'S A LOT OF DIFFERENT PLACES...
YOUR MAIN CAST SEEMS QUITE LARGE, TOO.
AH, YES. IT SEEMS BIGGER THAN MOST OTHER FAIRY TALES OUT THERE...
......
SO, WHAT DID YOUR COLLABORATOR SAY?
UM...
YOU TOLD HIM MY CONDITIONS FOR THIS EXCHANGE, CORRECT?
YES...
IT SEEMS, INSTEAD OF AN EXCHANGE, HE WANTS TO MEET UP WITH YOU AND SPEAK WITH YOU DIRECTLY...
BUT HE'S GOTTEN INJURED OVER HERE IN THIS WORLD...
SO HE WANTS US TO GO TO HIS AREA TO TALK.
AND HAVE YOU BEEN TO HIS AREA BEFORE?
NO, NOT YET.
HOW TRUSTWORTHY IS YOUR COLLABORATOR'S INFORMATION?

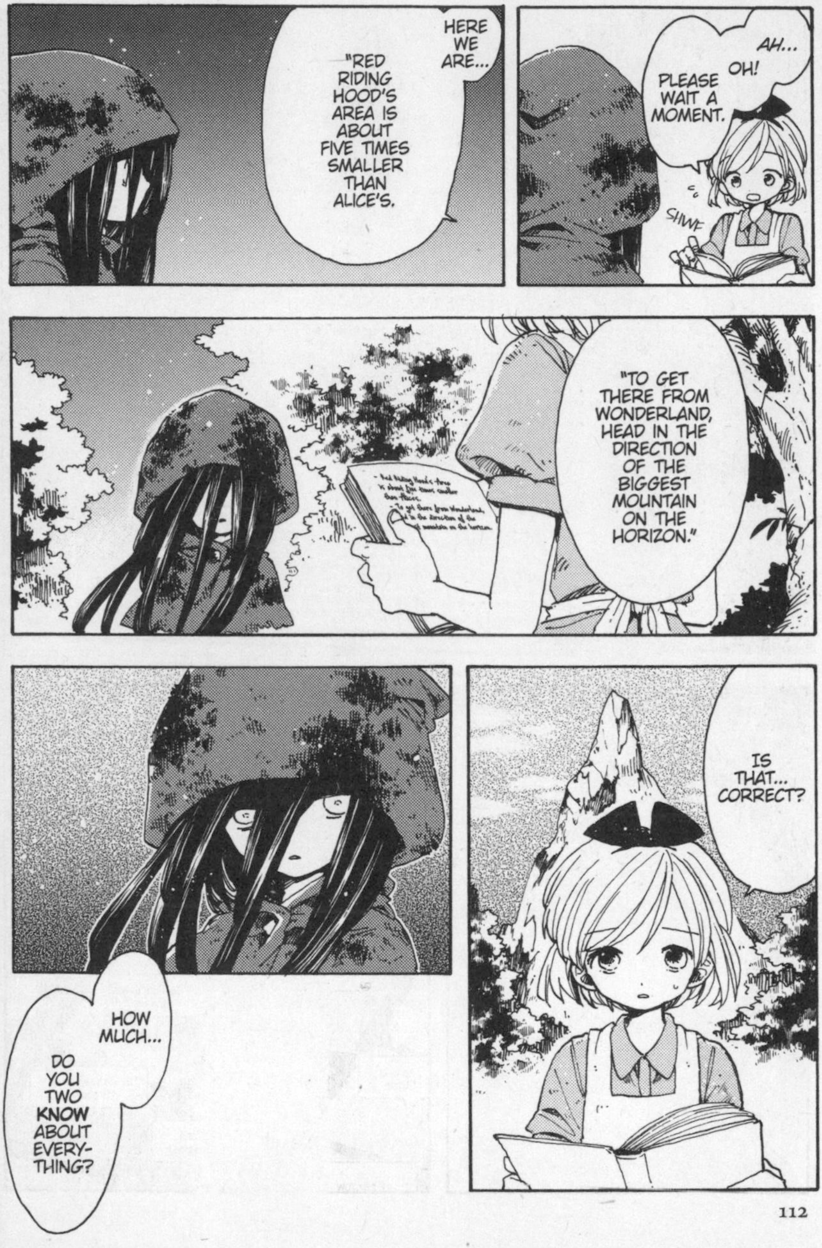
AH... OH!
PLEASE WAIT A MOMENT.
SHWF
HERE WE ARE...
"RED RIDING HOOD'S AREA IS ABOUT FIVE TIMES SMALLER THAN ALICE'S.
"TO GET THERE FROM WONDERLAND, HEAD IN THE DIRECTION OF THE BIGGEST MOUNTAIN ON THE HORIZON."
IS THAT... CORRECT?
HOW MUCH...
DO YOU TWO KNOW ABOUT EVERY-THING?

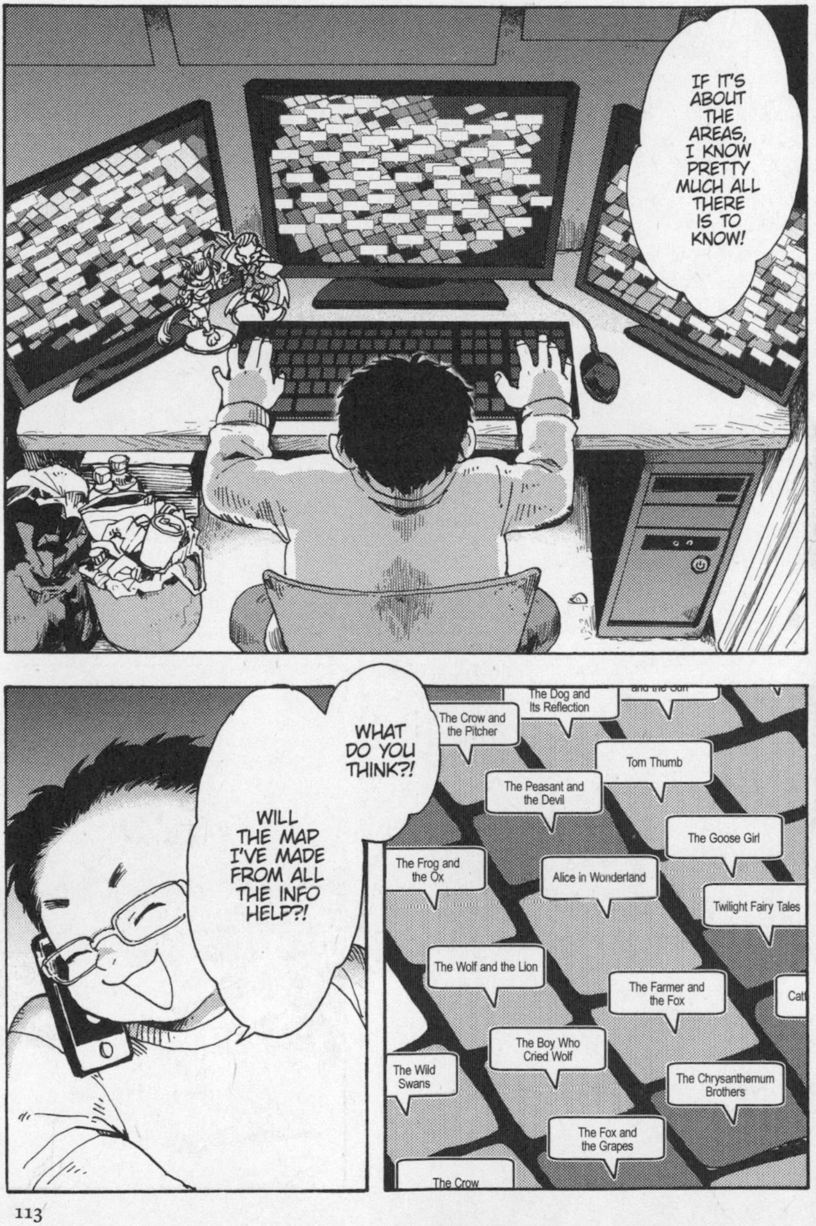
IF IT'S ABOUT THE AREAS, I KNOW PRETTY MUCH ALL THERE IS TO KNOW!
The Dog and Its Reflection
The Crow and the Pitcher
Tom Thumb
The Peasant and the Devil
The Goose Girl
Alice in Wonderland
The Frog and the Ox
Twilight Fairy Tales
The Wolf and the Lion
The Farmer and the Fox
The Boy Who Cried Wolf
The Chrysanthemum Brothers
The Wild Swans
The Fox and the Grapes
The Crow
WHAT DO YOU THINK?!
WILL THE MAP I'VE MADE FROM ALL THE INFO HELP?!

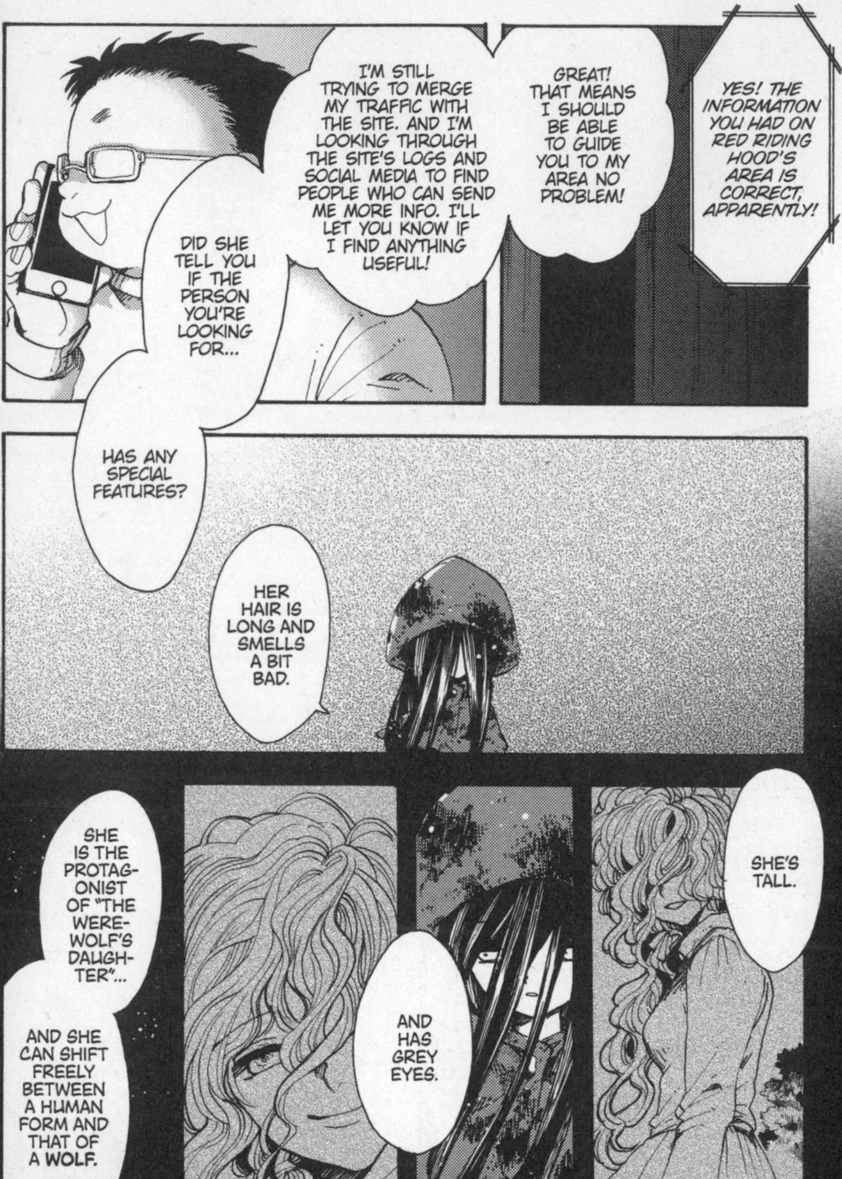
YES! THE INFORMATION YOU HAD ON RED RIDING HOOD'S AREA IS CORRECT, APPARENTLY!
GREAT! THAT MEANS I SHOULD BE ABLE TO GUIDE YOU TO MY AREA NO PROBLEM!
I'M STILL TRYING TO MERGE MY TRAFFIC WITH THE SITE. AND I'M LOOKING THROUGH THE SITE'S LOGS AND SOCIAL MEDIA TO FIND PEOPLE WHO CAN SEND ME MORE INFO. I'LL LET YOU KNOW IF I FIND ANYTHING USEFUL!
DID SHE TELL YOU IF THE PERSON YOU'RE LOOKING FOR...
HAS ANY SPECIAL FEATURES?
HER HAIR IS LONG AND SMELLS A BIT BAD.
SHE'S TALL.
AND HAS GREY EYES.
SHE IS THE PROTAG-ONIST OF "THE WERE-WOLF'S DAUGH-TER"...
AND SHE CAN SHIFT FREELY BETWEEN A HUMAN FORM AND THAT OF A **WOLF**.

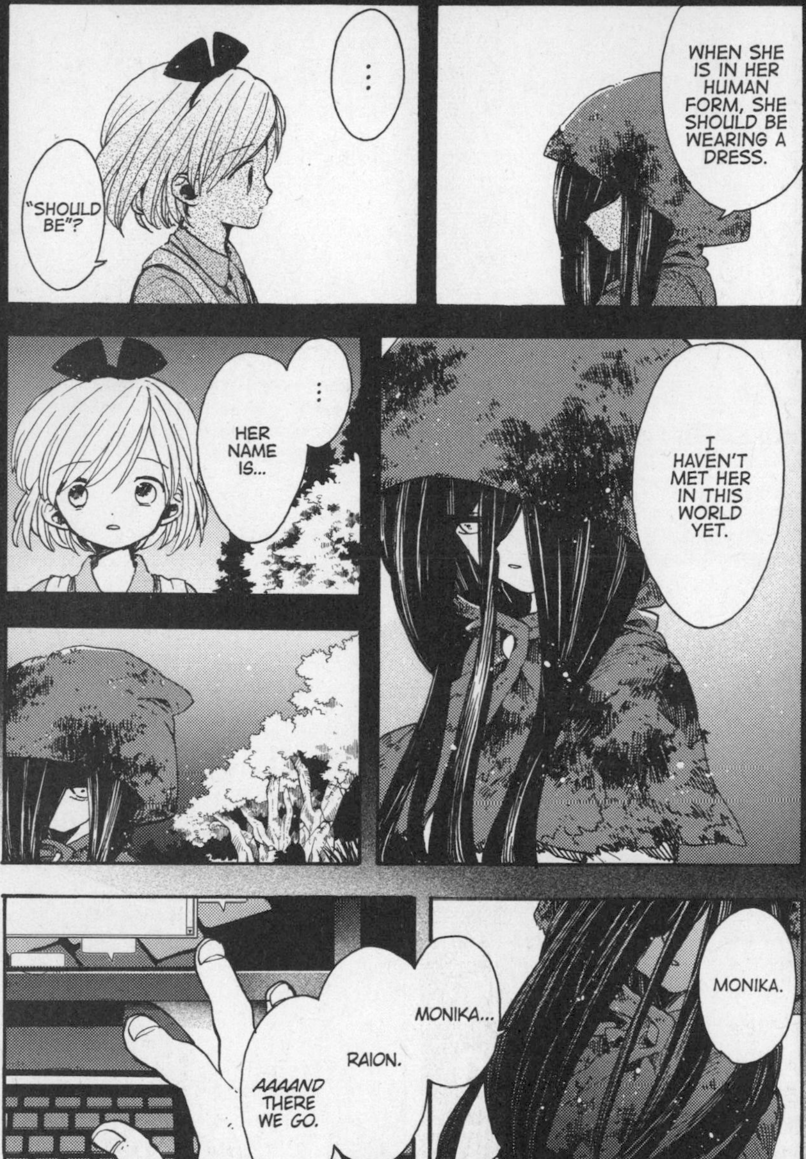
WHEN SHE IS IN HER HUMAN FORM, SHE SHOULD BE WEARING A DRESS.
...
"SHOULD BE"?
I HAVEN'T MET HER IN THIS WORLD YET.
... HER NAME IS...
MONIKA.
MONIKA...
RAION.
AAAAND THERE WE GO.

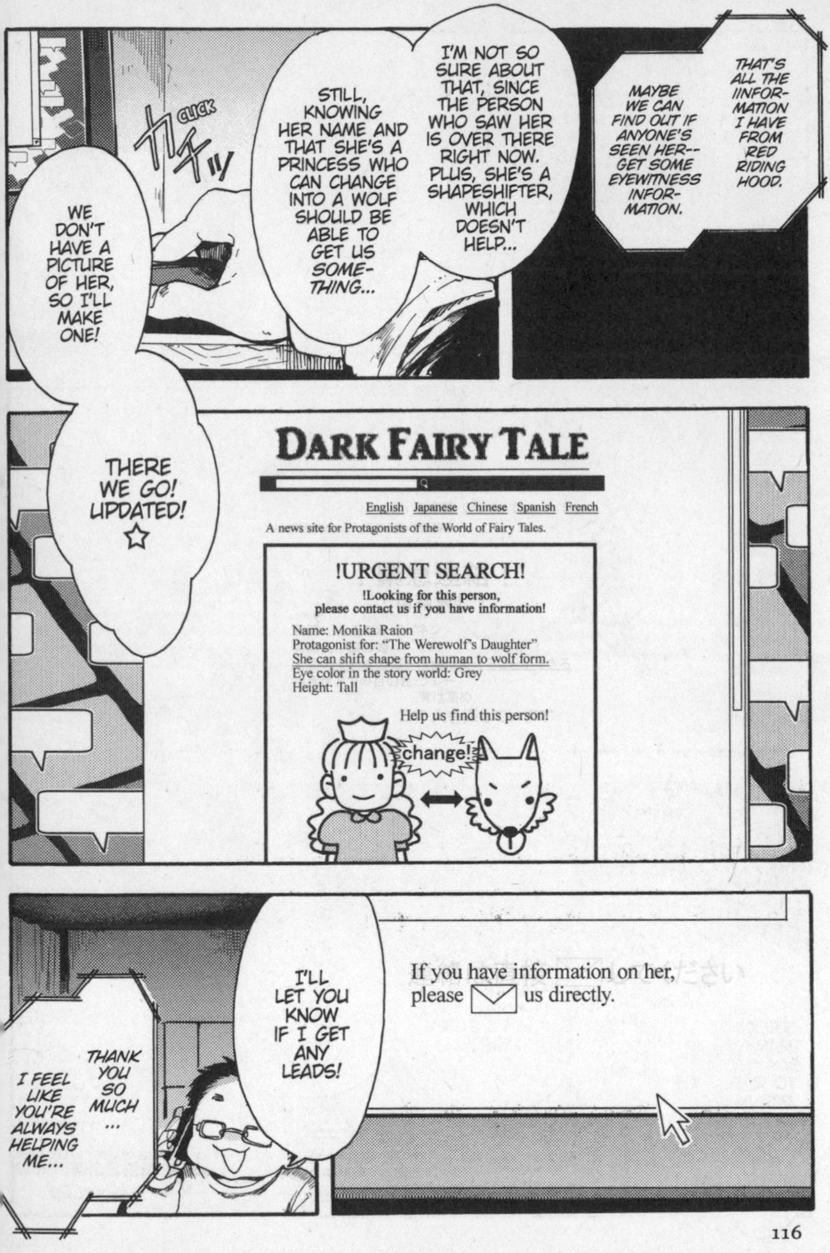
THAT'S ALL THE IINFORMATION I HAVE FROM RED RIDING HOOD.
MAYBE WE CAN FIND OUT IF ANYONE'S SEEN HER--GET SOME EYEWITNESS INFORMATION.
I'M NOT SO SURE ABOUT THAT, SINCE THE PERSON WHO SAW HER IS OVER THERE RIGHT NOW. PLUS, SHE'S A SHAPESHIFTER, WHICH DOESN'T HELP...
STILL, KNOWING HER NAME AND THAT SHE'S A PRINCESS WHO CAN CHANGE INTO A WOLF SHOULD BE ABLE TO GET US SOMETHING...
カチッ
CLICK
WE DON'T HAVE A PICTURE OF HER, SO I'LL MAKE ONE!
DARK FAIRY TALE
English Japanese Chinese Spanish French
A news site for Protagonists of the World of Fairy Tales.
!URGENT SEARCH!
!Looking for this person, please contact us if you have information!
Name: Monika Raion
Protagonist for: "The Werewolf's Daughter"
She can shift shape from human to wolf form.
Eye color in the story world: Grey
Height: Tall
Help us find this person!
change!
THERE WE GO! UPDATED! ☆
If you have information on her, please ✉ us directly.
I'LL LET YOU KNOW IF I GET ANY LEADS!
THANK YOU SO MUCH...
I FEEL LIKE YOU'RE ALWAYS HELPING ME...

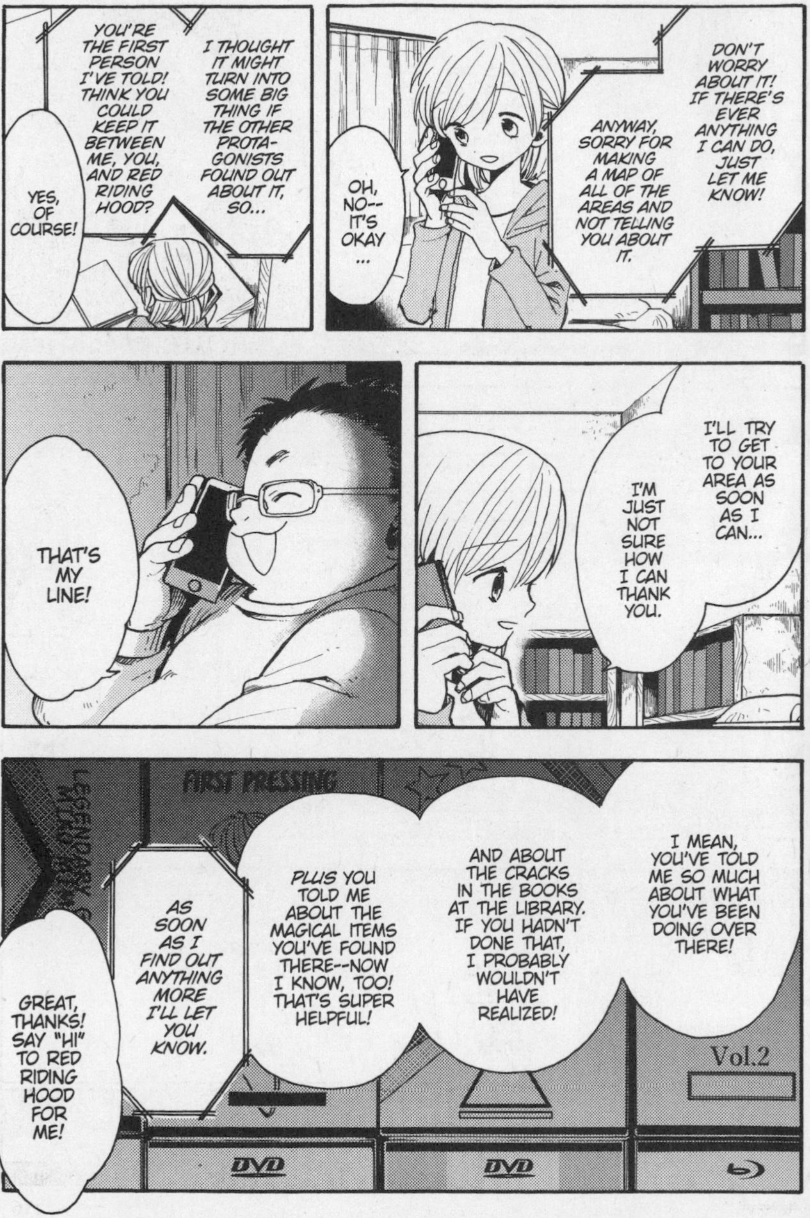
DON'T WORRY ABOUT IT! IF THERE'S EVER ANYTHING I CAN DO, JUST LET ME KNOW!
ANYWAY, SORRY FOR MAKING A MAP OF ALL OF THE AREAS AND NOT TELLING YOU ABOUT IT.
OH, NO-- IT'S OKAY ...
I THOUGHT IT MIGHT TURN INTO SOME BIG THING IF THE OTHER PROTAGONISTS FOUND OUT ABOUT IT, SO...
YOU'RE THE FIRST PERSON I'VE TOLD! THINK YOU COULD KEEP IT BETWEEN ME, YOU, AND RED RIDING HOOD?
YES, OF COURSE!
I'LL TRY TO GET TO YOUR AREA AS SOON AS I CAN...
I'M JUST NOT SURE HOW I CAN THANK YOU.
THAT'S MY LINE!
FIRST PRESSING
I MEAN, YOU'VE TOLD ME SO MUCH ABOUT WHAT YOU'VE BEEN DOING OVER THERE!
AND ABOUT THE CRACKS IN THE BOOKS AT THE LIBRARY. IF YOU HADN'T DONE THAT, I PROBABLY WOULDN'T HAVE REALIZED!
PLUS YOU TOLD ME ABOUT THE MAGICAL ITEMS YOU'VE FOUND THERE--NOW I KNOW, TOO! THAT'S SUPER HELPFUL!
AS SOON AS I FIND OUT ANYTHING MORE I'LL LET YOU KNOW.
GREAT, THANKS! SAY "HI" TO RED RIDING HOOD FOR ME!
Vol.2
DVD
DVD

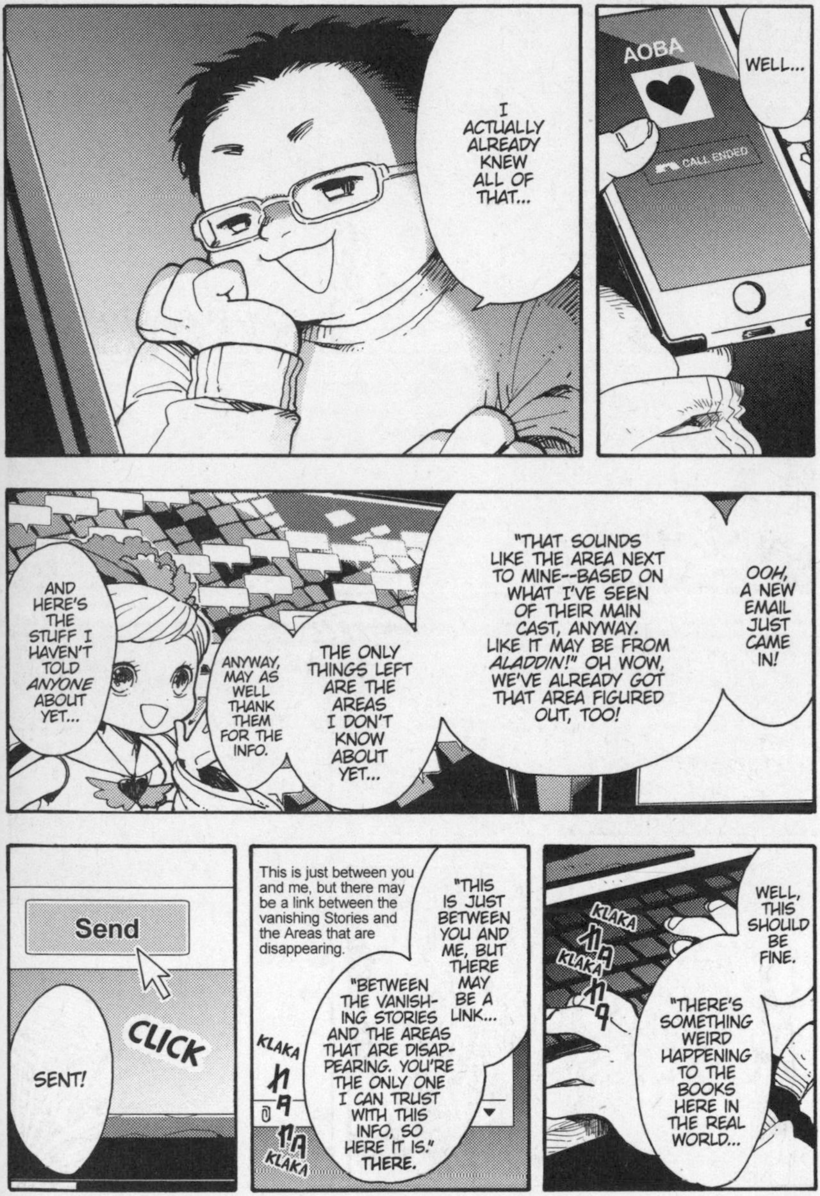
AOBA
CALL ENDED
WELL...
I ACTUALLY ALREADY KNEW ALL OF THAT...
OOH, A NEW EMAIL JUST CAME IN!
"THAT SOUNDS LIKE THE AREA NEXT TO MINE--BASED ON WHAT I'VE SEEN OF THEIR MAIN CAST, ANYWAY. LIKE IT MAY BE FROM *ALADDIN!*" OH WOW, WE'VE ALREADY GOT THAT AREA FIGURED OUT, TOO!
THE ONLY THINGS LEFT ARE THE AREAS I DON'T KNOW ABOUT YET...
ANYWAY, MAY AS WELL THANK THEM FOR THE INFO.
AND HERE'S THE STUFF I HAVEN'T TOLD *ANYONE* ABOUT YET...
WELL, THIS SHOULD BE FINE.
KLAKA
KLAKA
"THERE'S SOMETHING WEIRD HAPPENING TO THE BOOKS HERE IN THE REAL WORLD...
This is just between you and me, but there may be a link between the vanishing Stories and the Areas that are disappearing.
"THIS IS JUST BETWEEN YOU AND ME, BUT THERE MAY BE A LINK...
"BETWEEN THE VANISHING STORIES AND THE AREAS THAT ARE DISAPPEARING. YOU'RE THE ONLY ONE I CAN TRUST WITH THIS INFO, SO HERE IT IS." THERE.
KLAKA
KLAKA
Send
CLICK
SENT!

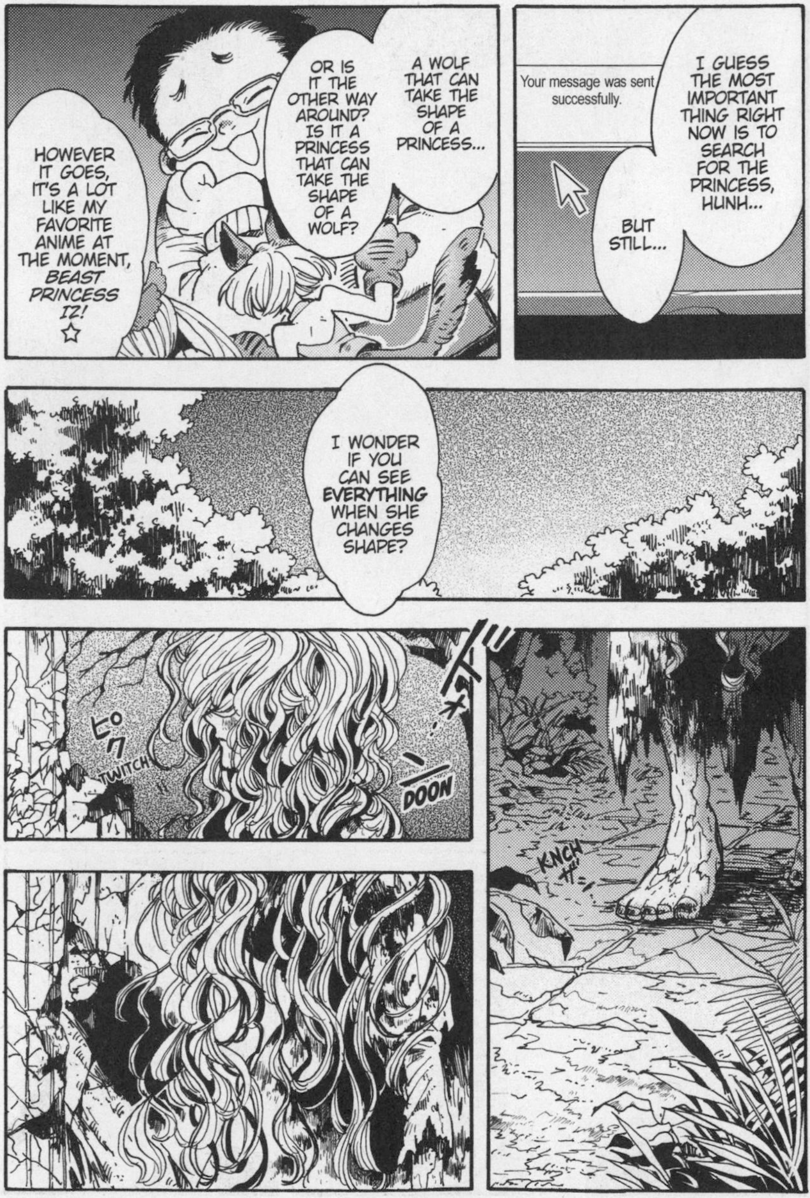
Your message was sent successfully.
I GUESS THE MOST IMPORTANT THING RIGHT NOW IS TO SEARCH FOR THE PRINCESS, HUNH...
BUT STILL...
A WOLF THAT CAN TAKE THE SHAPE OF A PRINCESS...
OR IS IT THE OTHER WAY AROUND? IS IT A PRINCESS THAT CAN TAKE THE SHAPE OF A WOLF?
HOWEVER IT GOES, IT'S A LOT LIKE MY FAVORITE ANIME AT THE MOMENT, *BEAST PRINCESS IZ!* ☆
I WONDER IF YOU CAN SEE **EVERYTHING** WHEN SHE CHANGES SHAPE?
KNCH
DOON
TWITCH

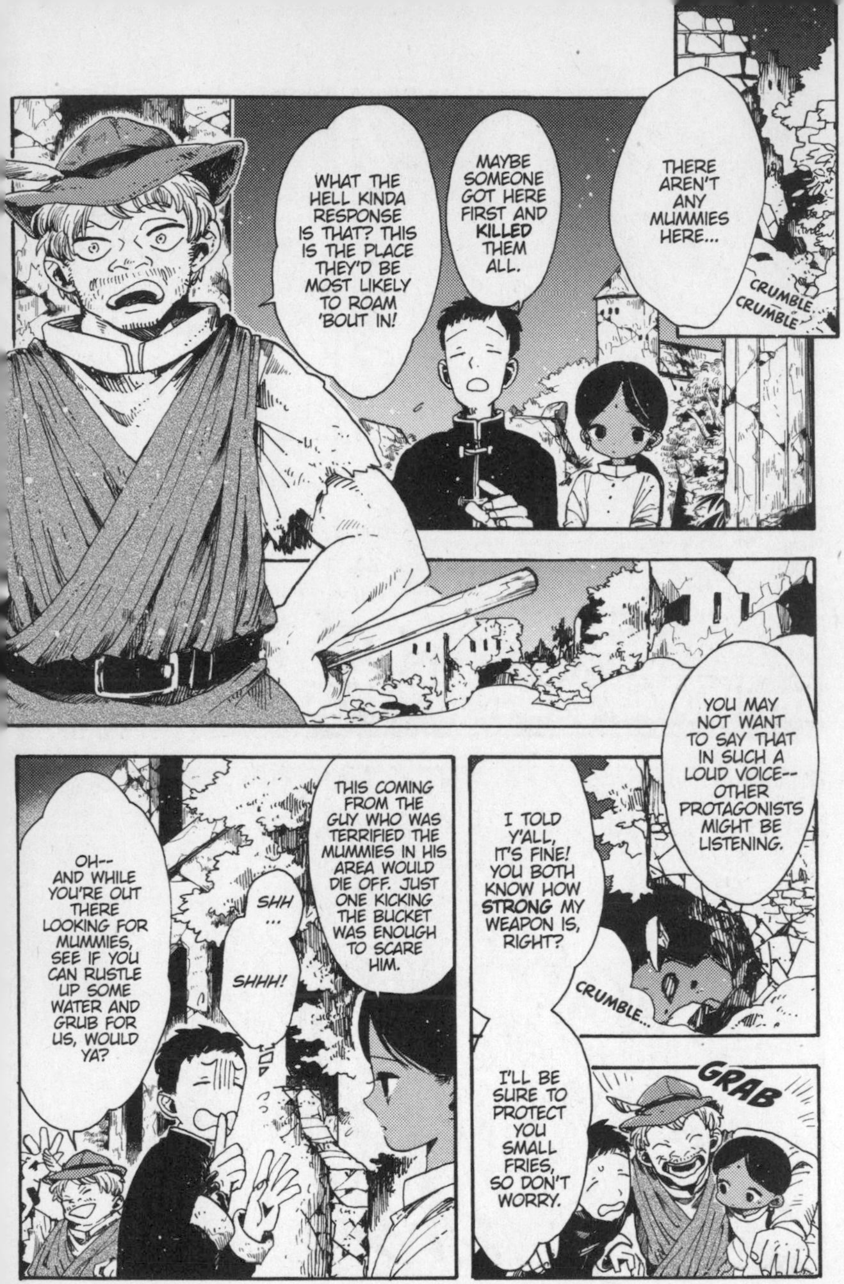
THERE AREN'T ANY MUMMIES HERE...
CRUMBLE CRUMBLE
MAYBE SOMEONE GOT HERE FIRST AND KILLED THEM ALL.
WHAT THE HELL KINDA RESPONSE IS THAT? THIS IS THE PLACE THEY'D BE MOST LIKELY TO ROAM 'BOUT IN!
YOU MAY NOT WANT TO SAY THAT IN SUCH A LOUD VOICE-- OTHER PROTAGONISTS MIGHT BE LISTENING.
I TOLD Y'ALL, IT'S FINE! YOU BOTH KNOW HOW STRONG MY WEAPON IS, RIGHT?
CRUMBLE...
GRAB
I'LL BE SURE TO PROTECT YOU SMALL FRIES, SO DON'T WORRY.
THIS COMING FROM THE GUY WHO WAS TERRIFIED THE MUMMIES IN HIS AREA WOULD DIE OFF. JUST ONE KICKING THE BUCKET WAS ENOUGH TO SCARE HIM.
SHH ...
SHHH!
OH-- AND WHILE YOU'RE OUT THERE LOOKING FOR MUMMIES, SEE IF YOU CAN RUSTLE UP SOME WATER AND GRUB FOR US, WOULD YA?

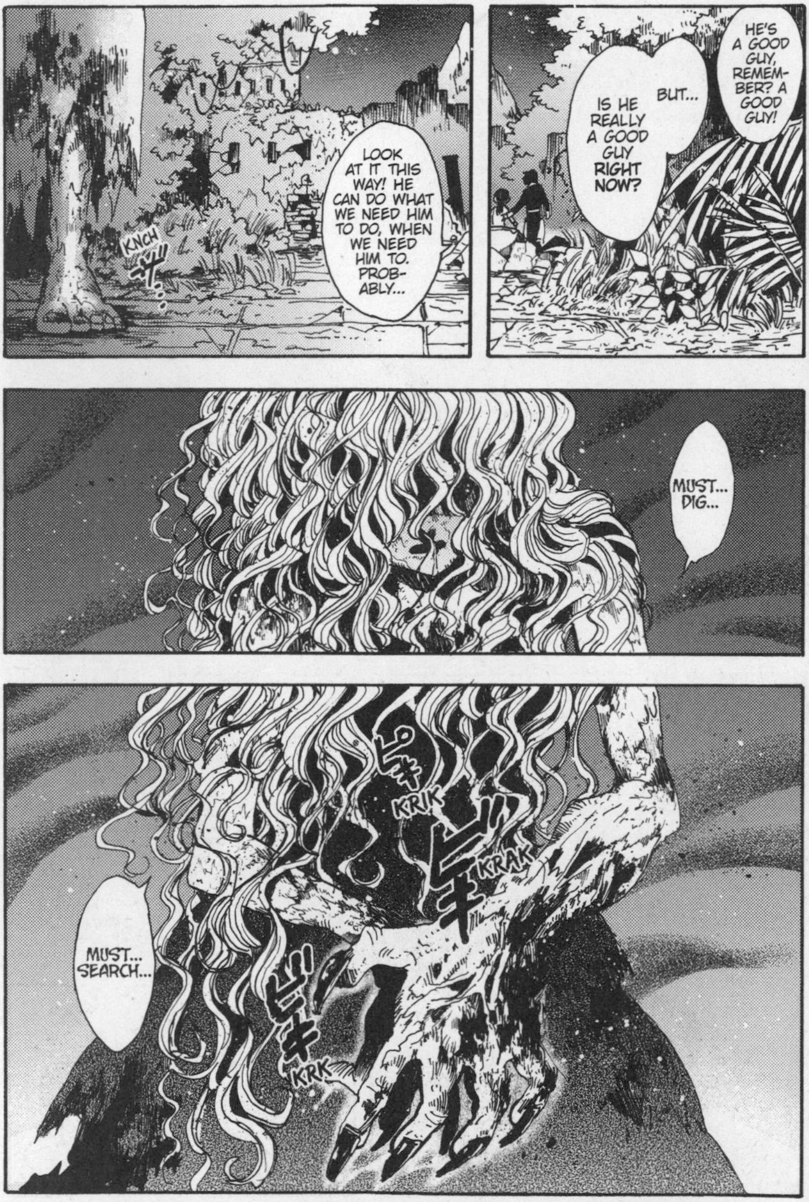
HE'S A GOOD GUY, REMEMBER? A GOOD GUY!
BUT...
IS HE REALLY A GOOD GUY RIGHT NOW?
LOOK AT IT THIS WAY! HE CAN DO WHAT WE NEED HIM TO DO, WHEN WE NEED HIM TO. PROBABLY...
KNCH
MUST... DIG...
KRIK
KRAK
MUST... SEARCH...
KRK

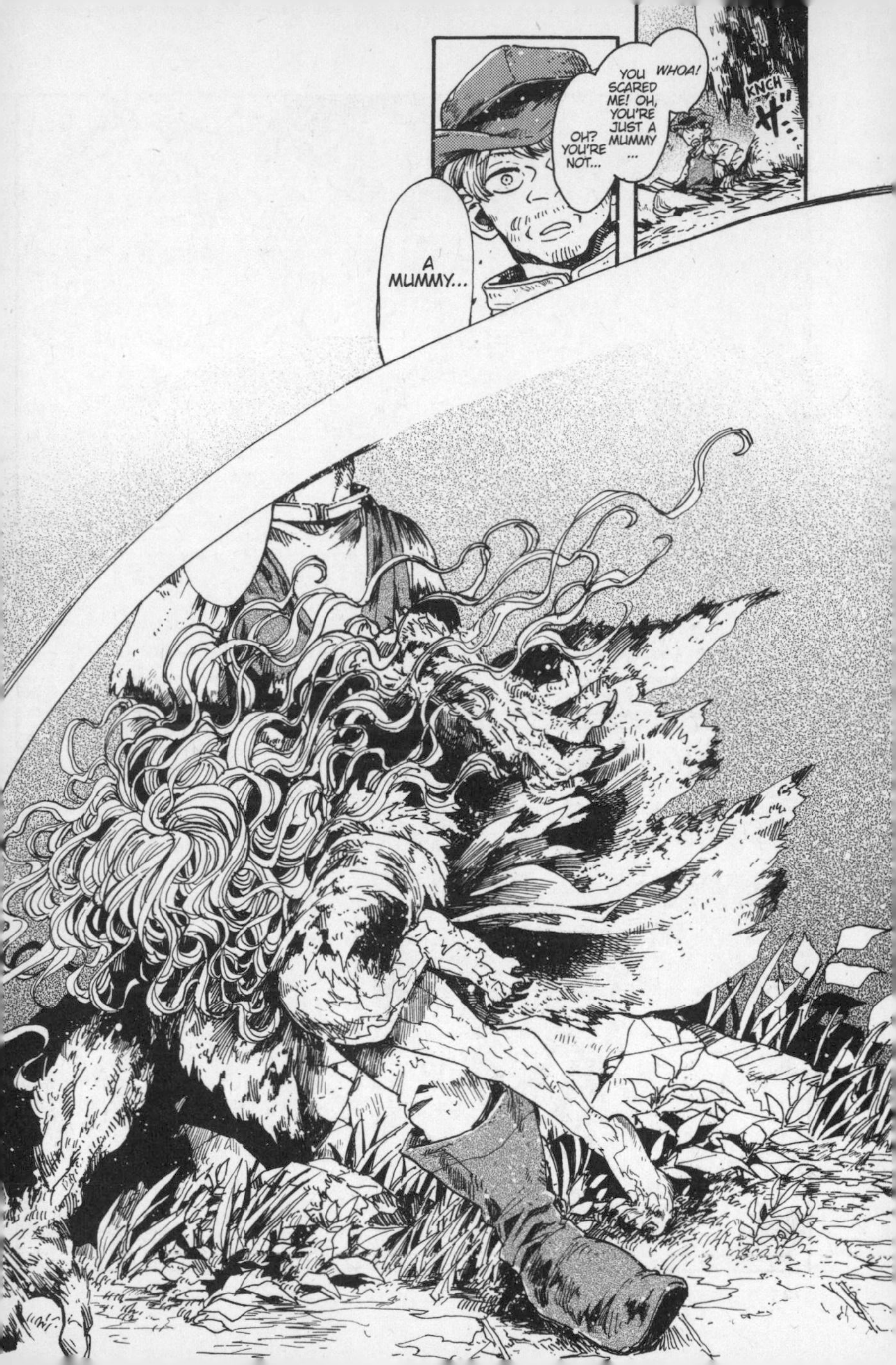
KNCH
WHOA!
YOU SCARED ME! OH, YOU'RE JUST A MUMMY ...
OH? YOU'RE NOT...
A MUMMY...

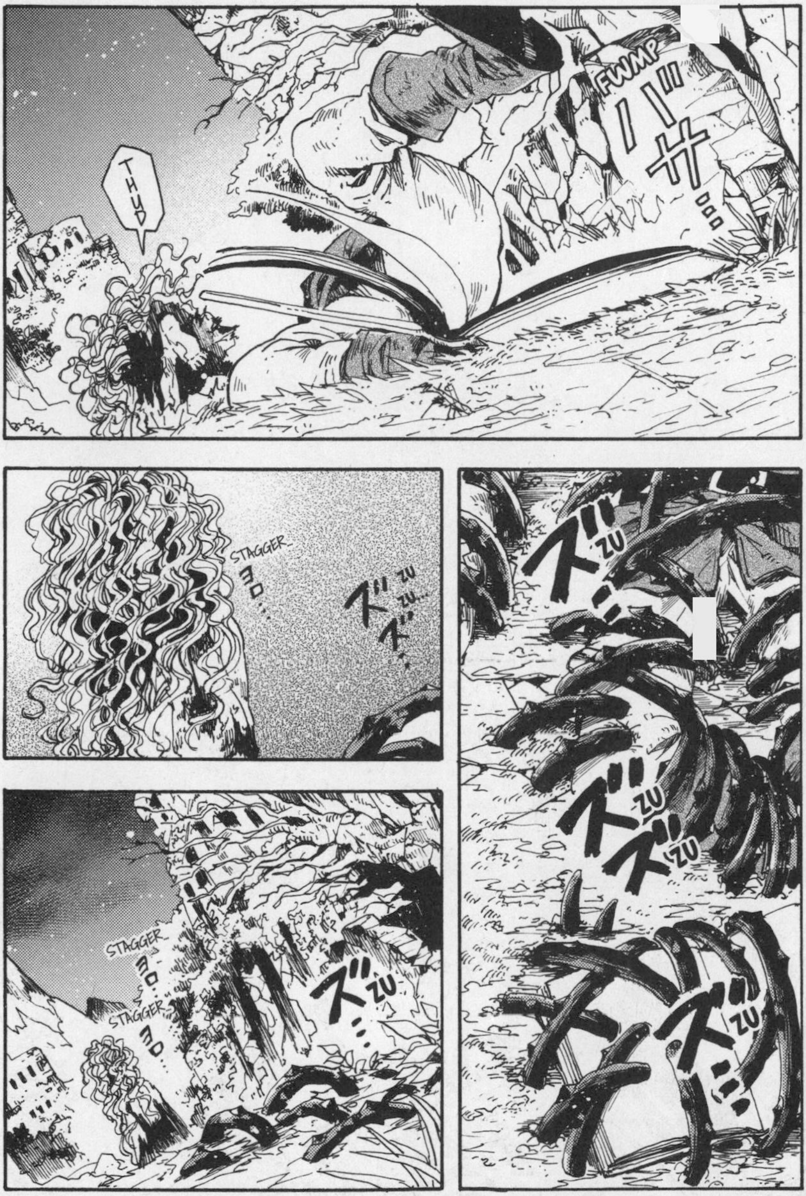

FWMP
バサ…
THUD
ズ ZU
ズ ZU
ズ ZU
ズ ZU…
ズズ… ZU ZU…
STAGGER
ヨロ…
ズ ZU…
STAGGER
ヨロ…
STAGGER
ヨロ…

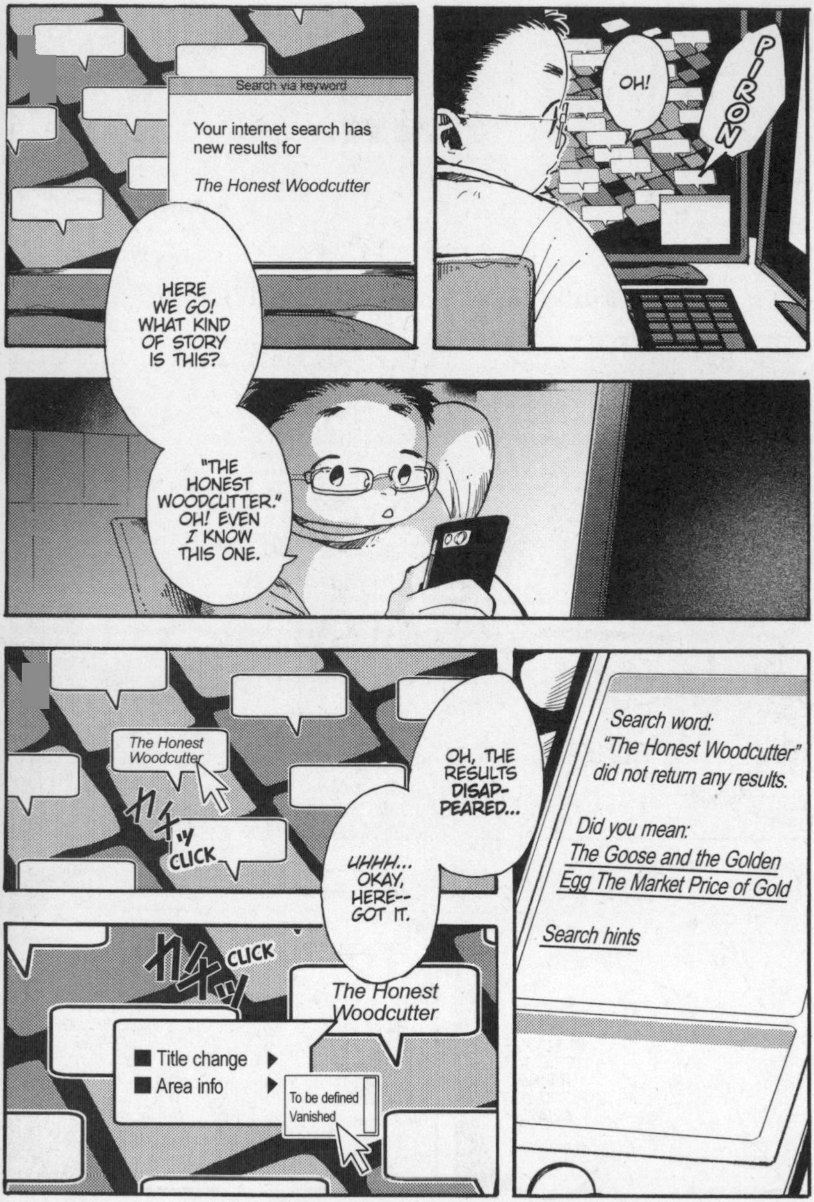
PIRON
OH!
Search via keyword
Your internet search has new results for
The Honest Woodcutter
HERE WE GO! WHAT KIND OF STORY IS THIS?
"THE HONEST WOODCUTTER." OH! EVEN I KNOW THIS ONE.
Search word: "The Honest Woodcutter" did not return any results.
Did you mean:
The Goose and the Golden Egg The Market Price of Gold
Search hints
OH, THE RESULTS DISAPPEARED...
The Honest Woodcutter
カチッ
CLICK
UHHH... OKAY, HERE-- GOT IT.
カチッ
CLICK
The Honest Woodcutter
Title change
Area info
To be defined
Vanished

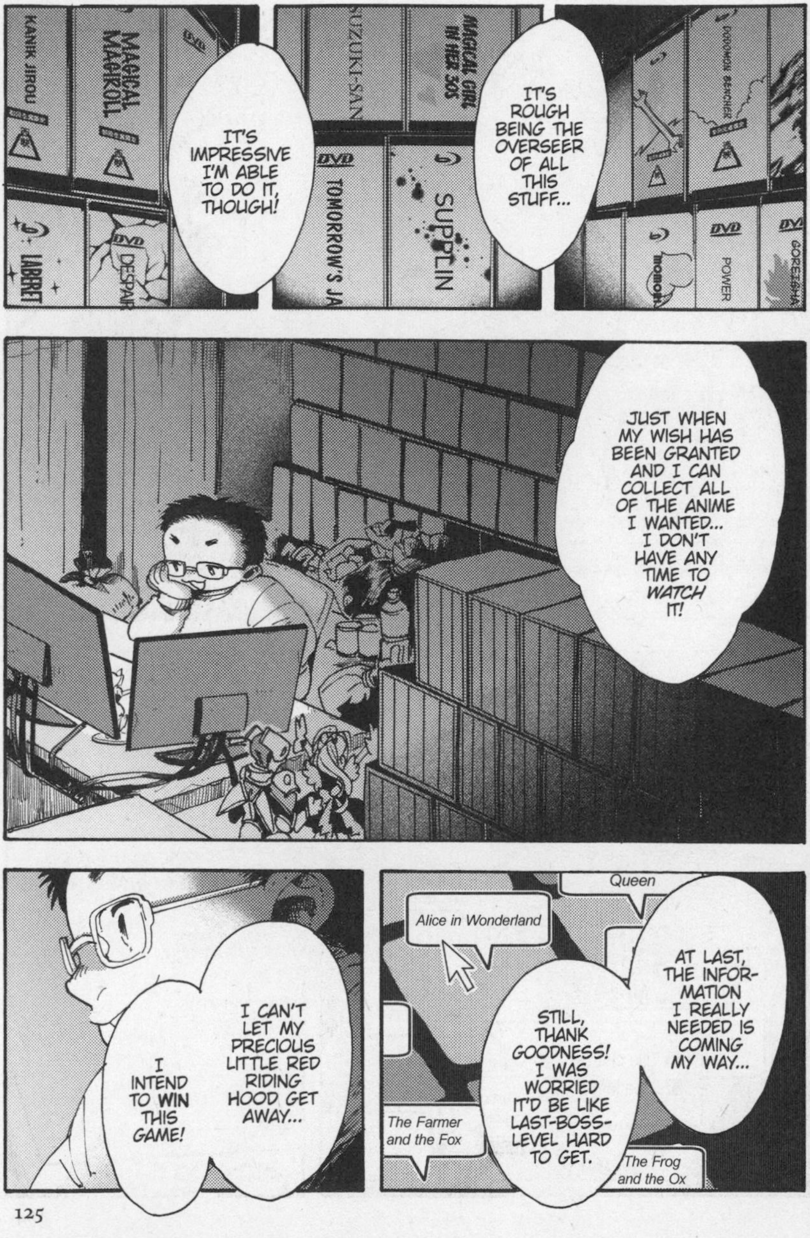
POWER
GOREISHA
SUZUKI-SAN
MAGICAL GIRL IN HER 30S
IT'S ROUGH BEING THE OVERSEER OF ALL THIS STUFF...
TOMORROW'S JA
SUPPLIN
KANIK JIROU
MAGICAL MAGIROLL
IT'S IMPRESSIVE I'M ABLE TO DO IT, THOUGH!
DESPAIR
JUST WHEN MY WISH HAS BEEN GRANTED AND I CAN COLLECT ALL OF THE ANIME I WANTED... I DON'T HAVE ANY TIME TO *WATCH* IT!
Queen
Alice in Wonderland
AT LAST, THE INFORMATION I REALLY NEEDED IS COMING MY WAY...
STILL, THANK GOODNESS! I WAS WORRIED IT'D BE LIKE LAST-BOSS-LEVEL HARD TO GET.
The Farmer and the Fox
The Frog and the Ox
I CAN'T LET MY PRECIOUS LITTLE RED RIDING HOOD GET AWAY...
I INTEND TO **WIN** THIS GAME!

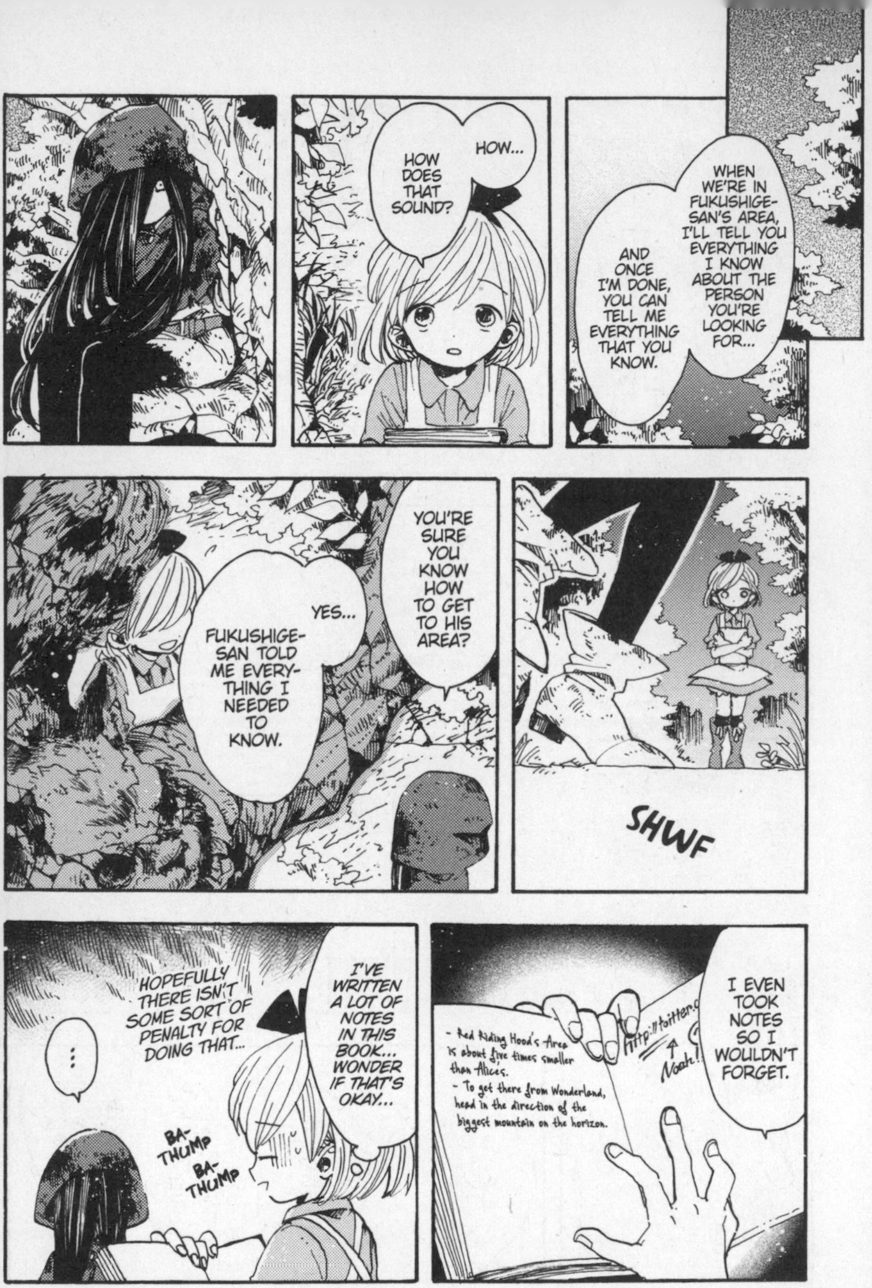
WHEN WE'RE IN FUKUSHIGE-SAN'S AREA, I'LL TELL YOU EVERYTHING I KNOW ABOUT THE PERSON YOU'RE LOOKING FOR...
AND ONCE I'M DONE, YOU CAN TELL ME EVERYTHING THAT YOU KNOW.
HOW...
HOW DOES THAT SOUND?
SHWF
YOU'RE SURE YOU KNOW HOW TO GET TO HIS AREA?
YES...
FUKUSHIGE-SAN TOLD ME EVERY-THING I NEEDED TO KNOW.
I EVEN TOOK NOTES SO I WOULDN'T FORGET.
- Red Riding Hood's Area is about five times smaller than Alice's.
- To get there from Wonderland, head in the direction of the biggest mountain on the horizon.
Noah!
I'VE WRITTEN A LOT OF NOTES IN THIS BOOK... WONDER IF THAT'S OKAY...
HOPEFULLY THERE ISN'T SOME SORT OF PENALTY FOR DOING THAT...
...
BA-THUMP
BA-THUMP

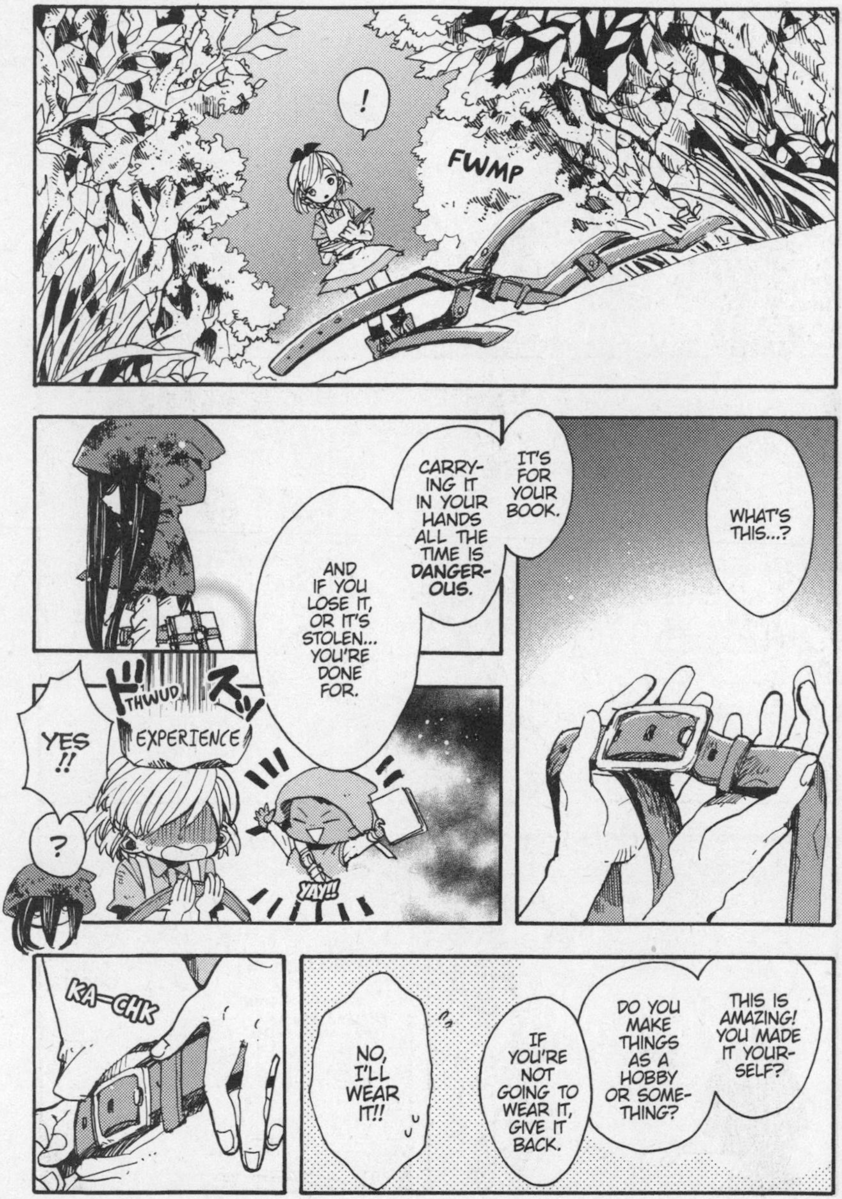
!
FWMP
WHAT'S THIS...?
IT'S FOR YOUR BOOK.
CARRYING IT IN YOUR HANDS ALL THE TIME IS DANGEROUS.
AND IF YOU LOSE IT, OR IT'S STOLEN... YOU'RE DONE FOR.
スッ
ド THWUD
EXPERIENCE
YES!!
YAY!!
?
THIS IS AMAZING! YOU MADE IT YOURSELF?
DO YOU MAKE THINGS AS A HOBBY OR SOMETHING?
IF YOU'RE NOT GOING TO WEAR IT, GIVE IT BACK.
NO, I'LL WEAR IT!!
KA-CHK

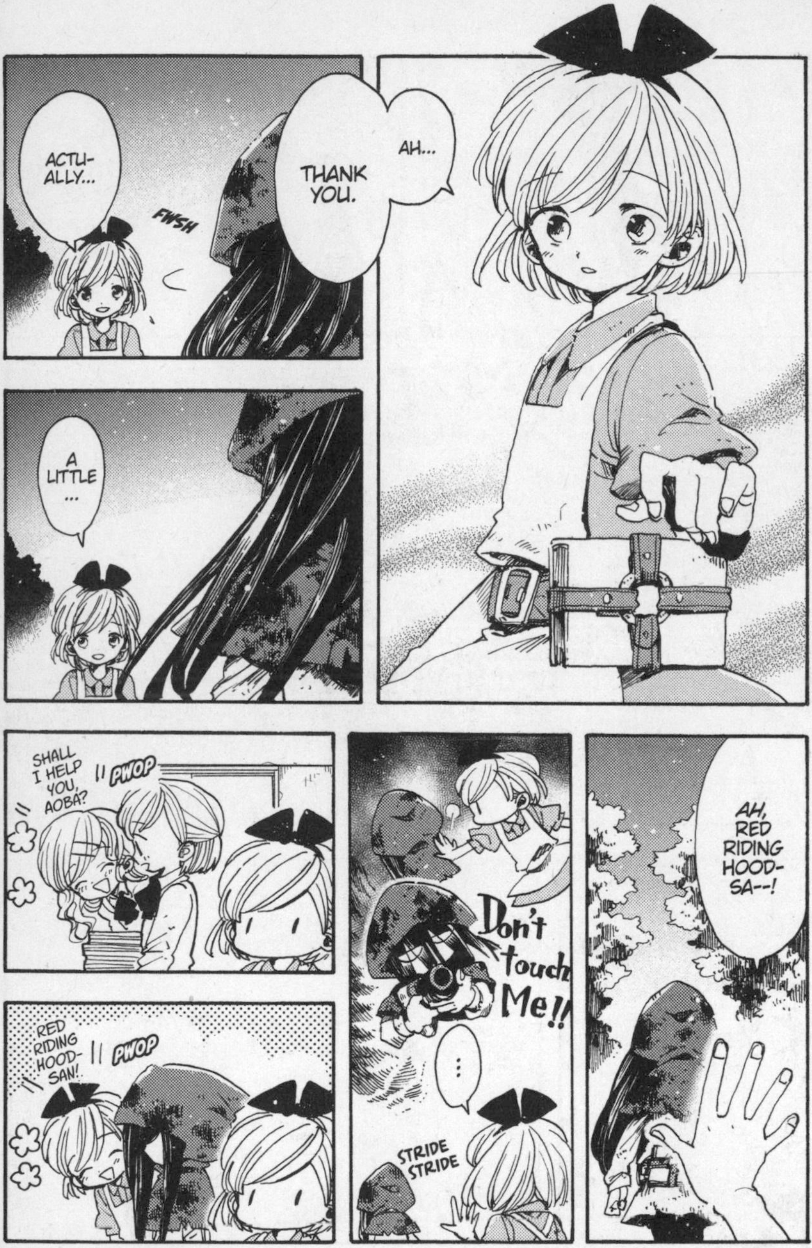
AH... THANK YOU.
FWSH
ACTU-ALLY...
A LITTLE ...
AH, RED RIDING HOOD-SA--!
Don't touch Me!!
...
STRIDE STRIDE
SHALL I HELP YOU, AOBA?
PWOP
RED RIDING HOOD-SAN!
PWOP

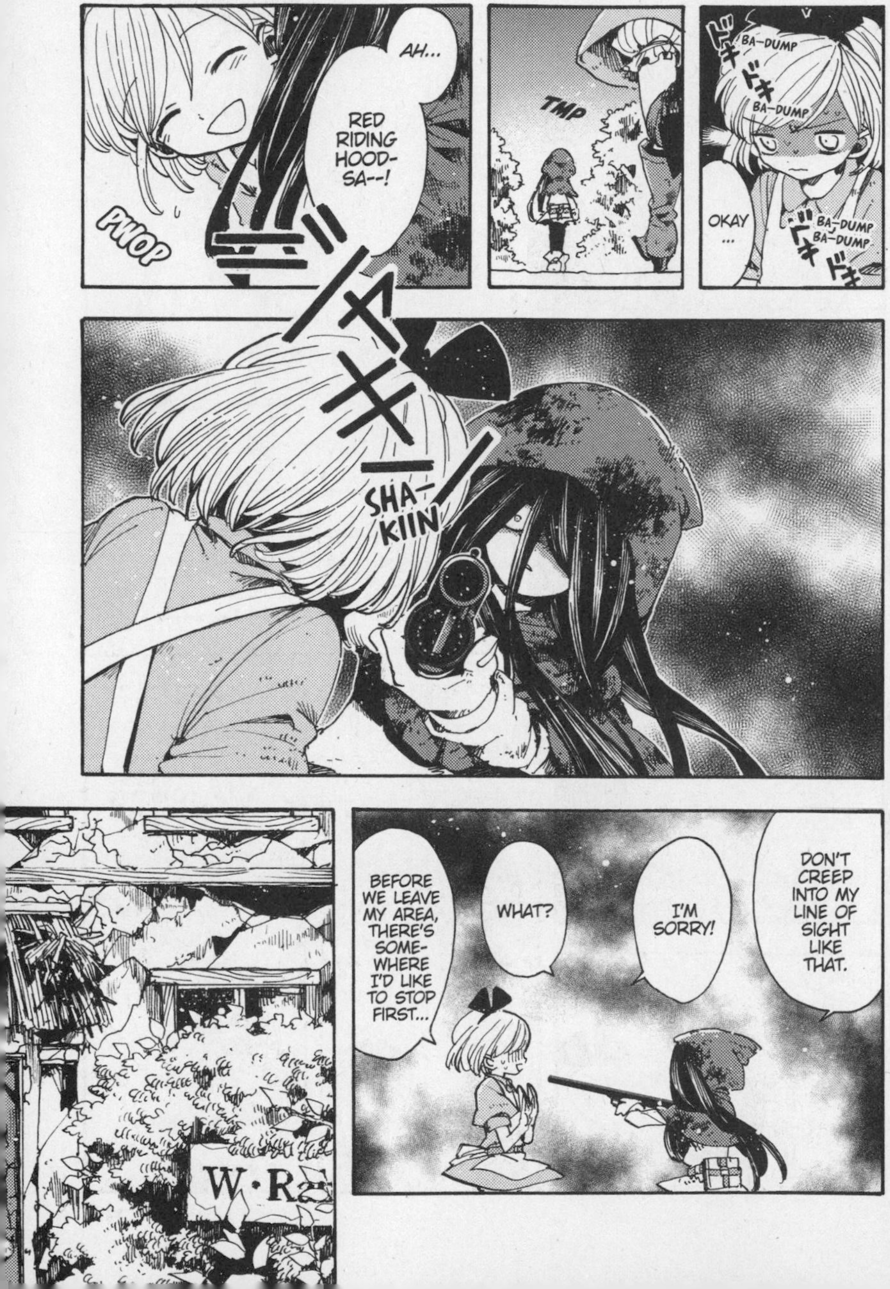
ドキ
BA-DUMP
ドキ
BA-DUMP
OKAY...
ドキ
BA-DUMP
ドキ
BA-DUMP
TMP
AH...
RED RIDING HOOD-SA--!
PWOP
SHA-KIIN
DON'T CREEP INTO MY LINE OF SIGHT LIKE THAT.
I'M SORRY!
WHAT?
BEFORE WE LEAVE MY AREA, THERE'S SOME-WHERE I'D LIKE TO STOP FIRST...
W·Ra

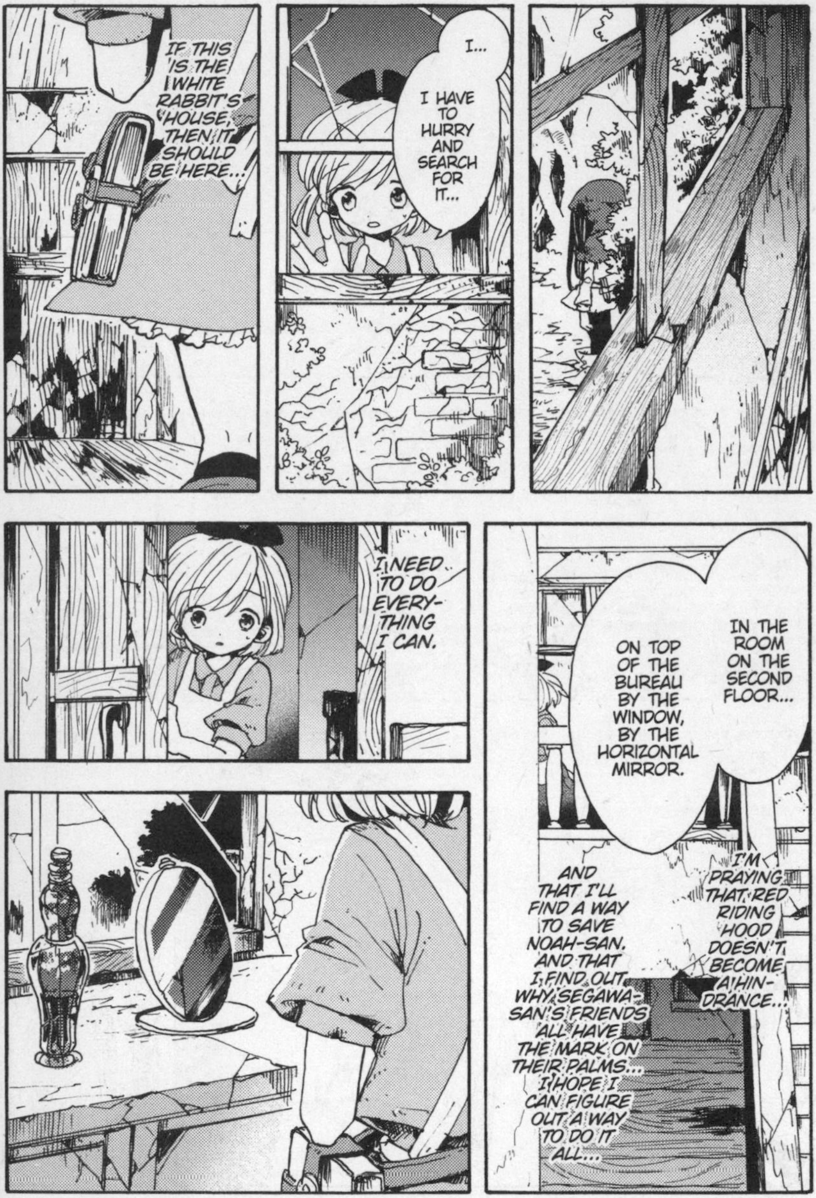
I...
I HAVE TO HURRY AND SEARCH FOR IT...
IF THIS IS THE WHITE RABBIT'S HOUSE, THEN IT SHOULD BE HERE...
IN THE ROOM ON THE SECOND FLOOR...
ON TOP OF THE BUREAU BY THE WINDOW, BY THE HORIZONTAL MIRROR.
I'M PRAYING THAT RED RIDING HOOD DOESN'T BECOME A HIN-DRANCE...
AND THAT I'LL FIND A WAY TO SAVE NOAH-SAN. AND THAT I FIND OUT WHY SEGAWA-SAN'S FRIENDS ALL HAVE THE MARK ON THEIR PALMS... I HOPE I CAN FIGURE OUT A WAY TO DO IT ALL...
I NEED TO DO EVERY-THING I CAN.

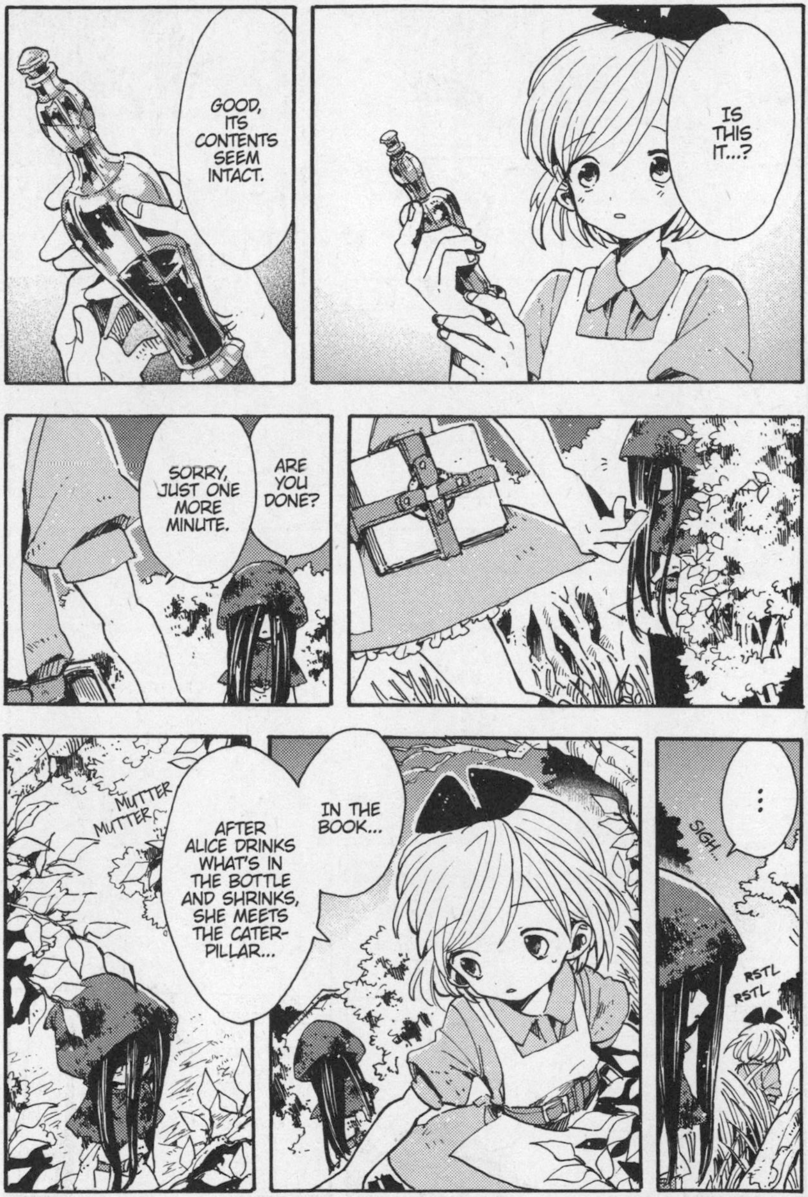
IS THIS IT...?
GOOD, ITS CONTENTS SEEM INTACT.
ARE YOU DONE?
SORRY, JUST ONE MORE MINUTE.
...
SIGH...
RSTL RSTL
IN THE BOOK...
AFTER ALICE DRINKS WHAT'S IN THE BOTTLE AND SHRINKS, SHE MEETS THE CATER-PILLAR...
MUTTER MUTTER

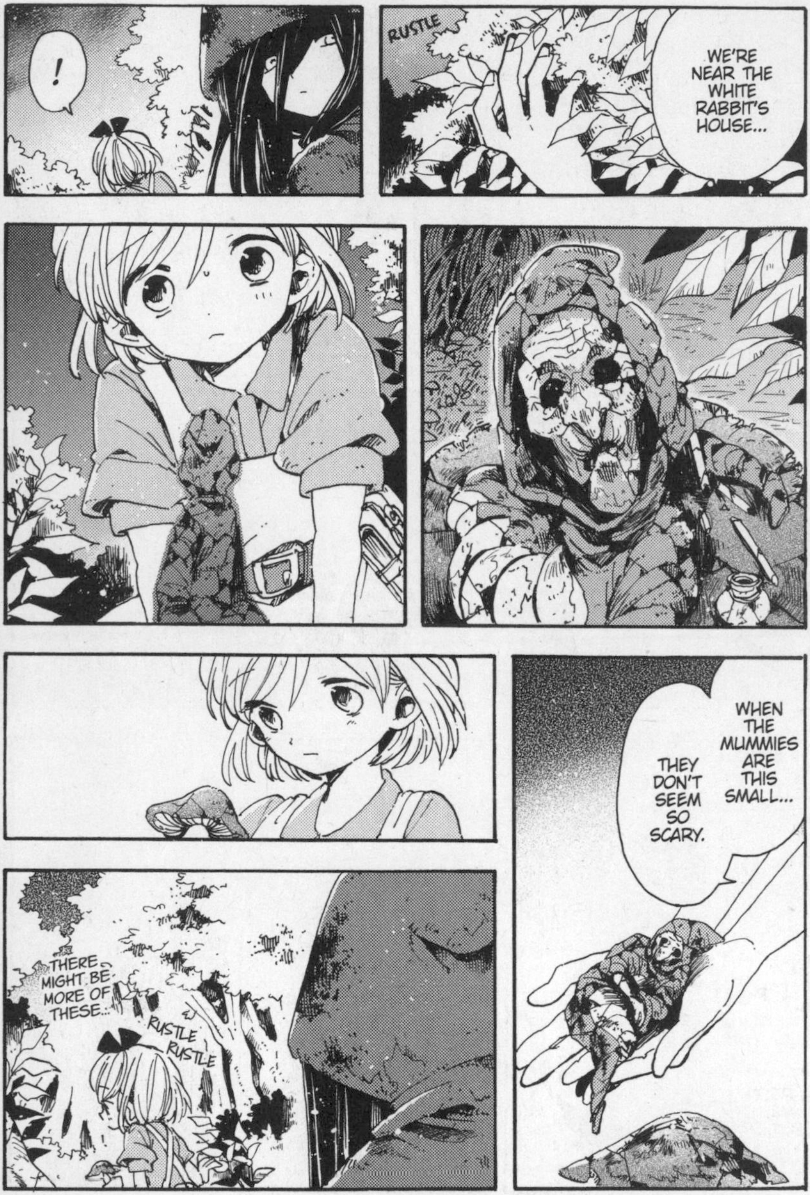
RUSTLE
WE'RE NEAR THE WHITE RABBIT'S HOUSE...
!
WHEN THE MUMMIES ARE THIS SMALL...
THEY DON'T SEEM SO SCARY.
THERE MIGHT BE MORE OF THESE...
RUSTLE RUSTLE
!

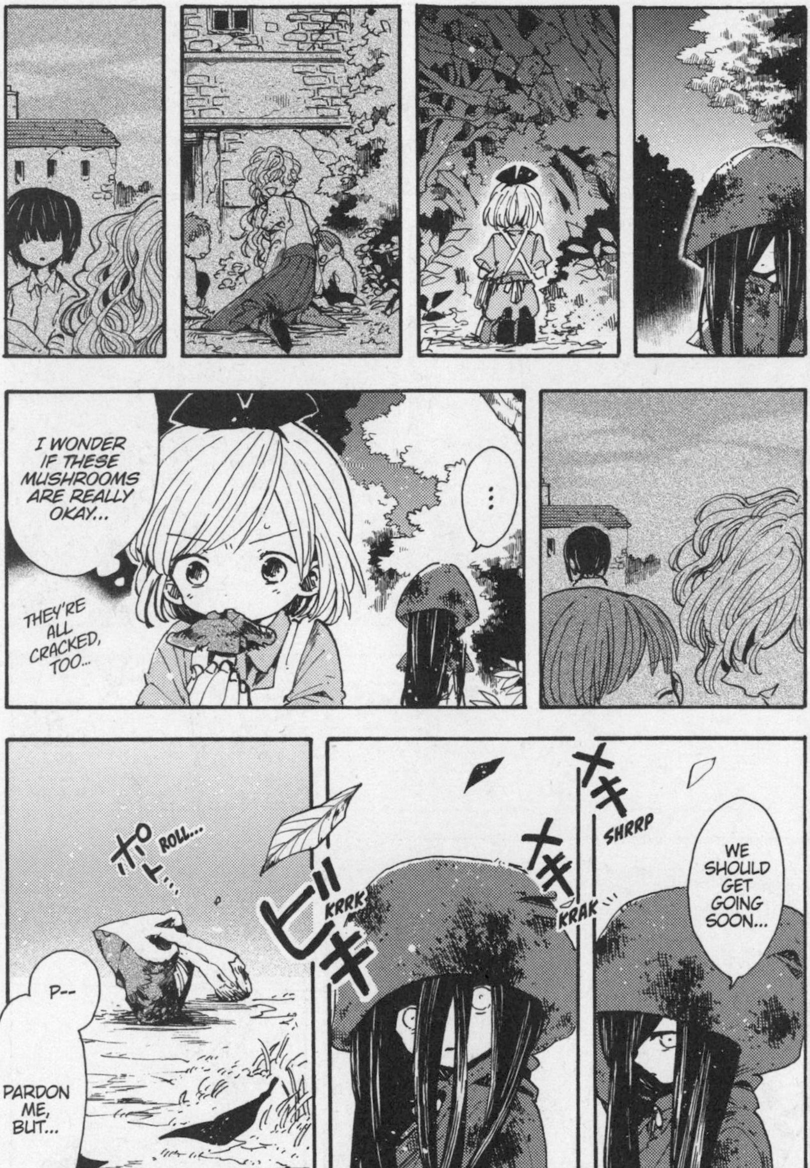
...
I WONDER IF THESE MUSHROOMS ARE REALLY OKAY...
THEY'RE ALL CRACKED, TOO...
WE SHOULD GET GOING SOON...
メキ
SHRRP
メキ
KRAK
ビキ
KRRK
ポト...
ROLL...
P--
PARDON ME, BUT...

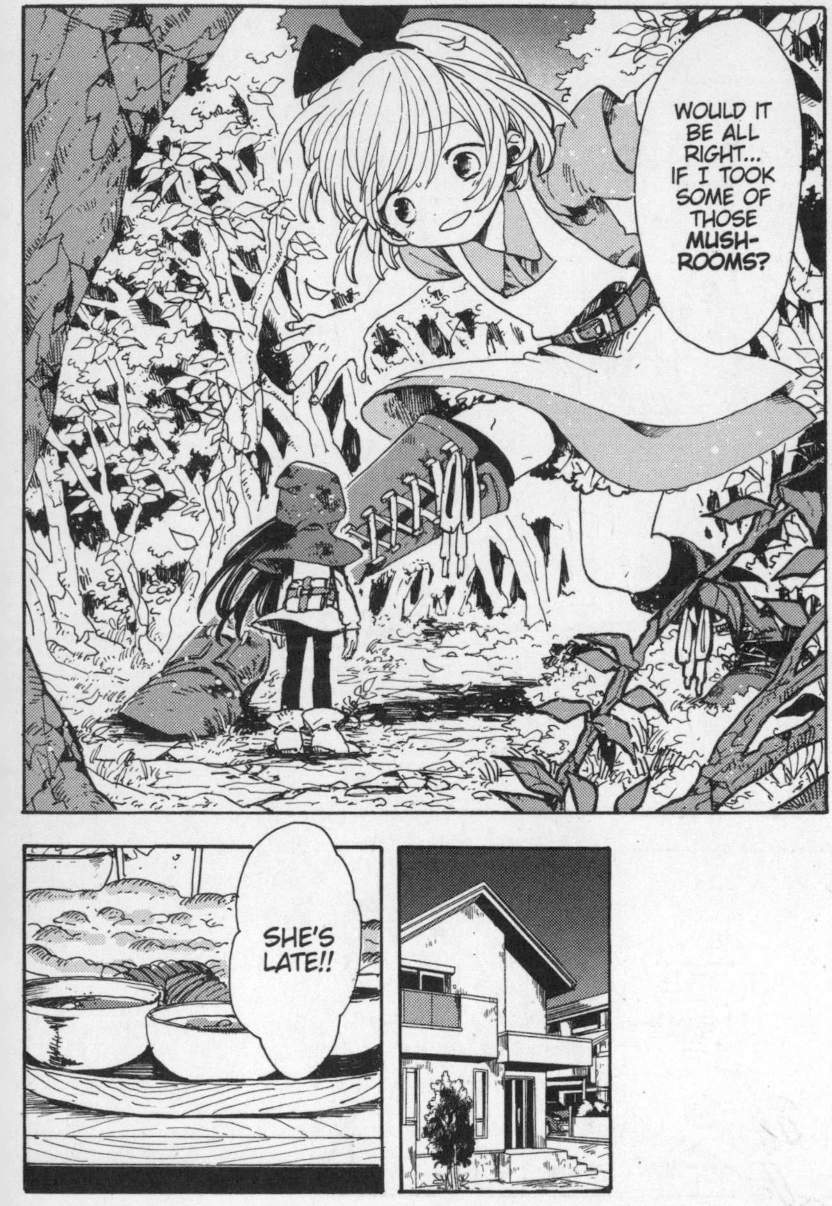
WOULD IT BE ALL RIGHT... IF I TOOK SOME OF THOSE MUSH-ROOMS?
SHE'S LATE!!

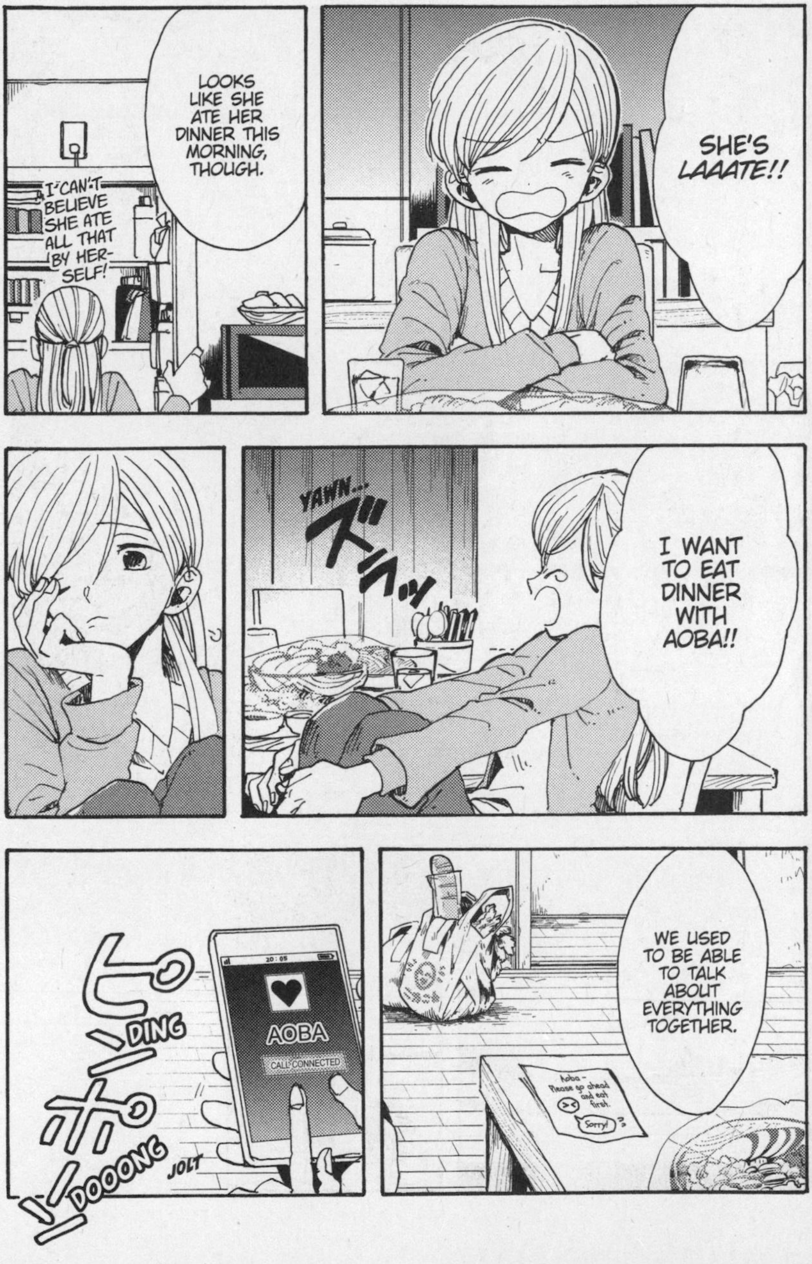
SHE'S LAAATE!!
LOOKS LIKE SHE ATE HER DINNER THIS MORNING, THOUGH.
I CAN'T BELIEVE SHE ATE ALL THAT BY HER-SELF!
I WANT TO EAT DINNER WITH AOBA!!
YAWN...
WE USED TO BE ABLE TO TALK ABOUT EVERYTHING TOGETHER.
Aoba - Please go ahead and eat first.
Sorry!
20:05
AOBA
CALL CONNECTED
DING
DOOONG
JOLT

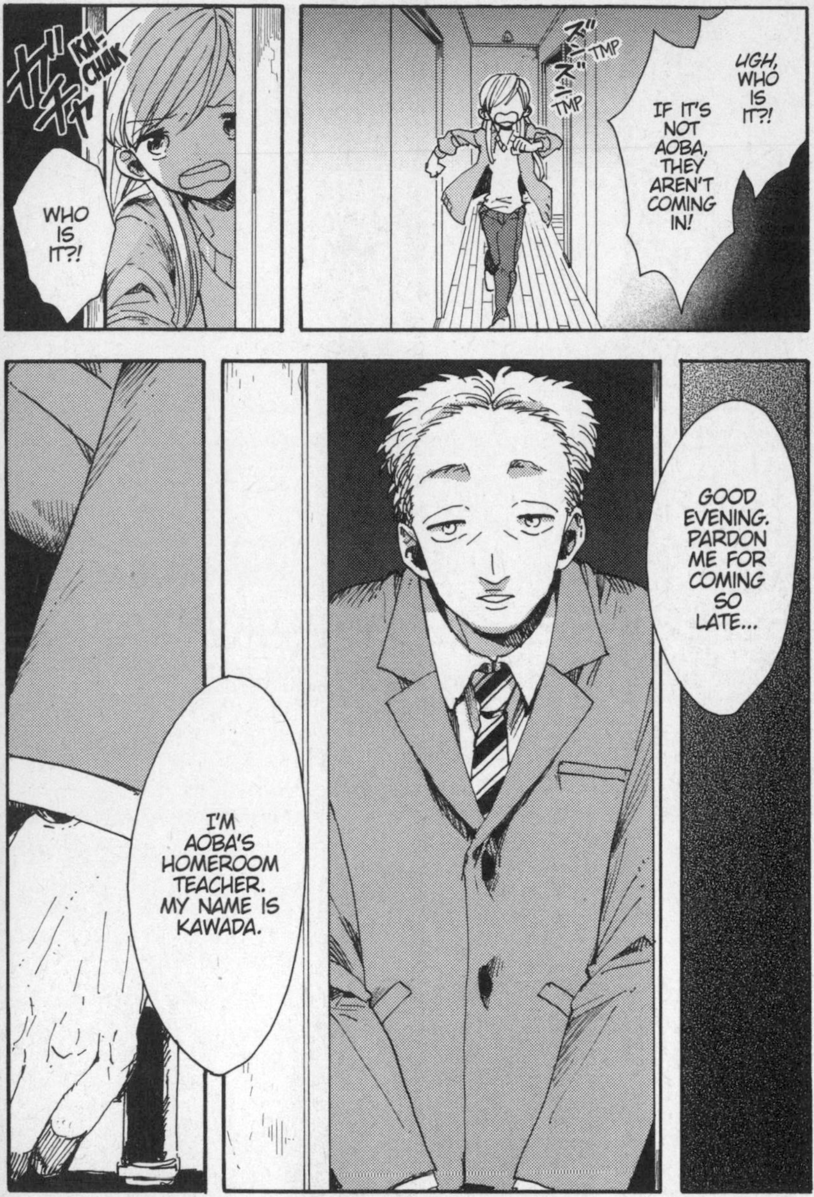
UGH, WHO IS IT?!
IF IT'S NOT AOBA, THEY AREN'T COMING IN!
TMP
TMP
ガチャ
KA-CHAK
WHO IS IT?!
GOOD EVENING. PARDON ME FOR COMING SO LATE...
I'M AOBA'S HOMEROOM TEACHER. MY NAME IS KAWADA.

FAIRY
TALE
BATTLE
ROYALE

FAIRY
TALE
BATTLE
ROYALE

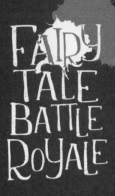

The Affairs of the Protagonists

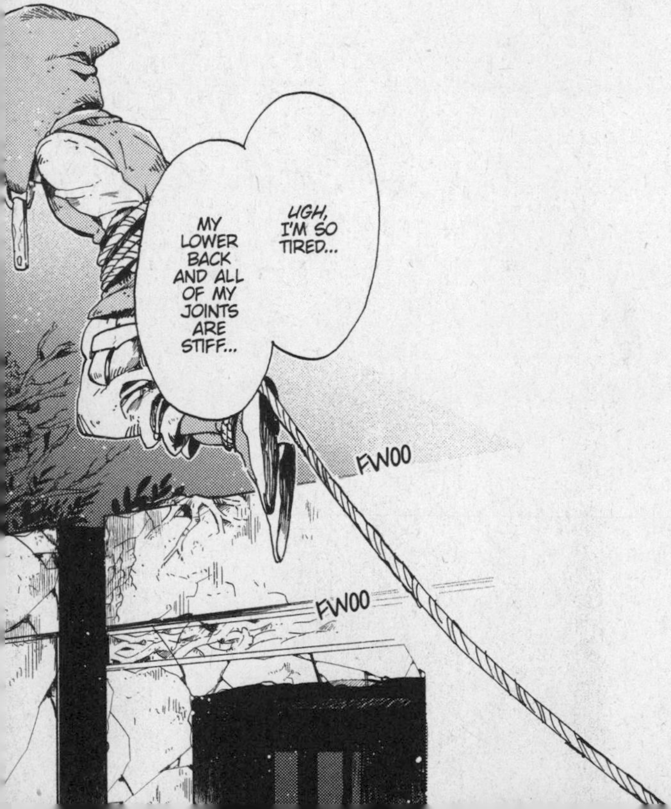
UGH, I'M SO TIRED...
MY LOWER BACK AND ALL OF MY JOINTS ARE STIFF...
FWOO
FWOO

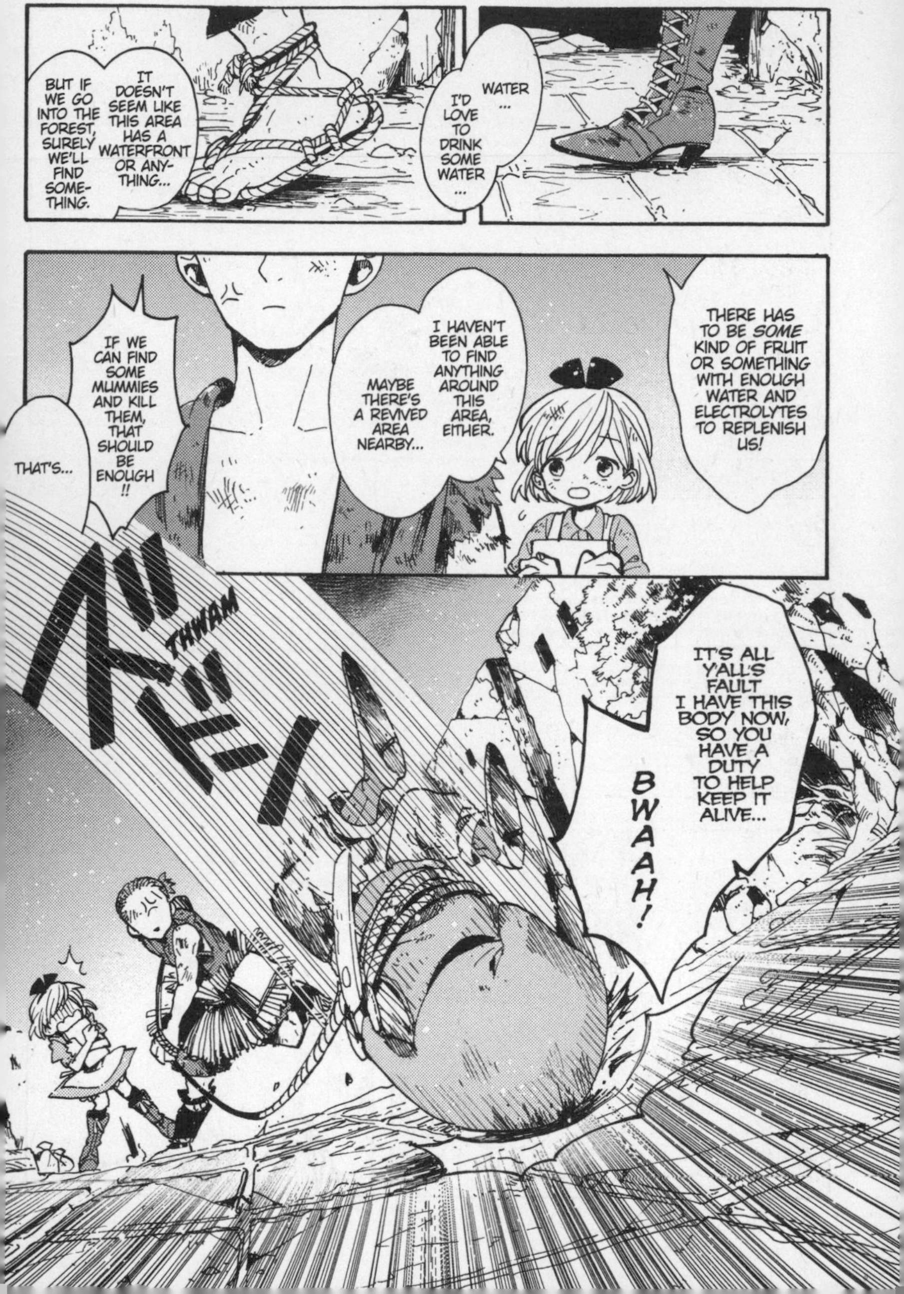
WATER ... I'D LOVE TO DRINK SOME WATER ...
IT DOESN'T SEEM LIKE THIS AREA HAS A WATERFRONT OR ANYTHING...
BUT IF WE GO INTO THE FOREST, SURELY WE'LL FIND SOMETHING.
THERE HAS TO BE *SOME* KIND OF FRUIT OR SOMETHING WITH ENOUGH WATER AND ELECTROLYTES TO REPLENISH US!
I HAVEN'T BEEN ABLE TO FIND ANYTHING AROUND THIS AREA, EITHER.
MAYBE THERE'S A REVIVED AREA NEARBY...
IF WE CAN FIND SOME MUMMIES AND KILL THEM, THAT SHOULD BE ENOUGH!!
THAT'S...
IT'S ALL Y'ALL'S FAULT I HAVE THIS BODY NOW, SO YOU HAVE A DUTY TO HELP KEEP IT ALIVE...
BWAAAH!
THWAM

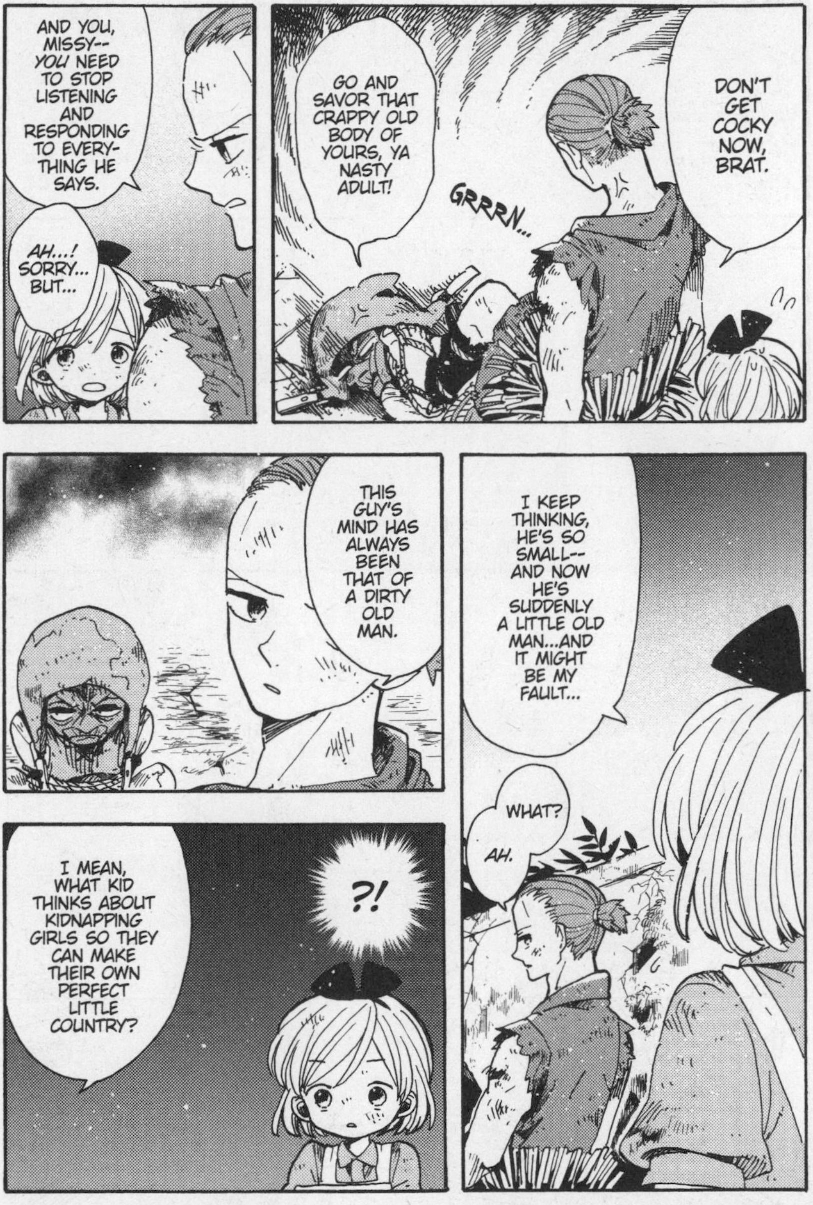
DON'T GET COCKY NOW, BRAT.
GO AND SAVOR THAT CRAPPY OLD BODY OF YOURS, YA NASTY ADULT!
GRRRN...
AND YOU, MISSY-- *YOU* NEED TO STOP LISTENING AND RESPONDING TO EVERY-THING HE SAYS.
AH...! SORRY... BUT...
I KEEP THINKING, HE'S SO SMALL-- AND NOW HE'S SUDDENLY A LITTLE OLD MAN...AND IT MIGHT BE MY FAULT...
WHAT?
AH.
THIS GUY'S MIND HAS ALWAYS BEEN THAT OF A DIRTY OLD MAN.
I MEAN, WHAT KID THINKS ABOUT KIDNAPPING GIRLS SO THEY CAN MAKE THEIR OWN PERFECT LITTLE COUNTRY?
?!

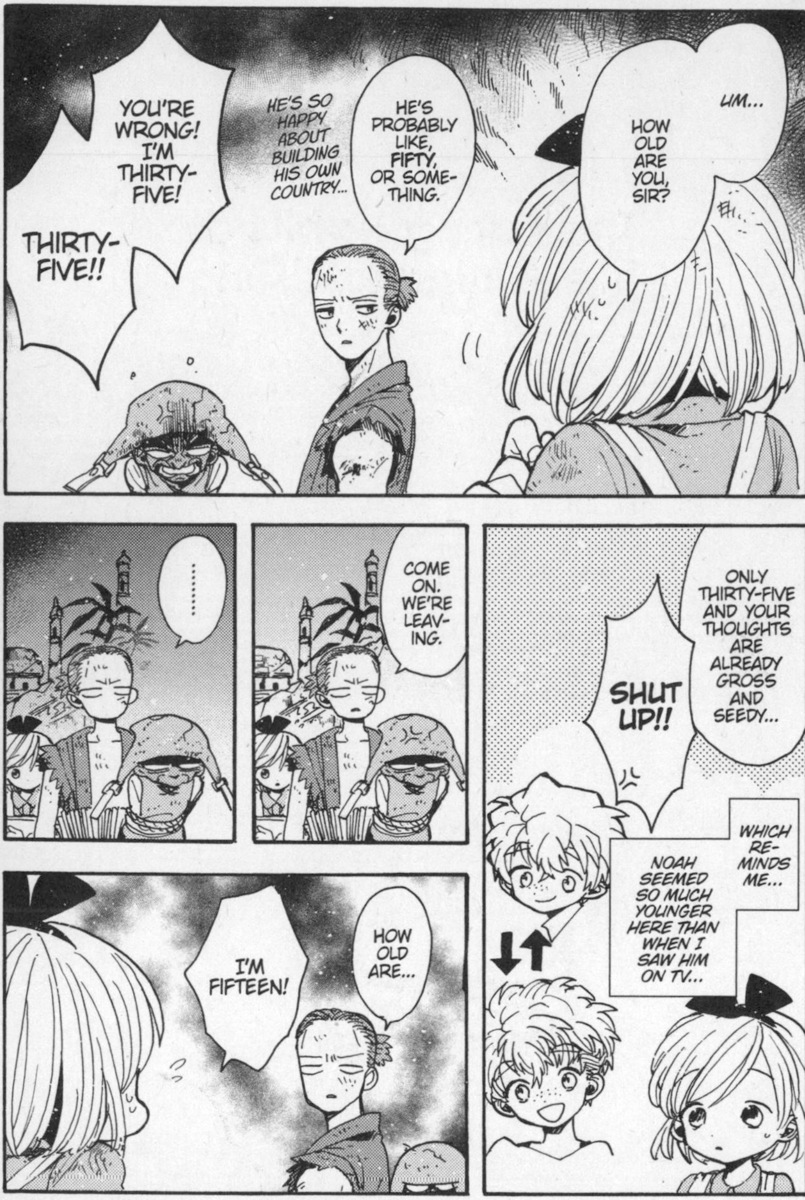
UM...
HOW OLD ARE YOU, SIR?
HE'S PROBABLY LIKE, FIFTY, OR SOME-THING.
HE'S SO HAPPY ABOUT BUILDING HIS OWN COUNTRY...
YOU'RE WRONG! I'M THIRTY-FIVE!
THIRTY-FIVE!!
ONLY THIRTY-FIVE AND YOUR THOUGHTS ARE ALREADY GROSS AND SEEDY...
SHUT UP!!
WHICH RE-MINDS ME...
NOAH SEEMED SO MUCH YOUNGER HERE THAN WHEN I SAW HIM ON TV...
COME ON. WE'RE LEAV-ING.
....
HOW OLD ARE...
I'M FIFTEEN!

The Eating Habits of the Kuninaka Sisters

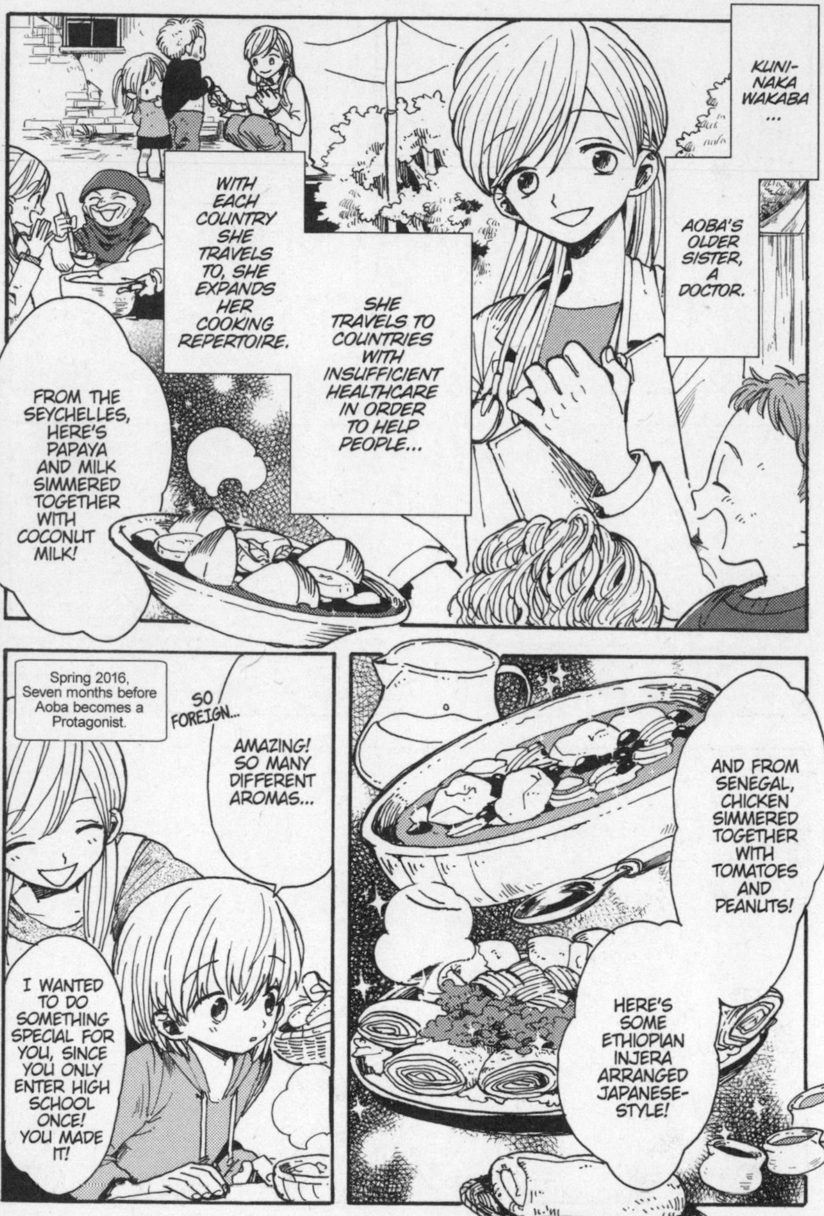
KUNI-NAKA WAKABA...
AOBA'S OLDER SISTER, A DOCTOR.
SHE TRAVELS TO COUNTRIES WITH INSUFFICIENT HEALTHCARE IN ORDER TO HELP PEOPLE...
WITH EACH COUNTRY SHE TRAVELS TO, SHE EXPANDS HER COOKING REPERTOIRE.
FROM THE SEYCHELLES, HERE'S PAPAYA AND MILK SIMMERED TOGETHER WITH COCONUT MILK!
AND FROM SENEGAL, CHICKEN SIMMERED TOGETHER WITH TOMATOES AND PEANUTS!
HERE'S SOME ETHIOPIAN INJERA ARRANGED JAPANESE-STYLE!
Spring 2016, Seven months before Aoba becomes a Protagonist.
SO FOREIGN...
AMAZING! SO MANY DIFFERENT AROMAS...
I WANTED TO DO SOMETHING SPECIAL FOR YOU, SINCE YOU ONLY ENTER HIGH SCHOOL ONCE! YOU MADE IT!

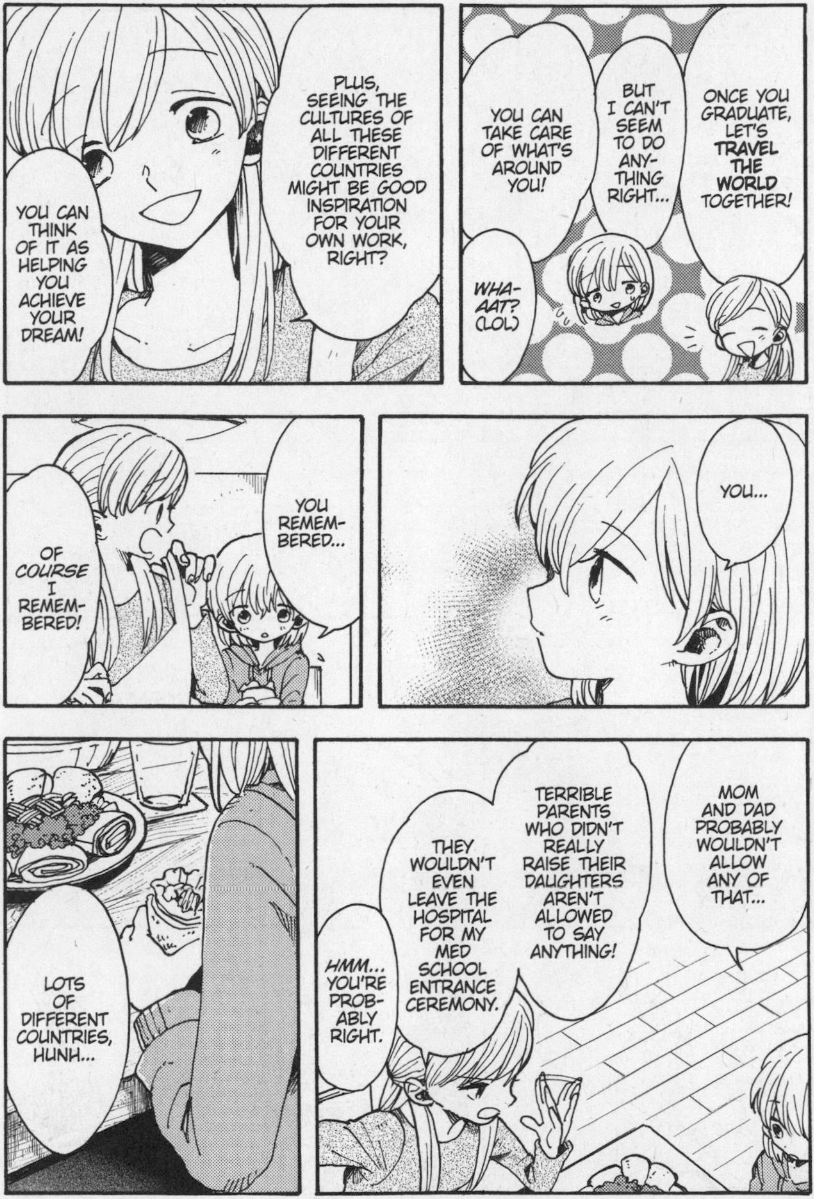
ONCE YOU GRADUATE, LET'S TRAVEL THE WORLD TOGETHER!
BUT I CAN'T SEEM TO DO ANYTHING RIGHT...
YOU CAN TAKE CARE OF WHAT'S AROUND YOU!
WHA-AAT? (LOL)
PLUS, SEEING THE CULTURES OF ALL THESE DIFFERENT COUNTRIES MIGHT BE GOOD INSPIRATION FOR YOUR OWN WORK, RIGHT?
YOU CAN THINK OF IT AS HELPING YOU ACHIEVE YOUR DREAM!
YOU...
YOU REMEMBERED...
OF COURSE I REMEMBERED!
MOM AND DAD PROBABLY WOULDN'T ALLOW ANY OF THAT...
TERRIBLE PARENTS WHO DIDN'T REALLY RAISE THEIR DAUGHTERS AREN'T ALLOWED TO SAY ANYTHING!
THEY WOULDN'T EVEN LEAVE THE HOSPITAL FOR MY MED SCHOOL ENTRANCE CEREMONY.
HMM... YOU'RE PROBABLY RIGHT.
LOTS OF DIFFERENT COUNTRIES, HUNH...

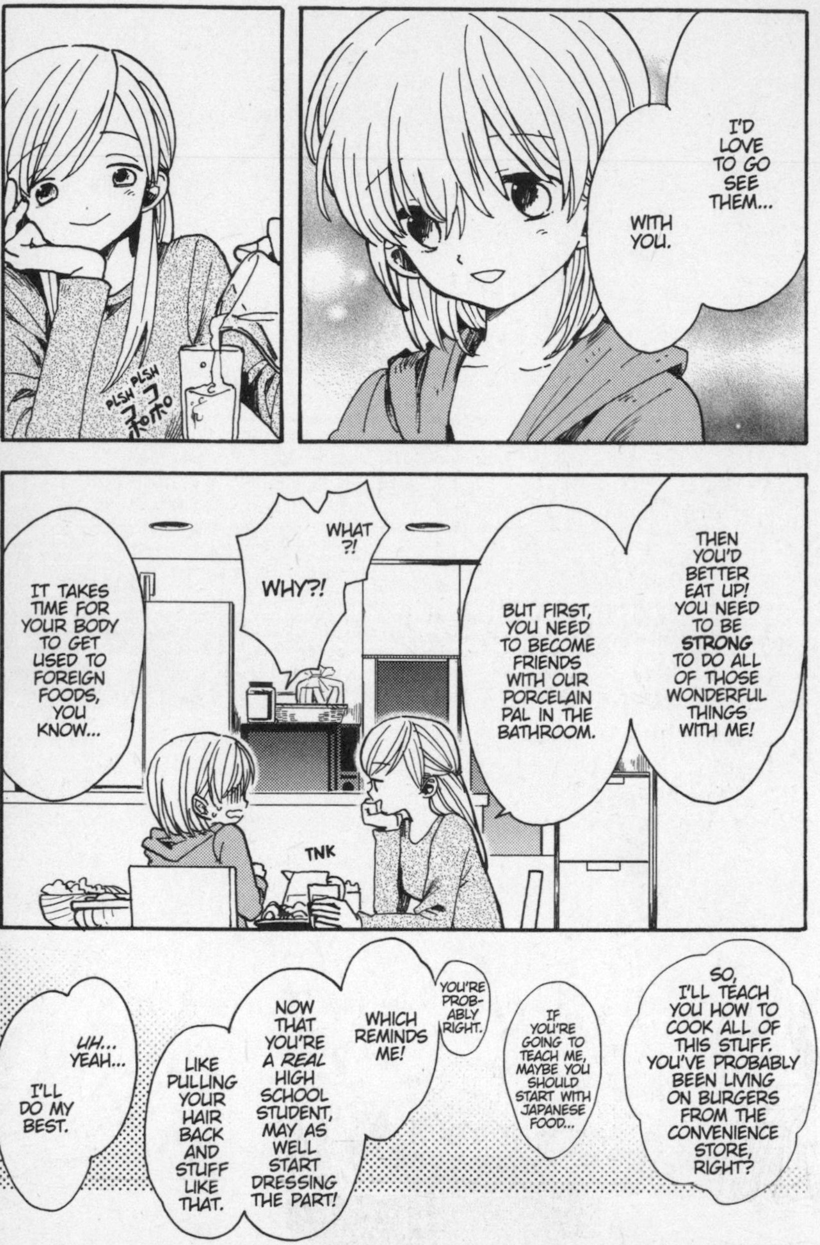
I'D LOVE TO GO SEE THEM...
WITH YOU.
PLSH PLSH
THEN YOU'D BETTER EAT UP! YOU NEED TO BE **STRONG** TO DO ALL OF THOSE WONDERFUL THINGS WITH ME!
BUT FIRST, YOU NEED TO BECOME FRIENDS WITH OUR PORCELAIN PAL IN THE BATHROOM.
WHAT?!
WHY?!
IT TAKES TIME FOR YOUR BODY TO GET USED TO FOREIGN FOODS, YOU KNOW...
TNK
SO, I'LL TEACH YOU HOW TO COOK ALL OF THIS STUFF. YOU'VE PROBABLY BEEN LIVING ON BURGERS FROM THE CONVENIENCE STORE, RIGHT?
IF YOU'RE GOING TO TEACH ME, MAYBE YOU SHOULD START WITH JAPANESE FOOD...
YOU'RE PROBABLY RIGHT.
WHICH REMINDS ME!
NOW THAT YOU'RE A *REAL* HIGH SCHOOL STUDENT, MAY AS WELL START DRESSING THE PART!
LIKE PULLING YOUR HAIR BACK AND STUFF LIKE THAT.
UH... YEAH...
I'LL DO MY BEST.

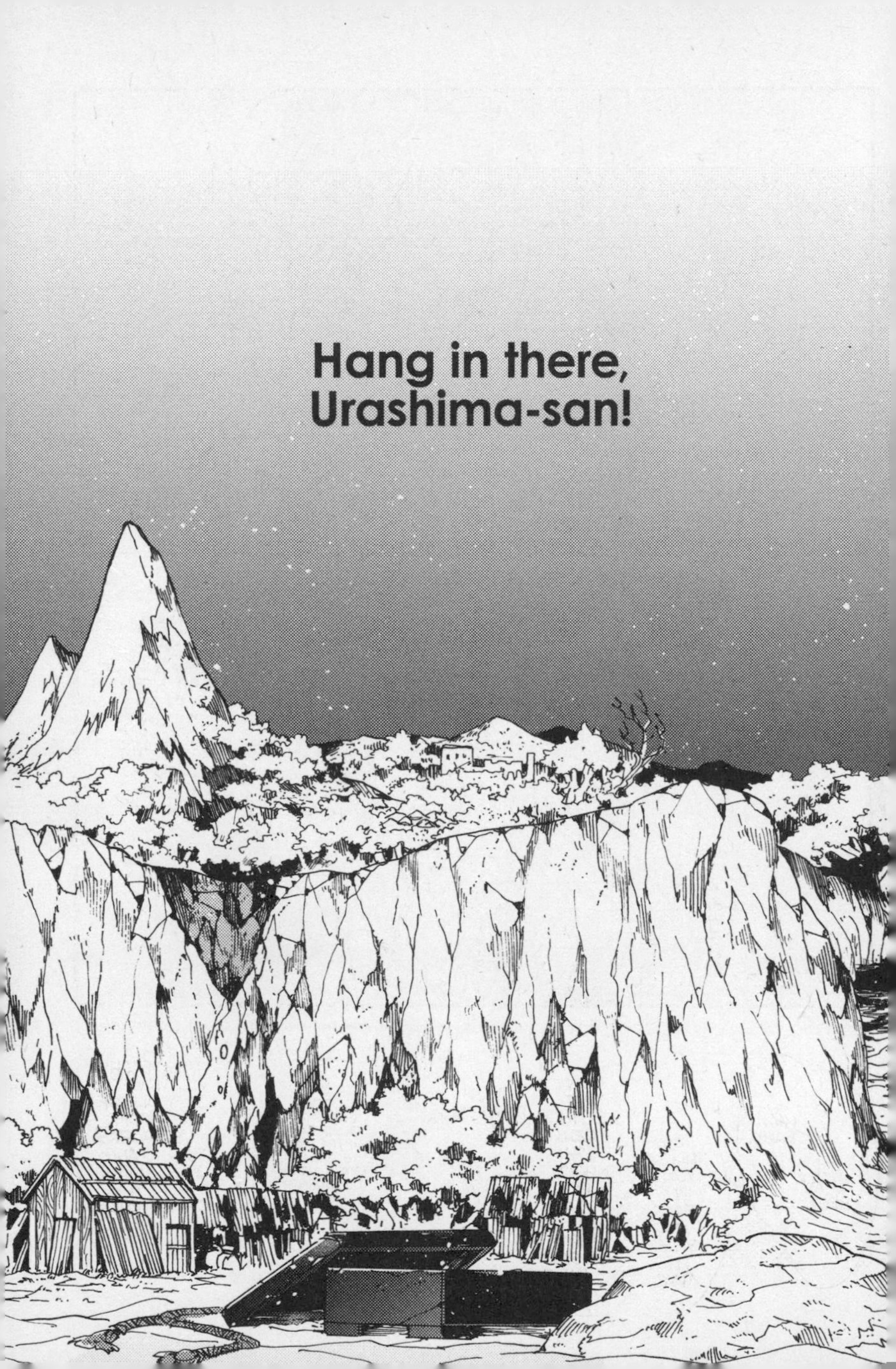
Hang in there,
Urashima-san!

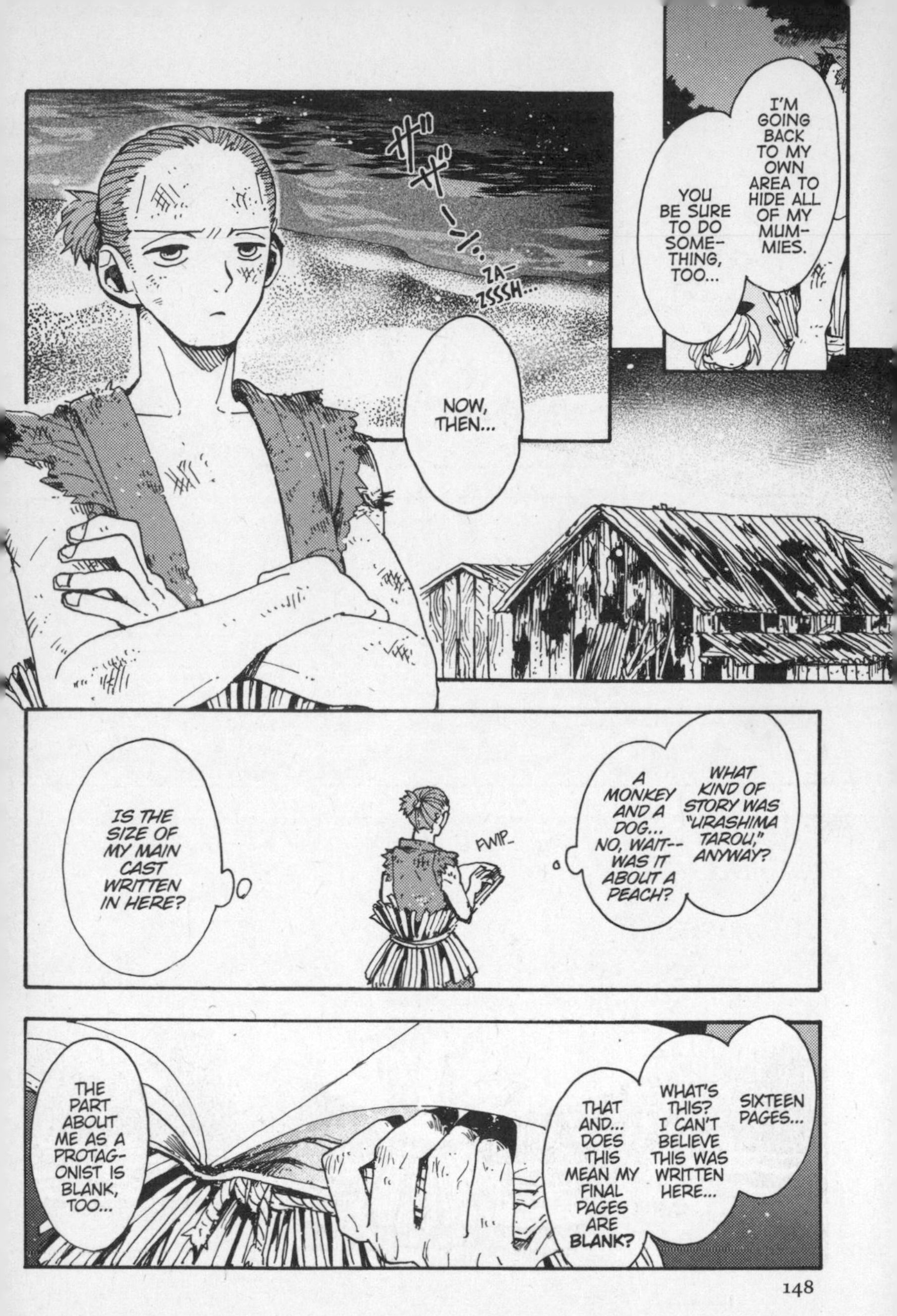
I'M GOING BACK TO MY OWN AREA TO HIDE ALL OF MY MUM-MIES.
YOU BE SURE TO DO SOME-THING, TOO...
ZA-ZSSSH...
NOW, THEN...
WHAT KIND OF STORY WAS "URASHIMA TAROU," ANYWAY?
A MONKEY AND A DOG... NO, WAIT-- WAS IT ABOUT A PEACH?
FWIP...
IS THE SIZE OF MY MAIN CAST WRITTEN IN HERE?
SIXTEEN PAGES...
WHAT'S THIS? I CAN'T BELIEVE THIS WAS WRITTEN HERE...
THAT AND... DOES THIS MEAN MY FINAL PAGES ARE BLANK?
THE PART ABOUT ME AS A PROTAGONIST IS BLANK, TOO...

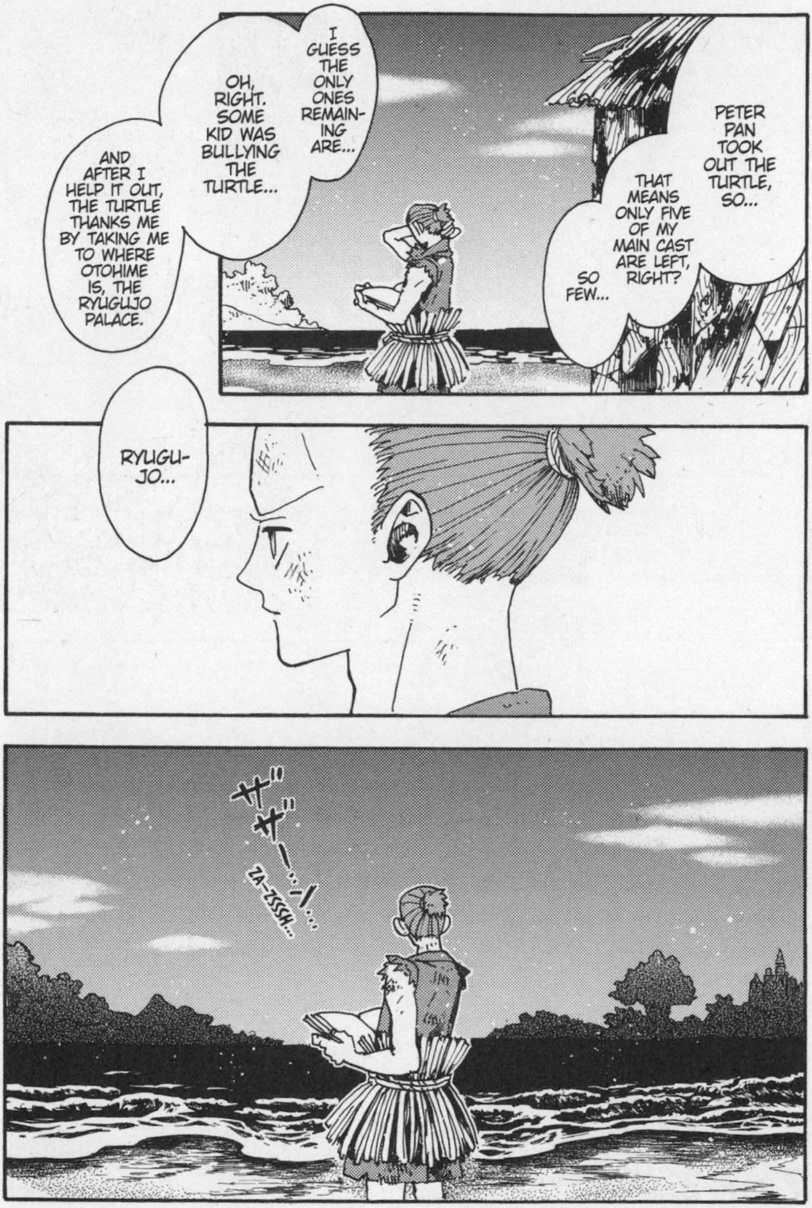
PETER PAN TOOK OUT THE TURTLE, SO...
THAT MEANS ONLY FIVE OF MY MAIN CAST ARE LEFT, RIGHT?
SO FEW...
I GUESS THE ONLY ONES REMAINING ARE...
OH, RIGHT. SOME KID WAS BULLYING THE TURTLE...
AND AFTER I HELP IT OUT, THE TURTLE THANKS ME BY TAKING ME TO WHERE OTOHIME IS, THE RYUGUJO PALACE.
RYUGU-JO...
ザザーン...
ZA-ZSSSH...

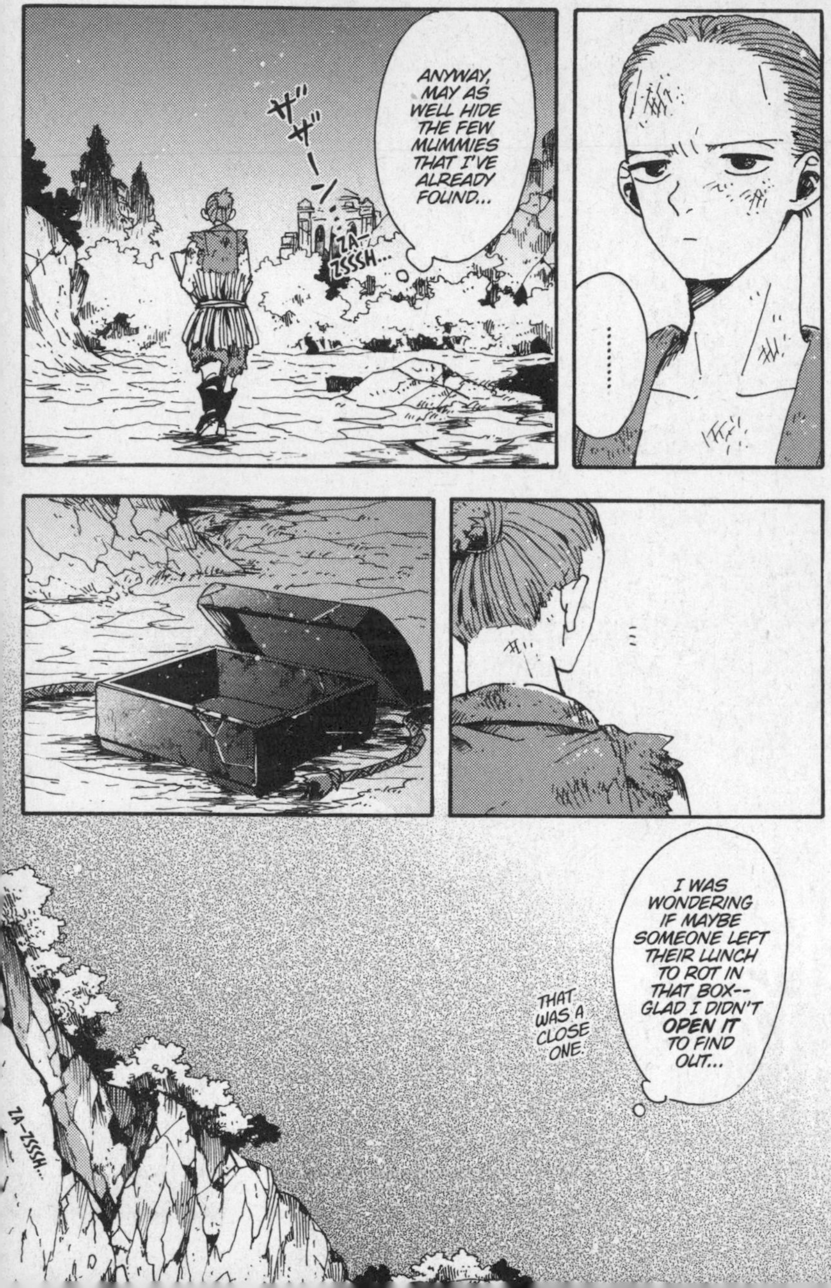
......
ANYWAY, MAY AS WELL HIDE THE FEW MUMMIES THAT I'VE ALREADY FOUND...
ZA-ZSSSH...
I WAS WONDERING IF MAYBE SOMEONE LEFT THEIR LUNCH TO ROT IN THAT BOX-- GLAD I DIDN'T OPEN IT TO FIND OUT...
THAT WAS A CLOSE ONE.
ZA-ZSSSH...

FAIRY
TALE
BATTLE
ROYALE

Little Red Riding Hood

First in Print: 1697
Retelling By: Charles Perrault

With many different authors and versions, "Red Riding Hood" is a story that has changed a lot since its humble origins as a folktale.

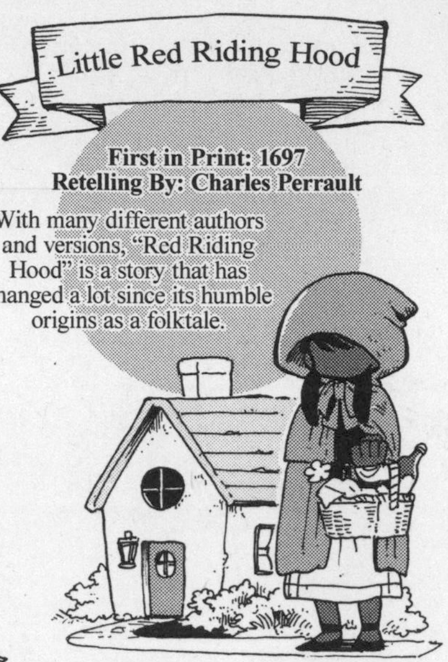

Peter Pan

First Published: 1902
Author: J. M. Barrie

Peter Pan originally debuted in a book called *The Little White Bird*. Barrie later developed parts of that book into a story for children--what is now known as *Peter Pan*.

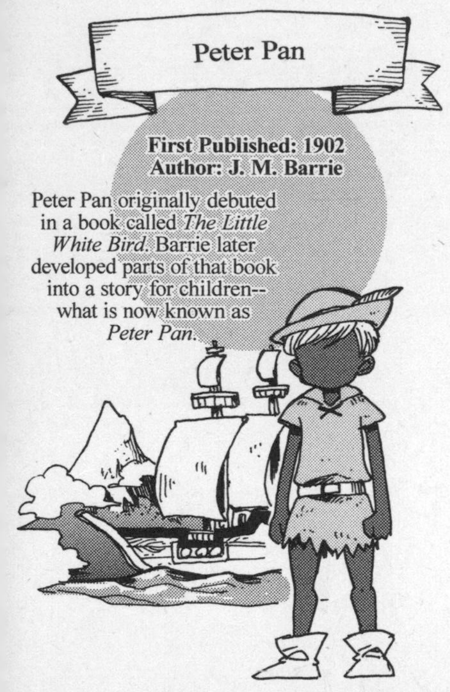

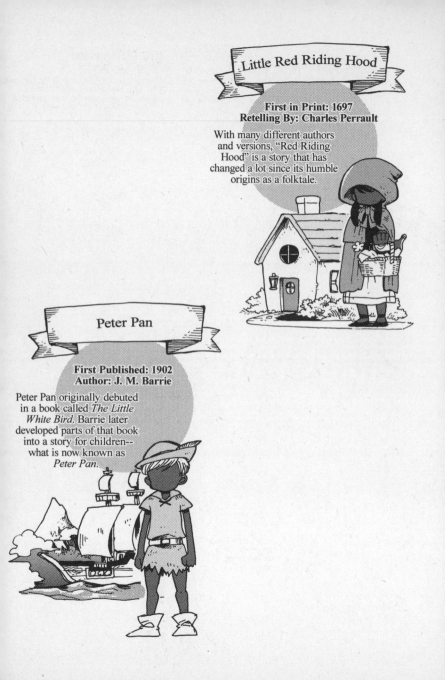

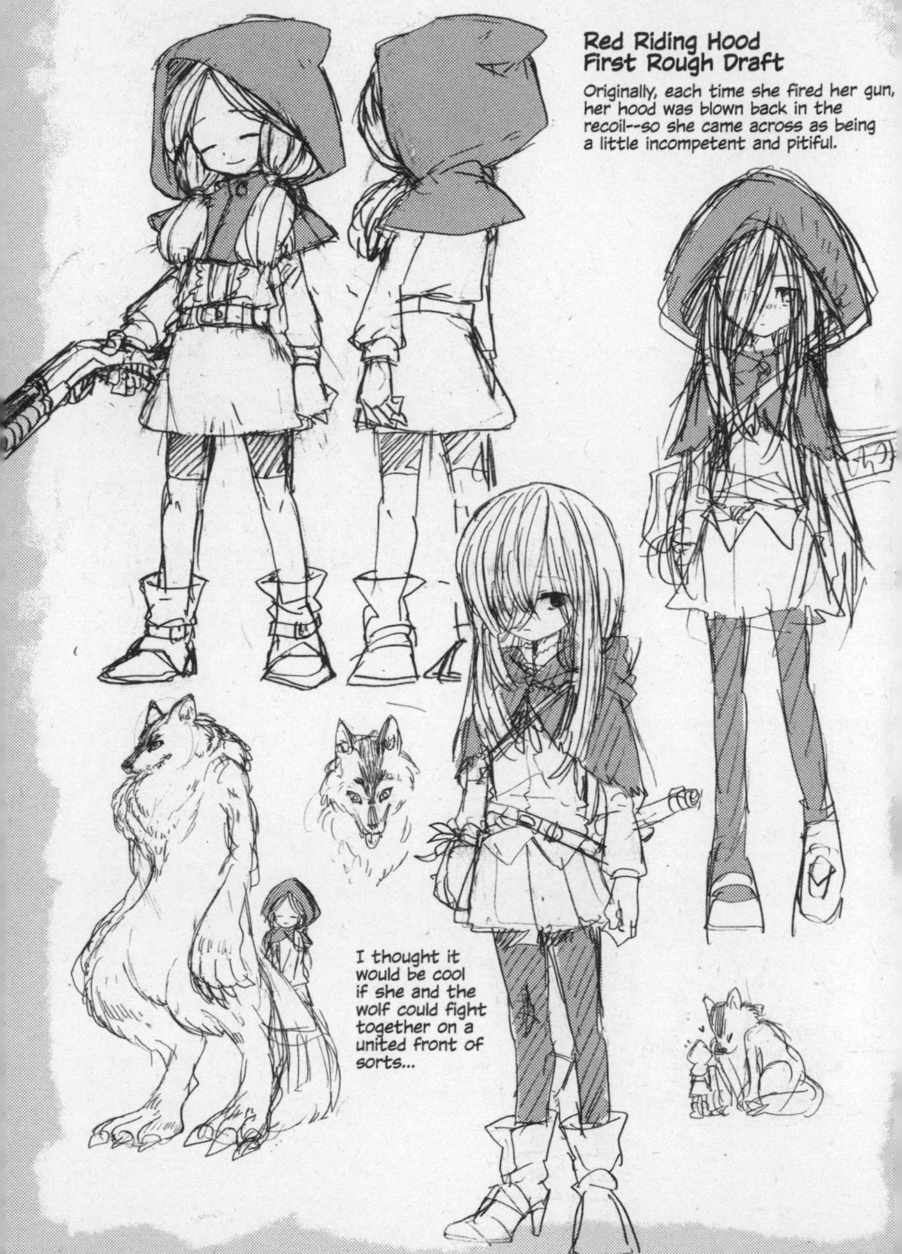
Red Riding Hood
First Rough Draft
Originally, each time she fired her gun, her hood was blown back in the recoil--so she came across as being a little incompetent and pitiful.
I thought it would be cool if she and the wolf could fight together on a united front of sorts...

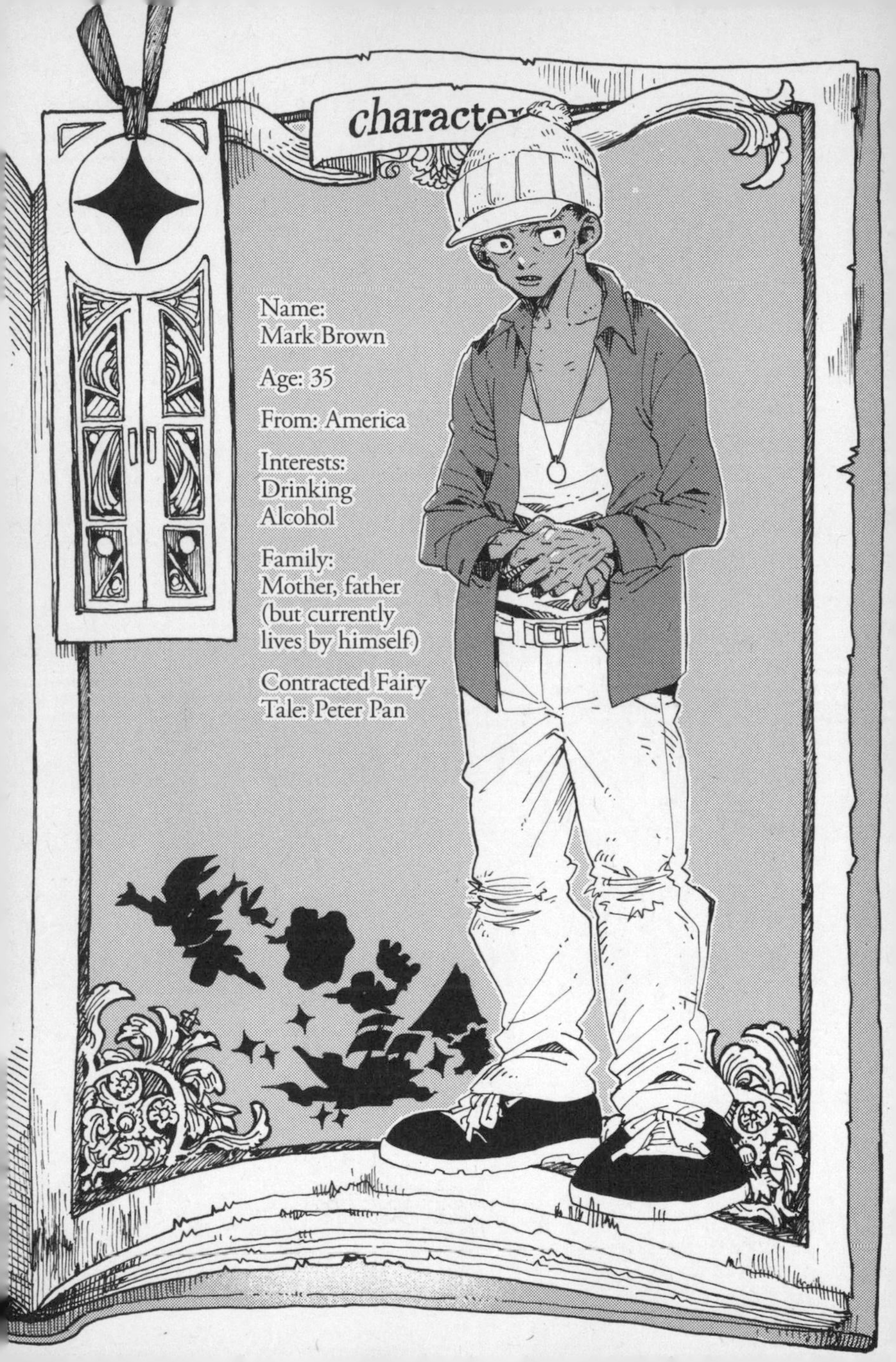
characte
Name:
Mark Brown
Age: 35
From: America
Interests:
Drinking
Alcohol
Family:
Mother, father
(but currently
lives by himself)
Contracted Fairy
Tale: Peter Pan

Peter Pan
Rough Conceptualization

My foremost concern was about Peter Pan's actual age and how old he'd be in real life.

I really did intend for him to be a child at first.

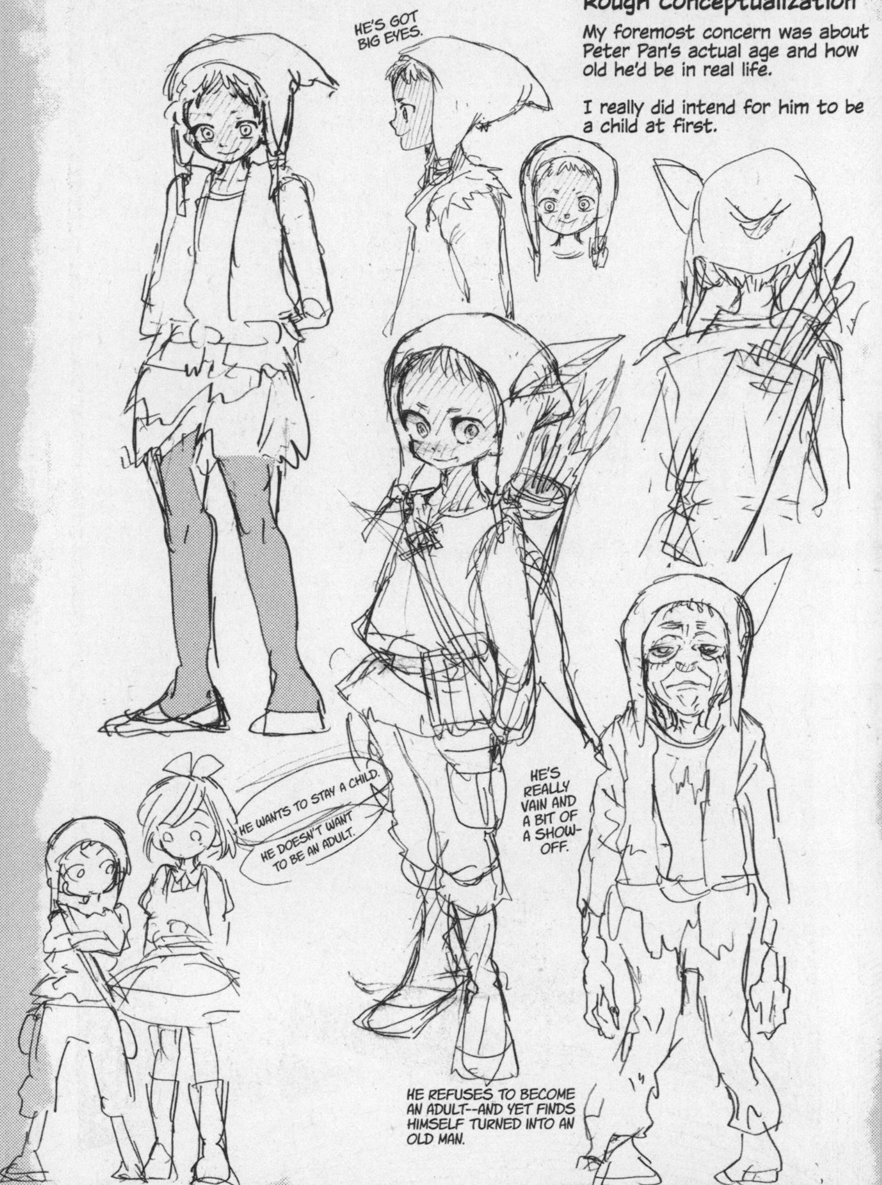

HE'S GOT BIG EYES.
HE WANTS TO STAY A CHILD.
HE DOESN'T WANT TO BE AN ADULT.
HE'S REALLY VAIN AND A BIT OF A SHOW-OFF.
HE REFUSES TO BECOME AN ADULT--AND YET FINDS HIMSELF TURNED INTO AN OLD MAN.

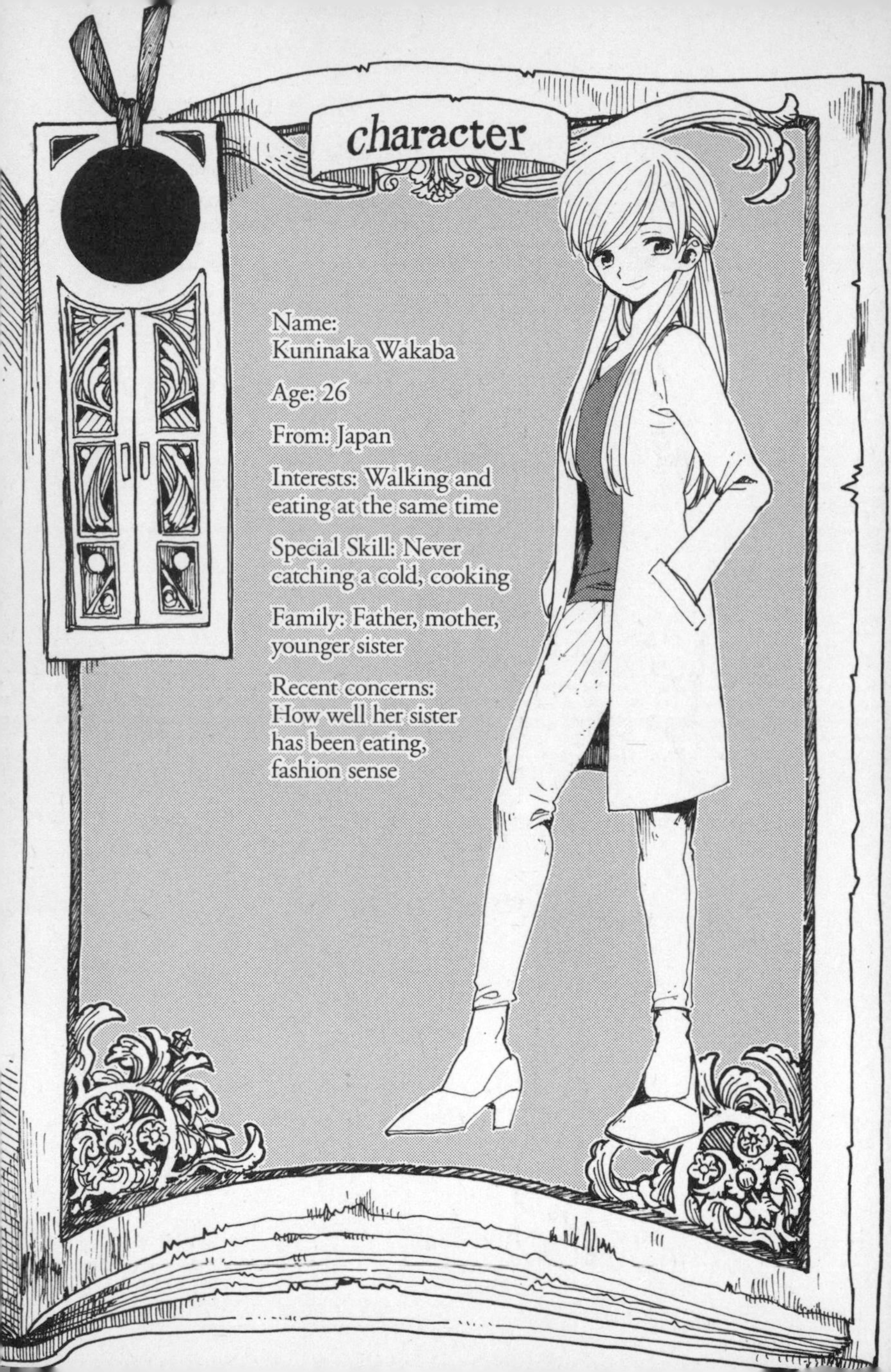
character
Name:
Kuninaka Wakaba
Age: 26
From: Japan
Interests: Walking and eating at the same time
Special Skill: Never catching a cold, cooking
Family: Father, mother, younger sister
Recent concerns: How well her sister has been eating, fashion sense

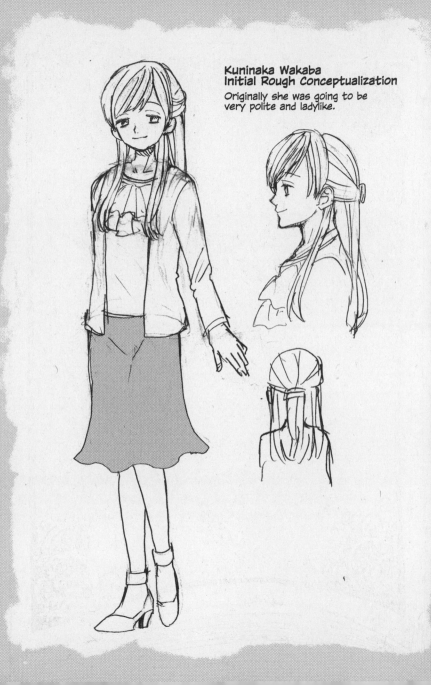

Kuninaka Wakaba
Initial Rough Conceptualization

Originally she was going to be very polite and ladylike.

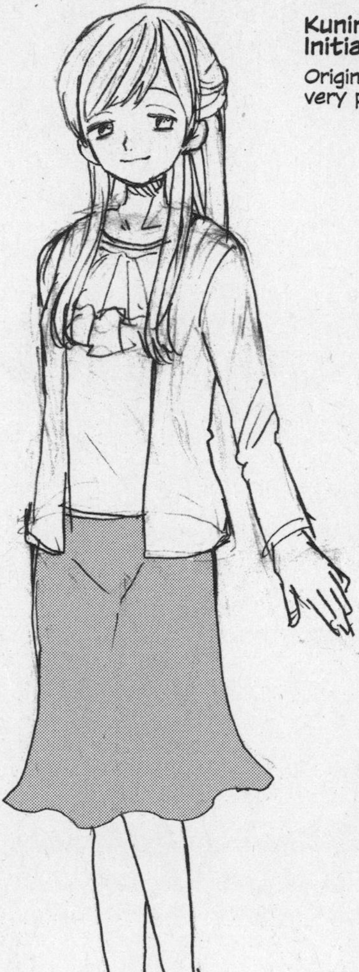

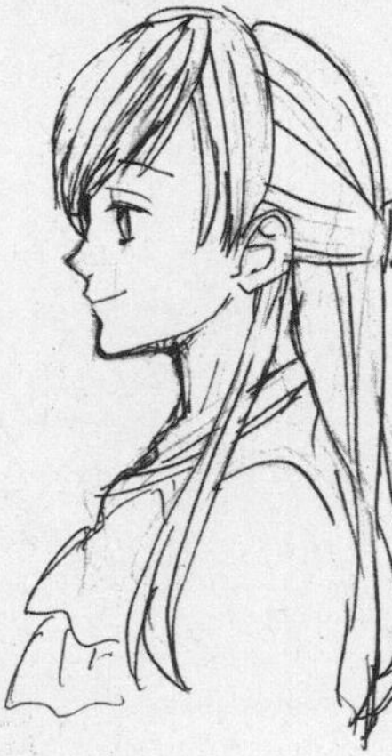

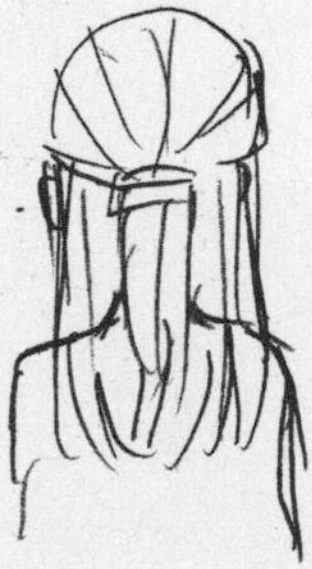

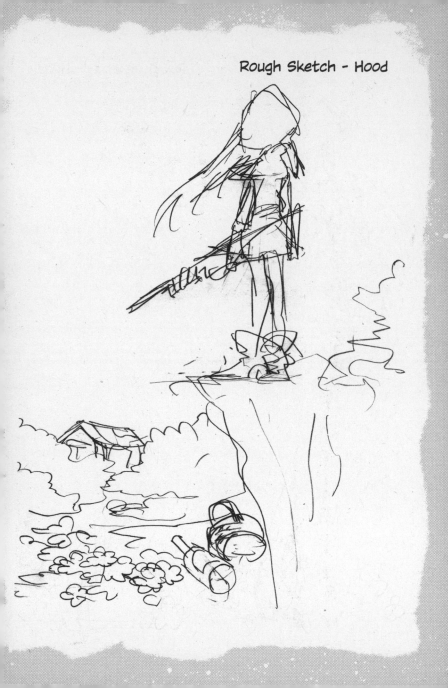

Rough Sketch - Hood

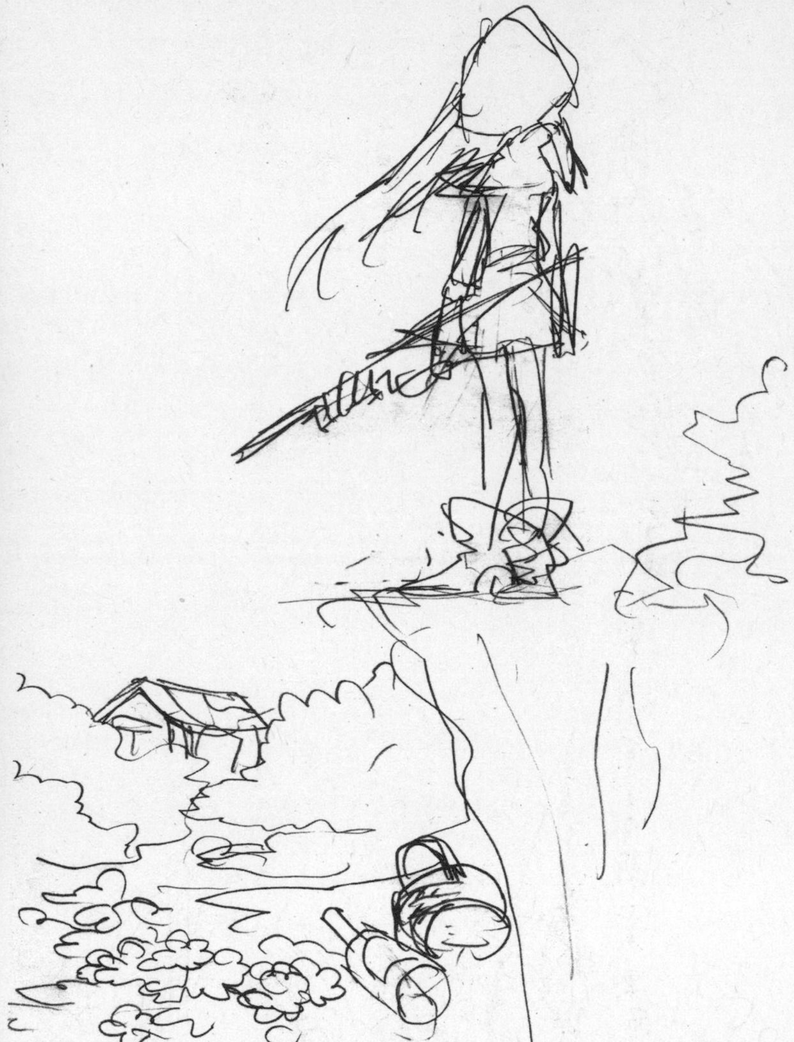

Rough Sketch - Hood

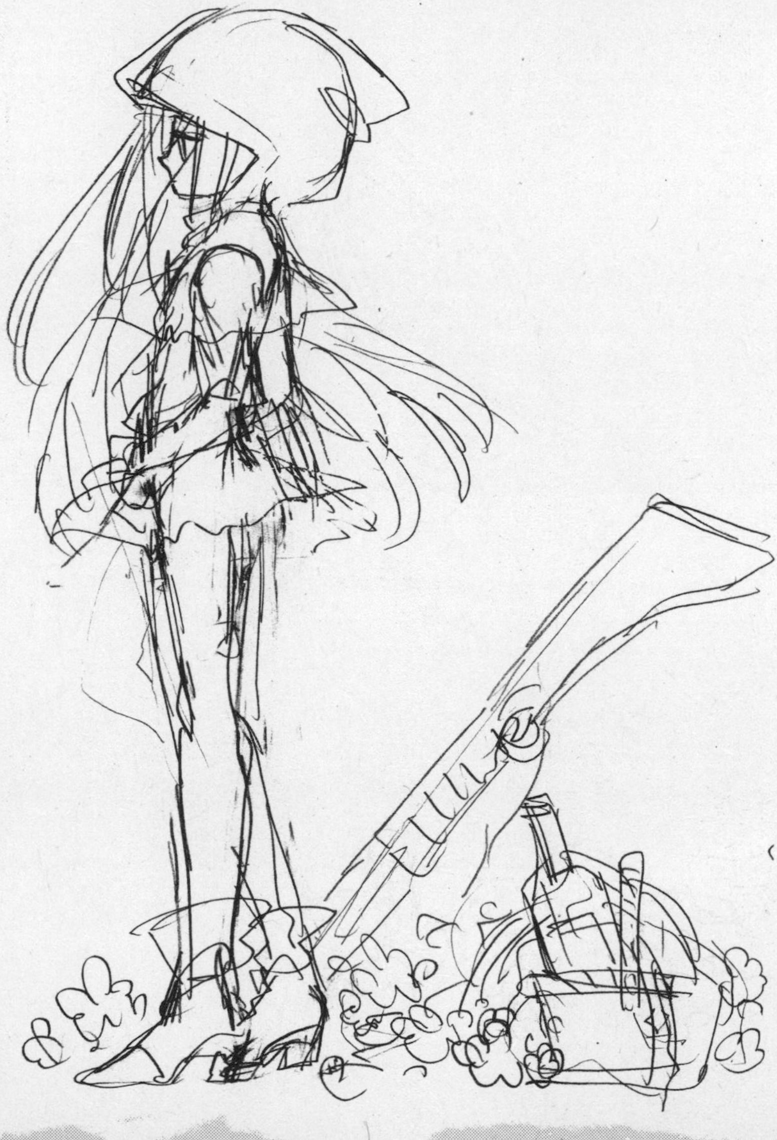

Rough Sketch - Hood

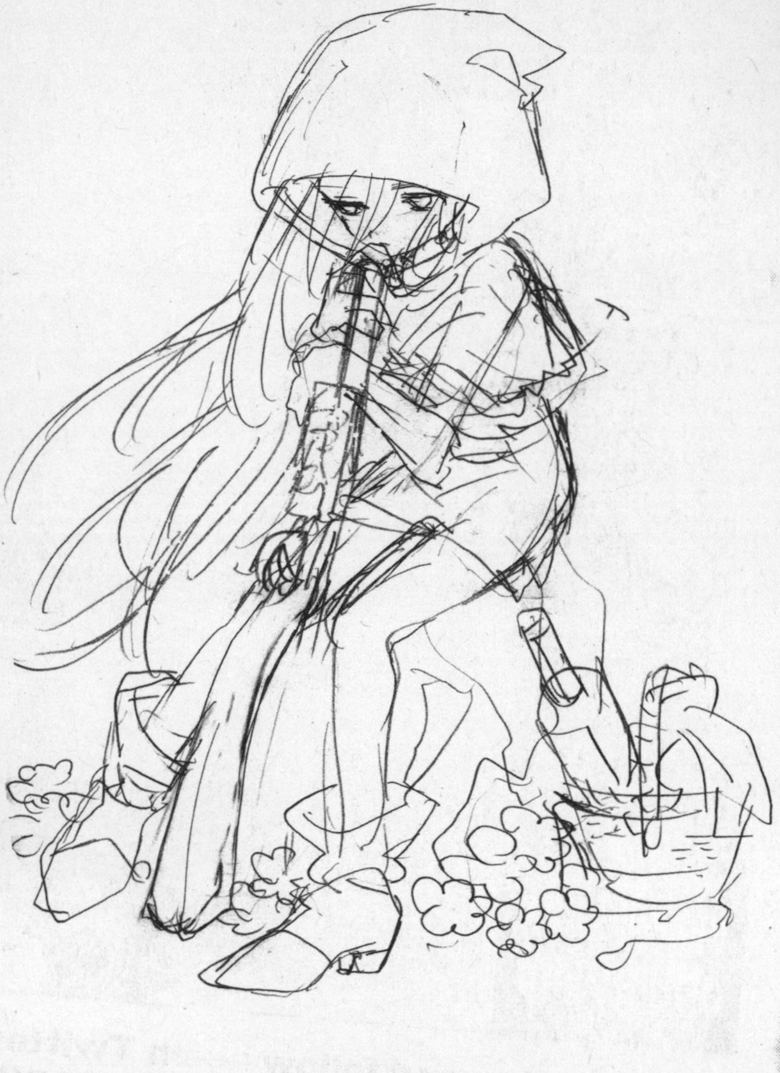

SEVEN SEAS ENTERTAINMENT PRESENTS

FAIRY TALE BATTLE ROYALE

Volume 3

story and art by SORAHO INA

TRANSLATION
Molly Rabbitt

ADAPTATION
Cae Hawksmoor

LETTERING AND RETOUCH
Alexandra Gunawan

COVER DESIGN
KC Fabellon

PROOFREADER
Kurestin Armada
Janet Houck

EDITOR
Shanti Whitesides

PRODUCTION MANAGER
Lissa Pattillo

MANAGING EDITOR
Julie Davis

EDITOR-IN-CHIEF
Adam Arnold

PUBLISHER
Jason DeAngelis

OTOGIBANASHI BATTLE ROYALE Volume 3
© Soraho Ina 2018
First published in Japan in 2018 by KADOKAWA CORPORATION, Tokyo.
English translation rights arranged with KADOKAWA CORPORATION, Tokyo.

Seven Seas press and purchase enquiries can be sent to Marketing Manager
Lianne Sentar at press@gomanga.com. Information regarding the distribution
and purchase of digital editions is available from Digital Manager CK Russell
at digital@gomanga.com.

Seven Seas and the Seven Seas logo are trademarks of
Seven Seas Entertainment. All rights reserved.

ISBN: 978-1-64275-110-9

Printed in Canada

First Printing: July 2019

10 9 8 7 6 5 4 3 2 1

FOLLOW US ONLINE: *www.sevenseasentertainment.com*

READING DIRECTIONS

This book reads from *right to left*, Japanese style.
If this is your first time reading manga, you start
reading from the top right panel on each page and
take it from there. If you get lost, just follow the
numbered diagram here. It may seem backwards at
first, but you'll get the hang of it! Have fun!!

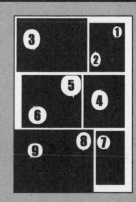